The Kodansha
KANJI USAGE GUIDE
An A to Z of *Kun* Homophones

The Kodansha

KANJI
USAGE
GUIDE

同訓使い分け辞典

An A to Z of *Kun* Homophones

Editor in Chief
Jack Halpern

Kodansha USA
New York

Published by Kodansha USA, Inc., 451 Park Avenue South, New York, NY 10016

Distributed in the United Kingdom and continental Europe by Kodansha Europe, Ltd.

Printed in South Korea through Dai Nippon Printing Co., Ltd.
24 23 22 21 20 19 18 17 16 15   12 11 10 9 8 7 6 5 4 3 2 1

Jacket design by Andrew Lee

Library of Congress Cataloging-in-Publication Data

The Kodansha Kanji usage guide : an A to Z of Kun homophones / Jack Halpern, Editor in Chief.
    pages cm
  Includes indexes.
  Text in English and Japanese.
  ISBN 978-1-56836-559-6
  1. Japanese language—Textbooks for foreign speakers—English. 2. Japanese language—Textbooks for foreign speakers—English. 3. Chinese characters—Textbooks for foreign speakers—Japanese. 4. Japanese language—Textbooks for foreign speakers—English.   I. Halpern, Jack, 1946- editor. II. Kodansha.
PL539.5.E5K550 2015
495.61'1—dc23

2014037381

www.kodanshausa.com

CONTENTS
目　次

PREFACE
序 言

The Kodansha Kanji Usage Guide (KKUG) is based on **The Kodansha Kanji Dictionary: Revised and Expanded** (KKD) published by Kodansha USA in 2013, originally published by Kenkyusha in 1990. These dictionaries have become standard reference works with a solid reputation in the Japanese-language education community throughout the world.

A unique feature of these dictionaries is their detailed treatment of the differences and similarities between closely related characters, including the differences between *kun homophones,* words like 開く 'open' and 空く 'become vacant', both of which are read あく. The ability to distinguish between such homophones is essential for mastering the Japanese writing system.

Unfortunately for learners of Japanese as a foreign language, dictionaries for native speakers sometimes disagree with each other on how to differentiate between such homophones, and in some cases they confuse the user by lumping their meanings into a single entry with no indication of how to distinguish between them.

The KKUG is a new type of reference work that enables learners to deepen their understanding of how *kun* homophones are used in contemporary Japanese. As the first Japanese-English dictionary devoted exclusively to *kun* homophones, the KKUG presents detailed usage articles that show the differences and similarities for 675 homophone groups consisting of approximately 1590 kanji headings and 4800 compound words and illustrative examples.

State-of-the-art typesetting technology was combined with computational lexicography to produce a work that aims to serve as a highly effective learning aid. Based on a systematic approach and in-depth research, this new work helps the serious student overcome the special problems posed by homophones by providing full guidance on the differences between the vast majority of single-character *kun* homophones in current use. Since homophones are a source of confusion to Japanese and non-Japanese alike, this is of great value to the student striving to gain a better understanding of Japanese texts or to write Japanese with greater precision.

It is my sincere hope that this unique work will help Japanese language learners deepen their knowledge of written Japanese.

ACKNOWLEDGMENTS

I wish to extend my heartfelt gratitude to the team of editors, programmers, and consultants for **The Kodansha Kanji Dictionary: Revised and Expanded** upon which this dictionary is based. Special recognition is due to the team of editors and programmers engaged in the editing, proofreading, and automated typesetting of this work, without whose contributions it would not have seen the light of day.

TOYOKO KON	Graphics Designer
NICOLA METTIFOGO	Typesetter, The CJK Dictionary Institute
KIMIKO MORISHITA	Senior Editor, The CJK Dictionary Institute
SHINYA MURAMATSU	Software Engineer, The CJK Dictionary Institute
TYLER REID	Software Engineer, The CJK Dictionary Institute
MICHAEL STALEY	CEO, The Michael Staley Agency, Inc.

November 2014
Saitama, Japan

JACK HALPERN
Editor in Chief

INTRODUCTION
序 説

1 KUN HOMOPHONES

As every learner of Japanese knows, kanji can have one or more Chinese-derived pronunciations, called *on* readings, and a bewildering variety of native Japanese pronunciations, referred to as *kun* readings. 上, for example, has such *on* readings as じょう and しょう and such *kun* readings as うえ, かみ, あげる, あがる, のぼる, and others.

A major obstacle faced by the learner is that Japanese has numerous **kun homophones.** These are *kun* words that are pronounced the same but written differently, and that usually differ in meaning, as shown below.

上る　のぼる　go up (steps, a hill)
登る　のぼる　climb, scale
昇る　のぼる　ascend, rise (up to the sky)

Because of the numerous homophones, students learning how to write Japanese are often at a loss when attempting to select the correct character in a particular context. Mary Noguchi, the author of the well-known column Kanji Clinic appearing in *The Japan Times,* points out that "Japanese surely qualifies for a first-place blue ribbon in the 'complex and irregular writing system' category. A major factor contributing to this complexity is the existence of two types of homophones." She goes on to say, "The distinctions between *kun*-homophones are often so subtle that even native speakers do not know how to use a particular homophone correctly."

Although *on* homophones, such as 機構 きこう 'mechanism' and 帰港 きこう 'returning to the harbor', are even more common, they are not likely to be confused since each character conveys a distinct meaning. *Kun* homophones, on the other hand, are easily confused even by native speakers, not to speak of learners.

Not only can each kanji have many *kun* readings, but many *kun* words can be written with a bewildering variety of kanji. Unlike *on* homophones, many *kun* homophones are close or even identical in meaning. For example, 解ける and 溶ける (とける) are interchangeable in the sense of 'melt, thaw' but not in the sense of 'come loose', which is always written 解ける. On the other hand, 柔らかい and 軟らかい (やわらかい) both have identical meanings (similar to variant spellings of such English words as *judgment* and *judgement,* which are identical in meaning).

2 IN-DEPTH UNDERSTANDING

Let us see how this dictionary helps the learner gain an in-depth understanding of the homophone groups **かわる** and **かえる** (see entries 154 and 204 for more details).

変わる: change, undergo change, be altered, be transformed
変える: change, alter, convert, transform, turn into

機械の機構が変わった
きかいのきこうがかわった
The machine's mechanism has undergone changes.

鉛を金に変える
なまりをきんにかえる
convert lead into gold

代わる: substitute, be substituted for (a person), take the place of
代える: substitute, use in place of, replace (something) with (another)

機械が人力に代わる
きかいがじんりょくにかわる
Machines take the place of human labor

BさんをAさんに代える
びーさんをえーさんにかえる
substitute Mr. A for Mr. B

換わる: be exchanged, become interchanged, be converted, change
換える: exchange, interchange, trade, barter, change (money), convert

この機械は金に換わる
このきかいはかねにかわる
This machine can be traded in for money

本を金に換える
ほんをかねにかえる
exchange a book for money

替わる: be replaced, change places with, replace, take turns, relieve, change
替える: replace (one thing or person by another), renew, change

機械が替わった
きかいがかわった
The (old) machine was replaced (by a new one)

畳の表を替える
たたみのおもてをかえる
replace the covers of old mats with new ones

As can be seen, the English equivalents, along with the illustrative examples, help the learner better understand how each homophone is used. By comparing the equivalents the learner can accurately grasp their differences and similarities, while the illustrative examples further clarify the shades of meaning.

Such in-depth information not only provides the learner with a better understanding of the often subtle differences between easily confused homophones, but also helps him/her write with greater precision. In addition, orthographic labels such as [sometimes also 唄う] show the degree of interchangeability between orthographic variants, while occasional supplementary notes, such as used esp. in reference to traditional Japanese songs in the example below, provide additional information.

3 ENTRY FORMAT

The term **homophone** as used here refers to a member of a group of *kun* words or word elements, often etymologically related, that are pronounced alike but written differently and that often have different meanings. **Homophone groups** consist of *kun* words or word elements that are pronounced the same but written differently and that usually differ in meaning, as in あく written as 開く, 空く, or 明く.

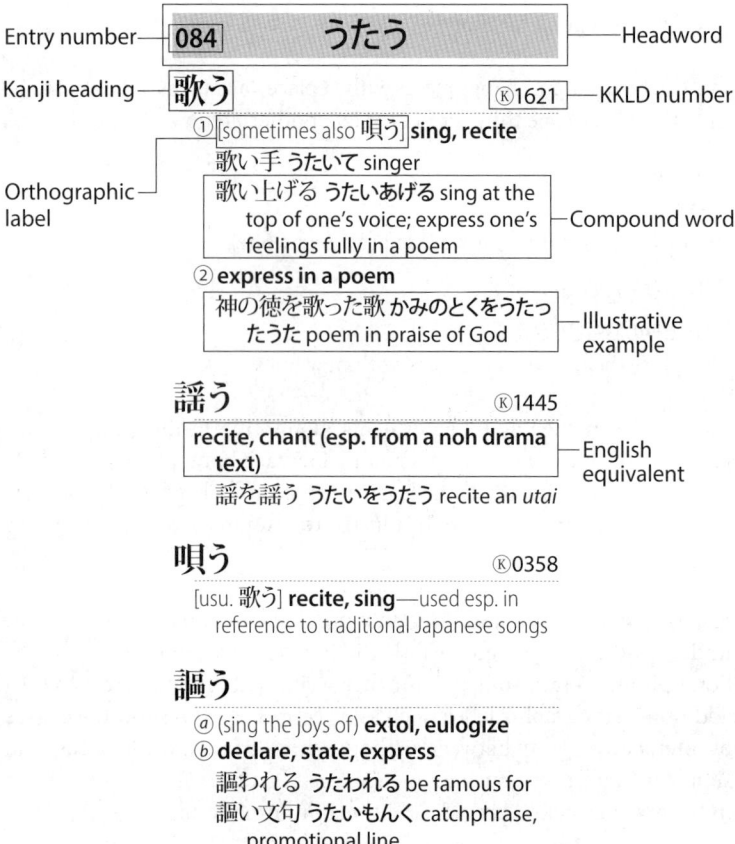

Entry number — **084** うたう — Headword

Kanji heading — **歌う** Ⓚ1621 — KKLD number

① [sometimes also 唄う] **sing, recite**

Orthographic label

歌い手 うたいて singer
歌い上げる うたいあげる sing at the top of one's voice; express one's feelings fully in a poem — Compound word

② **express in a poem**

神の徳を歌った歌 かみのとくをうたったうた poem in praise of God — Illustrative example

謡う Ⓚ1445

recite, chant (esp. from a noh drama text) — English equivalent

謡を謡う うたいをうたう recite an *utai*

唄う Ⓚ0358

[usu. 歌う] **recite, sing**—used esp. in reference to traditional Japanese songs

謳う

ⓐ (sing the joys of) **extol, eulogize**
ⓑ **declare, state, express**

謳われる うたわれる be famous for
謳い文句 うたいもんく catchphrase, promotional line

Each homophone group is treated in a separate entry that consists of the following elements:

1. The **headword** is the reading shared by the members of the homophone group (*okurigana* not shown). The headwords are numbered sequentially by boldface numerals.
2. The **kanji headings** are followed by the English equivalents.
3. The **KKLD number** refers to **The Kodansha Kanji Learner's Dictionary: Revised and Expanded.**
4. The many **compound words** and **illustrative examples** further clarify the differences between various homophones under each headword.
5. Sometimes an **orthographic label,** given in square brackets, indicates the degree of interchangeability between orthographic variants and shows in which sense(s) these variants are interchangeable. In the example, 歌う and 唄う are interchangeable in the sense of 'sing', but not in the sense of 'express in a poem'.
6. Occasionally a **supplementary note** provides additional information on the English equivalent(s), such as an analysis of the usage of various examples and an explanation of their differences and similarities.

-止める Ⓚ2545

[also -留める] **kill**

射止める いとめる shoot to death; win, acquire

突き止める つきとめる ascertain, run to the ground; [archaic] stab [thrust] to death

-留める Ⓚ2235

① **kill**

仕留める しとめる kill, shoot dead

② **write down, register**

書留 かきとめ registered mail

★ Both forms are used in compounds in the sense of kill, but -留める is preferred in the word 仕留める しとめる 'kill, shoot dead'. とめる is not used independently in this sense.

4 APPENDIXES AND INDEXES

A special feature of this dictionary is the **System of Kanji Indexing by Patterns** (SKIP), which enables even beginners to locate characters quickly and accurately. In all, this dictionary provides a choice of three methods for looking up entries:

1. In the main part of the dictionary, the headwords are listed in *a-i-u-e-o* order of their hiragana readings so that the user can locate the desired entry directly from its hiragana reading.
2. The **Radical Index** allows characters to be located from their traditional radicals.
3. The **Pattern Index** allows characters to be quickly located from their SKIP numbers.

Two appendixes explain in detail how the radical system and the SKIP system work.

5 ABBREVIATIONS AND SYMBOLS

biol	biology	( )	1. *okurigana* endings
colloq	colloquial		2. explanatory glosses
gram	grammar		3. optional omissions
hist	historical		$(A(B) = A$ or $AB)$
math	mathematics		4. alternative forms/
vi	intransitive verb		readings
vt	transitive verb	/	1. sometimes indicates
			alternatives
[1,2]	*kun* readings of exactly		2. separates sentences
	the same form	—	introduces supplemen-
①②...	numbered sense		tary glosses
ⓐⓑ...	subsense division letters	' '	encloses English equiva-
★	supplementary note		lents in explanatory text
[ ]	1. most labels	:	coordinates two parts of
	2. alternatives (*A[B]C =*		an English equivalent
	AC or *BC*)		

6 KIT

The Kodansha Kanji Usage Guide is the latest addition to **Kanji Integrated Tools** (KIT), a series of computer-edited dictionaries and software applications for the effective study of kanji. The use of the latest computational lexicography techniques ensures that all KIT dictionaries and applications are tightly integrated and of consistent quality. To date, the following dictionaries have been published:

1.	New Japanese-English Character Dictionary (NJECD)	Kenkyusha, 1990	Japanese market edition
2.	New Japanese-English Character Dictionary (NJECD-NTC)	NTC, 1993	international edition
3.	New Japanese-English Character Dictionary (NJECD-EB)	Nichigai Associates, 1995	electronic book edition
4.	The Kodansha Kanji Learner's Dictionary (KALD)	Kodansha International, 1999	learner's edition
5.	The Kodansha Kanji Learner's Dictionary (KALD-ED)	CASIO, 2007	electronic dictionary edition
6.	Japanese-Romanian Gakushu Kanji Dictionary (KALD-RM)	Polirom, 2008	Romanian edition
7.	The Kodansha Kanji Learner's Dictionary for iOS (iKALD)	The CJK Dictionary Institute, 2012	iOS edition
8.	The Kodansha Kanji Learner's Dictionary (KKLD)	Kodansha USA, 2013	revised and expanded
9.	The Kodansha Kanji Dictionary (KKD)	Kodansha USA, 2013	new edition of NJECD
10.	The Kodansha Kanji Learner's Dictionary for iOS (iKKLD)	The CJK Dictionary Institute, 2013	iOS edition of KKLD
11.	The Kodansha Kanji Learner's Dictionary (aKKLD)	The CJK Dictionary Institute, 2014	Android edition of KKLD
12.	The Kodansha Kanji Usage Guide (KKUG)	Kodansha USA, 2015	first edition
13.	The Kodansha Kanji Usage Guide for iOS (iKKUG)	The CJK Dictionary Institute, 2015	iOS edition of KKUG

The Kodansha
KANJI USAGE GUIDE
An A to Z of *Kun* Homophones

相-

®0808

① ⓐ **each other, mutually**
　ⓑ **together**
　相性 あいしょう affinity, congeniality
　相槌を打つ あいづちをうつ make (agreeable) responses (in a conversation)
　相手 あいて partner; opponent
　相乗り あいのり riding together
　相合傘で あいあいがさで sharing the same umbrella
　相棒 あいぼう pal, mate, companion
② **emphatic verbal prefix**
　相変わらず あいかわらず as usual, as before
　相次いで あいついで in succession

合い

®1740

① [in compounds]
　ⓐ **fitting**
　ⓑ **prearranged, agreed upon**
　合い鍵 あいかぎ duplicate key, passkey
　合図 あいず signal, sign
　合い言葉 あいことば password
② [also 間] (space between) **interval, space, opening**
　合いの戸 あいのと door between the rooms
③ [also 間]
　ⓐ (time between) **interval, intermission**
　ⓑ **between seasons**
　合の手 あいのて interlude
　合間 あいま interval
　合い服 あいふく between-season wear

④ [also 間] [in compounds] **mixed (blood)**
　合いの子 あいのこ *derogatory* person of mixed parentage; crossbreed
　合い挽き あいびき beef and pork ground together

間

®2836

① (space between) **interval, space, opening**
　間の戸 あいのと door between the rooms
② ⓐ [also prefix] (time between) **interval, intermission**
　ⓑ **between seasons**
　間の手 あいのて interlude
　間狂言 あいきょうげん interlude (in a noh drama)
　幕間 まくあい intermission, interval
　間服 あいふく between-season wear
③ [in compounds] **mixed (blood)**
　間の子 あいのこ *derogatory* person of mixed parentage; crossbreed

会う

®1741

(encounter by chance or arrangement)
meet, see, encounter, interview
　人に会う ひとにあう meet [see] a person
　立ち会う たちあう attend, take part in, witness
　出会い であい meeting, encounter

合う

®1740

① ⓐ **fit, suit**
　ⓑ **harmonize, agree with, coincide**

体に良く合う からだによくあう fit (a person) well

似合う にあう befit, suit; match well

② **come together, meet**

噛み合う かみあう gear [engage] with, be in gear [mesh]; bite each other

③ⓐ **be right [correct]**
ⓑ (of a clock) **indicate the right time**

合わない答え あわないこたえ incorrect answer

④ **pay, be profitable**

引き合う ひきあう pay (off), be profitable; pull against each other

遇う   Ⓚ2702

[also 遭う] (come upon, esp. by accident) **meet with, encounter, be confronted**

酷い目に遇う ひどいめにあう have a bad time

遭う   Ⓚ2725

[also 遇う] (come upon, esp. by accident) **meet with, encounter, be confronted**

酷い目に遭う ひどいめにあう have a bad time

逢う   Ⓚ2774

(encounter by chance or arrangement) **meet, see, encounter**—used esp. in reference to romantic encounters

逢わせる あわせる have (a person) meet (another), allow (a person) to see (someone)

逢い引き あいびき (lovers') date, rendezvous

逢瀬 おうせ meeting, date

出逢う であう meet (by chance), encounter

忍び逢い しのびあい clandestine meeting, rendezvous

003	あおい

青い   Ⓚ2152

①ⓐ **blue**
ⓑ **green**

青い旗 あおいはた blue flag

② [sometimes also 蒼い] (pale in appearance) **green, pale**

顔が青い かおがあおい look pale [green]

③ (not mature) **green, unripe**

青い果実 あおいかじつ unripe [green] fruit

蒼い   Ⓚ2050

[usu. 青い] **pale blue; pale; green**

顔が蒼い かおがあおい look pale [green]

004	あおぐ

扇ぐ   Ⓚ1704

[sometimes also 煽ぐ] **fan**

煽ぐ

[usu. 扇ぐ] **fan**

煽ぎ立てる あおぎたてる fan incessantly; agitate, instigate

005 あかい

赤い   Ⓚ1876

[sometimes also 紅い] **red, crimson,
scarlet**

紅い   Ⓚ1174

[usu. 赤い] **crimson, deep red**
紅組 あかぐみ red team

006 あかがね

銅   Ⓚ1533

[also 赤金] **copper**
銅の器 あかがねのうつわ copper
vessel

赤金   Ⓚ1876

[also 銅] **copper**

007 あからむ

赤らむ   Ⓚ1876

become red
赤らんだ あからんだ ruddy, florid

明らむ   Ⓚ0756

brighten

008 あがる

上がる   Ⓚ2876

① ⓐ **go up, come up, rise, climb**
   ⓑ **go up in price, rise, jump**
   ⓒ go up in rank or quality: **rise, be promoted; make progress, advance**

屋根に上がる やねにあがる go up on
the roof
風呂から上がる ふろからあがる step
out of the bath
月給が上がる げっきゅうがあがる get
a raise in salary
腕が上がる うでがあがる gain in skill

② ⓐ **be completed, be finished**
   ⓑ **come to an end, stop (raining);
die, die out**
   ⓒ (of games like Japanese parcheesi)
come to the finish

原稿が上がった げんこうがあがった
The manuscript is completed
雨が上がった あめがあがった It
stopped raining
商売が上がったりだ しょうばいがあ
がったりだ My business is ruined
一番で上がる いちばんであがる win
the first place

③ **issue, accrue, be derived**
効果が上がる こうかがあがる take
effect, bear fruit

④ **lose control of oneself, get excited,
be nervous, get stage fright**
試験で上がる しけんであがる get
nervous at an examination

⑤ [honorific] **take, have; eat, drink**
ワインを召し上がれ わいんをめしあ
がれ Please help yourself to the
wine

⑥ **be sufficient**
安く上がる やすくあがる cost little

⑦ ⓐ **come in, enter (a house), be
admitted to (a school)**
   ⓑ [honorific] **call on, visit**
上がり込む あがりこむ enter, come
in, step in
駅迄お迎えに上がります えきまでお
むかえにあがります I'll go to the
station to meet you

⑧ **land, go ashore**
上がり場 あがりば landing place
⑨ **be offered**
灯明が上がっている とうみょうが
あがっている Sacred candles
are lighted (before a household
shrine)

挙がる
®2169

① **be cited, be mentioned, be listed**
良い例が挙がっている よいれいが
あがっている A good example is
given
② **be arrested, be caught, be nabbed**
犯人が挙がった はんにんがあがった
The culprit was arrested
③ **become famous**
名が挙がる ながあがる become
famous
④ **come into possession, be recov-
ered**
証拠が挙がった しょうこがあがった
Evidence turned up

揚がる
®0542

① (rise high or float in the air) (of kites or
flags) **be up, fly, be flying;** (of fireworks) **be shot up, be set off**
旗が揚がっている はたがあがってい
る The flag is up
② **be fried, fry**
③ (of appearance) **stand out, improve**
風采が揚がらない ふうさいがあがら
ない make a poor appearance
④ **become elated, get into high
spirits**
意気が揚がっている いきがあがって
いる be in high spirits

空き
®1913

① [sometimes also 明き] **gap, aperture,
space; vacancy; free time**
空きを埋める あきをうめる fill a gap
② [prefix] **vacant, empty**
空き家 あきや vacant house
空き缶 あきかん empty can

明き
®0756

[usu. 空き] **gap, aperture, space; vacancy; free time**

飽きる
®1528

ⓐ [also suffix] **be satiated, be surfeited,
be fed up**
ⓑ [sometimes also 厭きる or 倦きる] **grow
tired of, lose interest in**
聞き飽きる ききあきる be fed up
listening to
快楽に飽きる かいらくにあきる be
satiated with pleasures
飽き あき weariness, tiresomeness
飽きっぽい あきっぽい be fickle [ca-
pricious], get soon wearied of
飽き飽きする あきあきする be sick
(of), be bored (with), be fed up

倦きる
®0099

[usu. 飽きる, sometimes also 厭きる] **grow
tired of, lose interest in**

厭きる

[usu. 飽きる, sometimes also 倦きる] **grow
tired of, lose interest in**

厭き厭きする あきあきする be sick (of), be bored (with)

厭き性 あきしょう fickle [capricious] nature, get soon wearied of

011　あく

明く　Ⓚ0756

① **one's eyes open, regain sight**
　目が明く めがあく regain sight
② **be settled, be put in order**
　埒が明かない らちがあかない remain unsettled, make no progress
③ (of clothing) **be opened (at the back)**
　背の明いた服 せのあいたふく garment open at the back
④ [usu. 空く] **have (a hole or aperture) in, (a gap) is open**
　明き あき gap, aperture space; vacancy; free time

空く　Ⓚ1913

① **become vacant, become vacated [empty]**
　空いている部屋 あいているへや vacant room
② **become available for use**
　辞書が空いたら貸して下さい じしょがあいたらかしてください Let me use the dictionary when available
③ **become free [unoccupied]**
　私は時間が空いている わたしはじかんがあいている I have time to spare
④ [sometimes also 明く] **have (a hole or aperture) in, (a gap) is open**
　穴が空いている あながあいている have [be pierced with] a hole

開く　Ⓚ2835

ⓐ **open, become open**
ⓑ (of a shop) **open, begin**
　ドアが開いている どあがあいている The door is open
　幕開き まくあき raising of the curtains; beginning
　十時に開く じゅうじにあく (the shop) opens ten o'clock

012　あけ

朱　Ⓚ2960

[sometimes also 緋] **red, blood red**
　朱に染まる あけにそまる welter in blood

緋　Ⓚ1250

[usu. 朱] **red, blood red**

013　あける

明ける　Ⓚ0756

① **dawn, become light, break**
　明け あけ dawn; expiration
　夜明け よあけ dawn, daybreak
② (of the new year) **begin, open**
　明けましておめでとうございます あけましておめでとうございます Happy New Year
　年明け としあけ beginning of the year
③ **expire, be over**
　冬が明けた ふゆがあけた Winter is over
④ [in compounds] **disclose, reveal**
　打ち明ける うちあける confide in (someone), reveal, disclose

空ける ⓚ1913

① **empty, clear, vacate, clear out**
部屋を空ける へやをあける clear a room

② **leave space, make room**
一字空ける いちじあける leave a space (between words)

③ **bore, make a hole**
穴を空ける あなをあける make a hole

④ **free oneself (to do), make spare time**
時間を空ける じかんをあける make oneself available [free]

開ける ⓚ2835

open, unlock
戸を開ける とをあける open the door

014 あげ

上げ ⓚ2876

① **rise in price**
② **making a tuck**

-揚げ ⓚ0542

ⓐ [also suffix] **fried food, fry**
ⓑ **fried bean curd**
精進揚げ しょうじんあげ fried vegetables
油揚げ あぶらあげ fried bean curd

015 あげる

上げる ⓚ2876

① ⓐ (cause to move upward) **raise, elevate, lift up**

ⓑ (increase the level of) **raise, increase, hike**

ⓒ (elevate in rank) **raise, promote, elevate**

ⓓ **raise one's voice, shout**

ⓔ (raise the quality of) **improve (one's skill), advance**

顔を上げる かおをあげる raise one's face

引き上げる ひきあげる draw [pull] up; promote; increase

棚上げする たなあげする shelve (up), pigeonhole

上げ あげ rise in price; making a tuck

値上げする ねあげする raise [increase] the price

賃上げ ちんあげ wage increase

格上げする かくあげする raise to higher status, promote to a higher rank

声を上げる こえをあげる raise one's voice

腕を上げる うであげる improve one's skill

② ⓐ **give, offer, present, hand (to a superior, equal or others, not the speaker)**

ⓑ **offer, make an offering (to a deity)**

彼に本を上げた かれにほんをあげた I gave him a book

仏壇に花を上げる ぶつだんにはなをあげる offer flowers before the family Buddhist altar

③ [following the TE-form of verbs] **perform an action for (the benefit of) someone, do for a person**

本を読んで上げよう ほんをよんであげよう I'll read a book for you

席を譲って上げる せきをゆずってあげる offer a seat to someone

④ **complete, finish**
　仕事を上げる　しごとをあげる finish the work
⑤ **achieve (results), gain (profits)**
　良い成績を上げる　よいせいせきをあげる achieve satisfactory results
　売り上げ　うりあげ sales, proceeds
⑥ **show in, usher in, admit**
　芸者を上げる　げいしゃをあげる call in a geisha
⑦ **send, enter (a child in school)**
　子供を学校に上げる　こどもをがっこうにあげる send one's child to school
⑧ **manage (to do something)**
　安く上げる　やすくあげる make it less expensive
⑨ **praise**
　上げたり下げたり　あげたりさげたり praising and blaming; raising and lowering
⑩ **dress up**
　髪を上げる　かみをあげる put up one's hair
⑪ **throw up, vomit**
　上げてしまった　あげてしまった I threw up
⑫ **(of tides) rise**
　上げ潮　あげしお rising [flowing] tide

挙げる
Ⓚ2169
①ⓐ (raise something and hold it up for display) **hold up, raise (one's hand or a wineglass)**
　ⓑ (gather together) **raise (an army), recruit**
　ⓒ (elevate in dignity) **raise oneself, raise one's reputation**

　手を挙げろ　てをあげろ Hold up!/Stick 'em up!
　兵を挙げる　へいをあげる raise an army
　名を挙げる　なをあげる make one's name, gain fame
② **cite, give (an example), mention**
　例を挙げる　れいをあげる cite an example
③ **hold (a function), perform (a ceremony)**
　式を挙げる　しきをあげる hold a ceremony
④ **arrest, round up, nab**
　挙げられる　あげられる be arrested, be caught
⑤ **give birth to, have children**
　三人の子を挙げる　さんにんのこをあげる have three children
⑥ **use fully**
　挙げて　あげて all, whole, en masse
⑦ **gain (points), score**
　先取点を挙げる　せんしゅてんをあげる score the first point
⑧ **unclassified compounds**
　挙げ句(=揚句)に　あげくに in the end; finally

揚げる
Ⓚ0542
① (cause to rise high or float in the air) **raise (a flag), send up, hoist, lift, fly (a kite), shoot up (fireworks)**
　旗を揚げる　はたをあげる raise [hoist] a flag
　凧揚げ　たこあげ kite flying
② **fry in deep fat**
　揚げ　あげ fried bean curd
　揚げ物　あげもの fried food, a fry
　魚を揚げる　さかなをあげる fry fish

③ **land, unload, disembark**

陸揚げ りくあげ landing, unloading

引き揚げる ひきあげる withdraw, leave, return, repatriate

016　　あこがれる

憧れる
Ⓚ0664

[sometimes also 憬れる] **yearn after; adore**

憧れ あこがれ yearning, longing

憧れの的 あこがれのまと object of envy; adored figure, idol

有名人に憧れる ゆうめいじんにあこがれる adore [be attracted to] a celebrity

憬れる
Ⓚ0663

[usu. 憧れる] **yearn after; adore**

憬れ あこがれ yearning, longing

017　　あさひ

旭
Ⓚ2571

[usu. 朝日] **rising sun, morning sun; rays of the morning sun**

朝日
Ⓚ1513

[sometimes also 旭] **rising sun, morning sun; rays of the morning sun**

018　　あし¹

足
Ⓚ1873

① ⓐ **leg, limb; foot, paw**
　ⓑ [also 脚] (leg-shaped support) **leg**
　ⓒ **foot (of something standing), base**

足腰 あしこし legs and loins

足首 あしくび ankle

足場 あしば scaffold, footing, foothold

足下(=足元) あしもと gait, pace, step

手足 てあし hands and feet, limbs

机の足 つくえのあし legs of a table

垂線の足 すいせんのあし foot of a perpendicular line

② ⓐ [also suffix] **walking, traveling**
　ⓑ **step, stride**
　ⓒ **means of transportation**

足取り あしどり one's manner of walking; trace (of a culprit's movement); (price) movement

足並み あしなみ pace, step

千鳥足 ちどりあし tottering gait

一足 ひとあし a step

通勤の足 つうきんのあし facilities for commutation

③ [also 脚] **movement, pace**

出足 であし start

雨足 あまあし density of the falling rain; pace (of the approaching shower)

④ **trace**

足が付く あしがつく be traced [tracked]

⑤ **deficit**

足が出る あしがでる exceed the budget, do not cover the expense

⑥ **relation**

足を洗う あしをあらう wash one's hands of, quit (the shady business); wash one's feet

足入れ あしいれ tentative marriage

脚
Ⓚ0887

① [also 足] (leg-shaped support) **leg**

三本脚の机 さんぼんあしのつくえ
three-legged table

② [also 足] **movement, pace**
雨脚 あまあし density of the falling
rain; pace (of the approaching
shower)

③ **bottom radical of Chinese charac-**
ters, leg radical
人脚 ひとあし *hitoashi*, 'bottom legs'
radical (儿)

019　あし²

葦　　　　　　　　　　　Ⓚ2041

common reed, reed
葦毛 あしげ gray (horse coat color)
葦笛 あしぶえ reed pipe
葦船 あしぶね papyrus boat
葦辺 あしべ reedy shore
葦鹿 あしか eared seal, sea lion

芦　　　　　　　　　　　Ⓚ1897

common reed, reed
芦毛 あしげ gray (horse coat color)

020　あずかる

預かる　　　　　　　　Ⓚ0954

① **receive on deposit, take charge**
of, keep
預かり あずかり custody; undecided
match, draw, tie
保護預かり ほごあずかり safe deposit

② **refrain from (doing something)**
批評は暫く預かる ひひょうはしばらく
あずかる I refrain from comment-
ing on it now

③ **leave (a game) undecided**

預かりにする あずかりにする call off
(a game) as a draw

与る　　　　　　　　　　Ⓚ2887

① **participate in, take part in, share in**
相談に与る そうだんにあずかる be
consulted

② **enjoy, receive**
招待に与る しょうたいにあずかる
receive an invitation

021　あたい

値　　　　　　　　　　　Ⓚ0091

ⓐ **value, worth, merit**
ⓑ *math* **value**
値する あたいする be worth, deserve,
merit
一読の値が有る いちどくのあたいが
ある be worth reading
Xの値 えっくすのあたい value of *x*

価　　　　　　　　　　　Ⓚ0067

price, cost
価千金の あたいせんきんの priceless,
invaluable

022　あたかも

宛も　　　　　　　　　　Ⓚ1908

[now usu. 恰も] **as if, just as, just like**
宛も月明の如し あたかもげつめいの
ごとし It is as bright as the moon

恰も　　　　　　　　　　Ⓚ0326

[formerly also 宛も] **just like, as if**

恰も好し あたかもよし luckily, fortu-
nately

023 あたたか

暖か Ⓚ0922

same as 暖かい あたたかい
暖かみ あたたかみ warmth
暖かな毛布 あたたかなもうふ warm
blanket

温か Ⓚ0554

same as 温かい あたたかい

024 あたたかい

暖かい Ⓚ0922

①ⓐ (of weather) **warm, mild, genial,
temperate**
ⓑ **warm (color)**
暖かさ あたたかさ warmth
今日は暖かい きょうはあたたかい It is
warm today
暖かい色 あたたかいいろ warm color
② **warmhearted, kindhearted, sympathetic**
暖かい人 あたたかいひと warmheart-
ed person

温かい Ⓚ0554

① **warm (to the touch), lukewarm**
温かい御飯 あたたかいごはん warm
rice
② **heartwarming, warm (feeling or
atmosphere)**
温かい歓迎 あたたかいかんげい
warm reception

★ Note the difference between sense
② of 暖かい and 温かい, roughly
equivalent to the difference between
warmhearted and *heartwarming*.
Study the equivalents and examples
carefully, as these words are easily
confused by Japanese and foreigners
alike. There is no difference between
the forms あたたかい and あたたかな,
except that the former is an adjective
and the latter a noun adjective.

025 あたたまる

暖まる Ⓚ0922

(surrounding air rises in temperature) **get
warm, be warmed, warm**
暖まった空気 あたたまったくうき
warmed air

温まる Ⓚ0554

① (of objects or persons) **warm oneself,
take warmth, get warm, be heated**
日光に温まる にっこうにあたたまる
bask in the sun, sun oneself
② **be heartwarming**
心温まる こころあたたまる heart-
warming

026 あたためる

暖める Ⓚ0922

(warm up the surrounding air) **warm,
warm up, heat**
部屋を暖める へやをあたためる heat
the room

温める ⓚ0554

① (raise the temperature of a thing) **warm, heat**

コーヒーを温める こーひーをあたためる warm up coffee

② **nurse (an idea), let (an idea) mellow**

アイディアを温める あいでぃあをあたためる nurse an idea in one's mind

③ **renew (an old friendship)**

027 あたり

当たり ⓚ1865

hit, on-target impact; hit, success; clue, guess; manners; batting average; a bite (in fishing)

辺り ⓚ2607

① ⓐ **vicinity, neighborhood, surroundings**

ⓑ [also suffix] (near that place or time) **thereabouts, about**

家の辺りに いえのあたりに around the house

一昨年辺り いっさくねんあたり the year before last or thereabouts

② **for instance**

ロンドン辺りなら ろんどんあたりなら in the case of London, for instance

028 あたる

当たる ⓚ1865

① ⓐ **hit, strike**

ⓑ **hit the mark**

ⓒ **strike against, touch, be touched, be exposed**

ⓓ (be struck by light or heat) **shine upon, strike; warm oneself, bask**

突き当たる つきあたる hit against, run into; come to the end of (a street)

体当たりする たいあたりする hurl oneself (at), dash oneself (against)

行き当たる いきあたる strike into, light on; come against

紛れ当たり まぐれあたり chance hit, fluke

当たり障りの無い あたりさわりのない harmless and inoffensive

口当たり くちあたり taste

手当たり次第 てあたりしだい at random

風に当たる かぜにあたる be exposed to wind

日当たり ひあたり exposure to the sun

火に当たる ひにあたる warm oneself at the fire

② ⓐ **hit on, guess rightly; come true**

ⓑ **make a hit, come off, succeed; win in a lottery**

思い当たる おもいあたる occur to, strike

見当たらない みあたらない not be found

心当たり こころあたり knowledge, idea, clue

当たり屋 あたりや lucky person, lucky batter; automobile accident faker

当たり役 あたりやく successful role

大当たり おおあたり big hit, great success, bonanza; bumper crop

籤が当たった くじがあたった I drew a prize

③ⓐ **be equivalent to, be equal, correspond to**
  ⓑ **be in relation to**
  一フィートは約一尺に当たる いちふぃーとはやくいっしゃくにあたる One foot is roughly equivalent to 1 *shaku*
  彼は私の叔父に当たる かれはわたしのおじにあたる He is my uncle

④ **be applicable to, apply**
  この解釈は当たっていない このかいしゃくはあたっていない This interpretation does not apply

⑤ **face, confront, attack**
  総当たり戦 そうあたりせん round robin event

⑥ [in the form of 当たり **あたり** or 当たって **あたって**] **on the occasion of, at, in**
  この時に当たって このときにあたって at this time [juncture]

⑦ **undertake, take charge of**
  任に当たる にんにあたる undertake a duty

⑧ [often in the form of 当たって見る **あたってみる**] **try, have a look, take a chance, feel out, sound**
  人の意向を当たって見る ひとのいこうをあたってみる sound out a person's thoughts
  別の辞書に当たって見る べつのじしょにあたってみる try another dictionary

⑨ **treat (unkindly)**
  当たり散らす あたりちらす find fault with everybody, make oneself disagreeable
  八つ当たりする やつあたりする snarl (at the wrong person), take it out on (someone)

⑩ **be assigned, be allotted; be selected**
  英語の時間に当たった えいごのじかんにあたった I was called on (to read aloud) in English class

⑪ **lie, be located (in the direction of)**
  京都は東京の西に当たる きょうとはとうきょうのにしにあたる Kyoto lies to the west of Tokyo

⑫ [formerly also 中る] **be poisoned, disagree with; suffer from**
  河豚に当たる ふぐにあたる get poisoned by swellfish

⑬ *theater jargon* **next, coming**
  当たる日曜日 あたるにちようび next Sunday

中る Ⓚ2902

[now usu. 当たる] **be poisoned, disagree with; suffer from**
  河豚に中る ふぐにあたる get poisoned by swellfish

029 あつい¹

熱い Ⓚ2495

① **hot (to the touch), heated**
  熱さ あつさ heat
  熱いコーヒー あついこーひー hot coffee

②ⓐ **hot (with excitement), passionate**
  ⓑ **be madly in love**
  熱い仲だ あついなかだ be sweet on each other

暑い Ⓚ2182

hot (weather), warm, sultry

暑さ あつさ heat, summer heat, hot weather

真夏の暑さ まなつのあつさ heat of high summer

蒸し暑い むしあつい sultry, sweltering

030 あつい²

厚い Ⓚ2588

① (great in depth) **thick, bulky, deep**

厚さ あつさ thickness

厚板 あついた thick board, plank

厚かましい あつかましい unabashed, brazen

厚着する あつぎする be heavily clothed

分厚い ぶあつい bulky, massive

② [formerly also 篤い] **cordial, kind, hearty, warm, deep**

厚い持てなし あついもてなし cordial reception

厚く礼を述べる あつくれいをのべる thank (a person) heartily

手厚い てあつい warm, hearty, cordial

下に厚く したにあつく more generously for the lower-paid

篤い Ⓚ2370

① [now usu. 厚い] **cordial, kind, hearty, warm, deep**

篤い持てなし あついもてなし cordial reception

篤い友情 あついゆうじょう warm friendship

篤い信仰 あついしんこう deep faith

② (of an illness) **critical, serious, dangerous**

病が篤い やまいがあつい be seriously ill

031 あて

当て Ⓚ1865

① **aim, end, goal**

当ても無く あてもなく aimlessly, at random

目当て めあて guide, aiming; aim

② **hopes, expectation**

当て事 あてごと expectations, hopes; guessing

当てが外れる あてがはずれる be disappointed

③ **reliance, confidence, trust**

当てにする あてにする rely upon, have trust in

④ [suffix] **pad**

肩当て かたあて shoulder pad

-宛て Ⓚ1908

① **addressed to**

A氏宛ての手紙 えーしあてのてがみ letter addressed to Mr. A

② **per, apiece**

オレンジを一人宛て三個 おれんじを ひとりあてさんこ three oranges apiece [per head]

032 あてる

当てる Ⓚ1865

① ⓐ **hit, strike; touch**

ⓑ **hit the mark**

ⓒ (cause to be struck) **expose**

当て逃げ あてにげ hit-and-run accident (causing property damage)

鞘当て さやあて rivalry ("touching of sheaths")

的を当てる まとをあてる hit the mark

日に当てる ひにあてる expose to the sun

② ⓐ **hit on, guess**
　ⓑ **make a hit, succeed**

言い当てる いいあてる guess right

掘り当てる ほりあてる strike, find, dig up

③ **apply (to), put (to), lay, place**

当て嵌まる あてはまる be applicable, come under (a category), fulfill (criteria)

当て嵌める あてはめる apply, fit, adapt

手当て てあて provision; medical care, treatment

手当 てあて allowance, compensation, benefits

双眼鏡に目を当てる そうがんきょうにめをあてる put binoculars to one's eyes

座布団を当てる ざぶとんをあてる sit on a cushion

④ [usu. 充てる, but in compounds always 当てる] **allot, assign, appropriate**

割り当てる わりあてる assign, allot

⑤ [usu. 宛てる, but in compounds also 当てる] **assign Chinese characters to a word (as phonetic substitutes)**

当前は当て字だ とうぜんはあてじだ 当前 is written in phonetic substitute characters

⑥ **call on (a pupil to answer a question)**

問題を三人に当てる もんだいをさんにんにあてる ask three pupils to solve a problem

⑦ [in the form of 当てられる **あてられる**]

ⓐ **be poisoned by, agree badly with, be affected by**
ⓑ **be annoyed by (flirtation)**

暑さに当てられる あつさにあてられる be affected by heat

充てる   Ⓚ1737

[sometimes also 当てる, but in compounds always 当てる] **allot, assign, appropriate**

金を借金の返済に充てる かねをしゃっきんのへんさいにあてる allot money to the payment of debts

宛てる   Ⓚ1908

① **address (a letter), direct**

宛て先 あてさき destination, address

宛名 あてな address

手紙を宛てる てがみをあてる address [direct] a letter to a person

② [sometimes also 当てる] **assign Chinese characters to a word (as phonetic substitutes)**

宛て字 あてじ phonetic substitute, false substitute character

外来語に字を宛てる がいらいごにじをあてる assign Chinese characters to a foreign word

★ Both 当てる and 宛てる are used in the sense 'assigning Chinese characters', but the latter is preferred. However, in the compound あてじ 'phonetic substitute, etc.', 当て字 is the preferred form.

あと

後 ⓚ0321

① ⓐ [also suffix] (subsequent in time) **after, afterward, later, subsequent**
ⓑ (subsequent in order) **after, latter, next, following**
ⓒ **after death**

後の あとの later, subsequent; the next [following]; back

後で あとで after, afterwards, later, later on

後片付け あとかたづけ cleaning up, clearing (the table); putting in order

後始末 あとしまつ settlement; cleaning up; putting in order

髭剃り後 ひげそりあと after shaving

三日後に みっかあとに three days after [later]

後払い あとばらい deferred payment

後書き あとがき postscript, afterword

後回し あとまわし deferment, postponement

後作 あとさく second crop

後を弔う あとをとむらう perform religious rites for the repose of a soul

② **back, rear**

後足 あとあし hind leg

後戻りする あともどりする go backward, move back, turn back; retrograde

③ ⓐ **descendant, posterity**
ⓑ **future**

源氏の後 げんじのあと descendant of the Genji family

後後 あとあと distant future

④ ⓐ **rest, remainder**

ⓑ **and, and also**

後金 あときん rest of the payment

後十分 あとじっぷん ten minutes more

鉛筆と後消しゴム えんぴつとあとけしごむ pencil and also eraser

⑤ **consequences, results, conclusion**

後を濁す あとをにごす leave a bad impression behind

後を引く あとをひく The effects linger [remain]

跡 ⓚ1395

① ⓐ (mark left by something) **trace(s), track, mark, footprint, trail, sign;** [also 痕] **scar**
ⓑ (sign of former presence) **ruins, remains, aftermath**

跡形も無く あとかたもなく without leaving any trace

傷跡 きずあと scar, cicatrix

足跡 あしあと footprint, footmark

跡始末(=後始末)する あとしまつする settle, take remedial measures

城跡 しろあと ruins of a castle

② **succession**

跡を絶たない あとをたたない (there) be no end to

跡を絶つ あとをたつ put an end to, wipe out

③ **inheritance, headship of a family**

跡継ぎ あとつぎ successor, heir

跡目 あとめ headship of a family, family property

蹟 ⓚ1473

ⓐ (mark left by something) **trace(s), track, mark, footprint, trail, sign**

ⓑ (sign of former presence) **ruins, remains, aftermath**

痕 ⓚ2795

[also 跡] **scar**

傷痕 きずあと scar, cicatrix
爪痕 つめあと scratch, nail mark; ravages, after effects

穴 ⓚ1852

① ⓐ **hole, opening, gap; hollow, cavity**
  ⓑ [sometimes also 孔] **open or bottomless hole, opening, aperture, perforation**
  ⓒ **cave, lair; pit**

ボタンの穴 ぼたんのあな buttonhole
落とし穴 おとしあな pit, trap
洞穴 ほらあな cave, cavern, den

② ⓐ **fault, flaw, defect**
  ⓑ **deficit, loss**

穴だらけだ あなだらけだ be full of holes; hold no water
穴を開ける あなをあける cause a loss

③ **good place known to few**

穴場 あなば good place known to few people

④ **long shot, dark horse**

大穴 おおあな big hole; *horse racing* dark horse

孔 ⓚ0158

[usu. 穴] **open or bottomless hole, opening, aperture, perforation**

針の孔 はりのあな needle's eye
毛孔 けあな pores (of the skin)

暴く ⓚ2194

[sometimes also 発く] **disclose (a secret), expose (a crime), lay bare, divulge**

秘密を暴く ひみつをあばく disclose a secret

発く ⓚ2222

[usu. 暴く] **disclose (a secret), expose (a crime), lay bare, divulge**

秘密を発く ひみつをあばく disclose a secret

油 ⓚ0303

oil, animal oil, vegetable oil

油絵 あぶらえ oil painting
油気 あぶらけ greasiness, oiliness
油を売る あぶらをうる loaf, idle away one's time
油を絞る あぶらをしぼる extract oil by pressing; give a person a severe talking-to
胡麻油 ごまあぶら sesame (seed) oil
大豆油 だいずあぶら soy bean oil

脂 ⓚ0861

[formerly also 膏] **fat, grease, lard, blubber; greasy substance**

脂ぎった あぶらぎった greasy, oily
脂が乗る あぶらがのる be in good table quality; get into the swing of (as one's work)
脂性 あぶらしょう fatty constitution

膏 Ⓚ1839

[now usu. 脂] **fat, grease; greasy substance**

膏汗 あぶらあせ cold sweat, greasy sweat

膏薬 あぶらぐすり(=こうやく) plaster; ointment

豚の膏 ぶたのあぶら lard, grease of a hog

037 あまねく

普く Ⓚ2028

[also 遍く] *literary* **all over, everywhere, widely, universally**

普く捜す あまねくさがす make a wide search

普く世界に知られる あまねくせかいにしられる be known all over the world

遍く Ⓚ2703

[also 普く] *literary* **all over, everywhere, widely, universally**

遍く捜す あまねくさがす make a wide search

遍く世界に知られる あまねくせかいにしられる be known all over the world

038 あや

綾 Ⓚ1258

①ⓐ [in compounds] **twill, twilled fabric**
ⓑ **twilled silk**
ⓒ [in compounds] **as beautiful or intricate as twilled silk**

綾織り あやおり twill

綾錦 あやにしき twill damask and brocade

綾取り あやとり cat's cradle

目も綾な めもあやな dazzlingly beautiful, brilliant

② [also 文] **figure, design, pattern (as of cloth)**

綾を成して あやをなして in beautiful patterns

③ [also 文]
ⓐ **figure of speech, rhetorical flourish**
ⓑ **intricate and subtle details, intricacies**

言葉の綾 ことばのあや figure of speech

事件の綾 じけんのあや web of the case

文 Ⓚ1708

① **figure, design, pattern (as of cloth)**

美しい文 うつくしいあや beautiful design

②ⓐ **figure of speech, rhetorical flourish**
ⓑ **intricate and subtle details, intricacies**

文の無い文体 あやのないぶんたい plain style

039 あやしい

怪しい Ⓚ0264

ⓐ **doubtful; suspicious**
ⓑ [also 妖しい] **strange, mysterious; uncanny**
ⓒ **clumsy, awkward**

怪しげな あやしげな questionable, doubtful, suspicious

怪しい手付きで あやしいてつきで
with clumsy hands, clumsily

妖しい   Ⓚ0212

[also 怪しい] **strange, mysterious; uncanny**

040   あやまる

謝る   Ⓚ1465

apologize
  謝り あやまり apology, excuse
  平謝り ひらあやまり humble apology

誤る   Ⓚ1403

① [formerly also 謬る] **mistake, make a mistake, err**
  誤り あやまり mistake, error, slip
  誤って あやまって by mistake, accidentally
② **mislead, lead astray**
  人を誤る ひとをあやまる mislead a person

謬る

[now usu. 誤る] **mistake, make a mistake, err**
  謬り あやまり mistake, error, slip

041   あら

荒-   Ⓚ1950

① (in a natural state) **wild, barren, desolate**
  荒野(=曠野) あらの(=あれの) wilderness, deserted land

②ⓐ (of natural phenomena) **wild, violent, rough**
 ⓑ [prefix] (of behavior) **wild, rough, rude, savage**
  荒海 あらうみ rough sea, stormy sea
  荒武者 あらむしゃ daredevil, rowdy
③ [also 粗-] (not elaborate) **coarse, rough, crude, gross**
  荒削りの あらけずりの roughhewn; unrefined
④ **unrestrained, extravagant**
  荒稼ぎ あらかせぎ making easy money; robbery

粗-   Ⓚ1214

①ⓐ [also 荒-] (not elaborate) **coarse, rough, crude, gross**
 ⓑ (in the natural state) **crude, raw, unrefined, unprocessed**
  粗筋 あらすじ outline, summary
  粗造り あらづくり rough work
  粗金 あらがね ore
② **sparse, scattered**
  粗播き あらまき sparse sowing [seeding]

042   あらい

荒い   Ⓚ1950

①ⓐ (of natural phenomena) **wild, violent, rough**
 ⓑ (of behavior) **wild, rough, rude, savage**
  荒さ あらさ wildness, roughness; extravagance
  荒い波 あらいなみ wild [raging] waves, stormy seas
  荒荒しい あらあらしい wild, violent; rough, rude, gruff

荒っぽい あらっぽい rough, wild, rude

手荒な てあらな violent, rough

② **unrestrained, lavish**

金遣いの荒い かねづかいのあらい wasteful of money, extravagant

粗い
Ⓚ1214

① ⓐ (not fine) **coarse, rough, gross**

ⓑ (not smooth) **coarse, rough, rugged**

ⓒ (not elaborate) **coarse, rough, crude, gross**

粗 あら fault, defect; bony parts (of a fish)

粗い網 あらいあみ coarse net

粗い肌 あらいはだ rough skin

粗い細工 あらいさいく rough workmanship

② **sparse, scattered**

種を粗く播く たねをあらくまく sow sparsely

043　　　あらわす

表す
Ⓚ2151

① **express, manifest (one's feelings), indicate (one's character), show (anger)**

喜びを顔に表す よろこびをかおにあらわす express one's happiness, show happiness on one's face

② (put in words) **express, convey**

言葉に表せない ことばにあらわせない inexpressible, ineffable

③ **express in symbols, represent, stand for, symbolize**

記号で表す きごうであらわす represent by signs

現す
Ⓚ0879

① **cause to appear, show, display, reveal**

姿を現す すがたをあらわす make an appearance

② **attain distinction, become famous**

名を現す なをあらわす distinguish oneself

著す
Ⓚ1993

author, write, publish

書き著す かきあらわす publish (a book)

044　　　あらわれ

表れ
Ⓚ2151

expression, manifestation, indication

現れ
Ⓚ0879

embodiment, materialization

045　　　あらわれる

表れる
Ⓚ2151

be expressed, find expression in, show, become manifest

表れ あらわれ expression, manifestation, indication

地方色の表れた小説 ちほうしょくのあらわれたしょうせつ novel with local color

現れる
Ⓚ0879

① **appear, emerge, come out, become visible, materialize**

現れ あらわれ embodiment, materialization
雲間に現れた月 くもまにあらわれた
つき moon peeping from behind
the clouds

② **become known, attain distinction;
be exposed [found out]**
悪事が現れた あくじがあらわれた
The evil deed was discovered

---

046   ある

有る
Ⓚ2576

① **be, exist, be present, there is**
有り様 ありさま condition, state of
affairs; sight
有り難う ありがとう thank you
有り難い ありがたい welcome, ap-
preciated; precious
有りの儘の ありのままの as it is, plain,
bare
有り合わせの ありあわせの available,
in [on] hand
有り触れた ありふれた common, run-
of-the-mill, trite
月にはクレーターが有る つきにはく
れーたーがある There are craters
on the moon

② **have, possess, own**
有り金 ありがね money on hand,
ready cash
彼女には子供が二人有る かのじょに
はこどもがふたりある She has two
children

③ **have the experience of doing
something**
フランスに行った事が有るか ふらん
すにいったことがあるか Have you
ever been to France?

④ (have a magnitude of) **number, cover,
weigh, measure**
あの農場は二百平方メートル有る あ
ののうじょうはにひゃくへいほう
めーとるある That farm covers 200
sq. meters

⑤ **happen, occur, take place**
事故が有った じこがあった There
was an accident
昨日会議が有った きのうかいぎが
あった The conference was held
yesterday

⑥ **consist [lie] in, depend on**
幸福は満足に有る こうふくはまんぞ
くにある Happiness consists in
contentment

⑦ [in the form of transitive verb followed
by て有る てある] **describes a state
resulting from an action**
部屋が暖めて有る へやがあたためて
ある The room is kept [has been
made] warm

在る
Ⓚ2577

① (exist in a specified place) **be at [in], be
situated in, be sited**
机の上に本が在る つくえのうえにほ
んがある There is a book on the
desk

② **be alive, live**
在りし日 ありしひ the days when one
was alive; bygone days

---

047   あわ

泡
Ⓚ0296

[sometimes also 沫] **bubble, foam**
泡立つ あわだつ bubble, foam
泡盛 あわもり millet brandy

石鹸の泡 せっけんのあわ lather, soapsuds

沫 ⓀR0301

[usu. 泡] **bubble, foam**

048　あわせる

合わせる ⓇR1740

① ⓐ (make into one) **combine, unite, join**
　　ⓑ [usu. 併せる] (bring two or more things together) **join together, combine, merge**
　組み合わせる くみあわせる combine, assort, join together, match
　合わせ技 あわせわざ *judo* combined trick
② ⓐ **juxtapose, put side by side [on top]**
　　ⓑ **make (persons) confront each other**
　背中合わせに せなかあわせに back to back
　詰め合わせ つめあわせ combination, assortment
　顔合わせ かおあわせ meeting, introduction; being matched against each other
③ **mix, compound**
　薬を合わせる くすりをあわせる compound a medicine
④ ⓐ **make fit, adjust, tune**
　　ⓑ **harmonize, match**
　ラジオを合わせる らじおをあわせる tune in the radio
　音楽に合わせて踊る おんがくにあわせておどる dance to the music
⑤ **sum [add] up**

合わせて百個 あわせてひゃっこ a hundred in total
⑥ **collate, tally with**
　照らし合わせる てらしあわせる check by comparison, collate, verify
　問い合わせ といあわせ reference, request for information
　打ち合わせ うちあわせ preliminary [previous] arrangement, preliminaries
　申し合わせる もうしあわせる make arrangement, mutually agree

併せる ⓀR0064

[sometimes also 合わせる] (bring two or more things together) **join together, combine, merge**
　併せて あわせて collectively, all together; in addition, besides
　併せ持つ あわせもつ own (something) as well
　二つの会社を併せる ふたつのかいしゃをあわせる merge two companies

会わせる ⓇR1741

have (a person) meet (another), allow (a person) to see (someone)
　社長に会わせる しゃちょうにあわせる arrange a meeting with the company president

遭わせる ⓀR2725

subject to (an unfavorable experience), expose to
　痛い目に遭わせる いたいめにあわせる make (a person) pay for (something)

049 あわれ

哀れ ⓚ1781

- ⓐ [formerly also 憐れ] **pity, sympathy**
- ⓑ **pathos**
- ⓒ **Alas! (in aesthetic sense)**

哀れな あわれな pitiable; miserable

憐れ ⓚ0692

[now usu. 哀れ] **pity, sympathy**

憐れな あわれな pitiable; miserable

050 あわれむ

哀れむ ⓚ1781

① [formerly also 憐れむ] **pity, sympa-thize, feel compassion**

哀れみ あわれみ pity, compassion

② **feel the pathos of things, appreci-ate the beauties (of nature)**

月を哀れむ つきをあわれむ enjoy the beauty of the moon

憐れむ ⓚ0692

[now usu. 哀れむ] **pity, sympathize, feel compassion**

憐れみ あわれみ pity, compassion

同病相憐れむ どうびょうあいあわれむ Fellow sufferers pity each other

051 い

猪 ⓚ0489

[in compounds] **wild boar**

猪首 いくび bull neck

亥 ⓚ1735

twelfth sign of the Oriental zodiac: the Boar—(time) 9-11 p.m., (direction) NNW, (season) October (of the lunar calendar)

亥の刻 いのこく 10 o'clock in the evening

052 いい

良い ⓚ2980

[sometimes also 好い] **colloquial form of** 良い よい

良い資料 よいしりょう valuable material

良い気味だ いいきみだ Serves you right!

良いですか いいですか Is it all right?/ You see?

天気が良くなってくれれば良いのだが てんきがよくなってくれればいいのだが I wish the weather would improve

車をお借りして良いですか くるまをおかりしていいですか May I use your car?

行っても良い いってもいい I wouldn't mind going there

好い ⓚ0184

[now usu. 良い] **colloquial form of** 好い よい

好い加減 いいかげん moderate, right; random, not thorough, vague

053 いう

言う ⓚ1698

- ①ⓐ **say, speak, talk (about)**
- ⓑ **tell, relate**

言わば いわば so to speak, in a sense; in short

言い回し いいまわし expression, manner [turn] of expression

言い方 いいかた way of speaking, expression

言い表わす いいあらわす express, say

言い換える いいかえる express in different words

言い出す いいだす begin to speak; suggest, propose

物言い ものいい manner of speaking; objection

② **state, declare, affirm**

言い分 いいぶん one's say [claim]; objection, complaint

言い渡す いいわたす announce, tell; sentence; order

言いなり いいなり doing as one is told

言い掛かり いいがかり false accusation [charge]

言い付ける いいつける tell, order

意見を言う いけんをいう state one's opinion

③ⓐ **call, name; express (in a foreign language)**

ⓑ [sometimes also 謂う] **refer to, call**—used chiefly in certain set expressions

典子と言う人 のりこというひと person called Noriko

これを音素と言う これをおんそというTo this is given the term "phoneme"

言うに言われぬ いうにいわれぬ inexpressible, indescribable

④ **sound, be heard**

ガタガタ言う音 がたがたいうおと rattling sound

謂う Ⓚ1441

[usu. 言う] **refer to, call**—used chiefly in certain set expressions

謂わば いわば as it were, so to call it

これを音素と謂う これをおんそという To this is given the term "phoneme"

ここで船とは宇宙船を謂う ここでふねとはうちゅうせんをいう By "ship" here is meant a spaceship

云う Ⓚ1692

such, such as, like, of this kind

そう云う物 そういうもの thing such as this

こう云った話 こういったはなし this kind of story

生かす Ⓚ2933

①ⓐ **let live, keep alive**

ⓑ **revive; stet**

あいつは生かして置けない あいつはいかしておけない I can't let him live

死者を生かす ししゃをいかす revive the dead

② [formerly also 活かす] **make the most of**

学問を生かす がくもんをいかす put one's learning to practical use

③ [formerly also 活かす] **put life [vividness] into, vivify**

絵を生かす えをいかす put life into a painting

活かす

Ⓚ0345

① **make the most of**

学問を活かして使う がくもんをいかしてつかう put one's knowledge to practical use

② **put life [vividness] into, vivify**

絵を活かす えをいかす put life into a painting

055　　いきる

生きる

Ⓚ2933

① ⓐ (be alive) **live, exist**

　ⓑ (make a living) **live (on), subsist**

生き いき freshness; stet

生き物 いきもの living creature

生き方 いきかた way of life, lifestyle

生き甲斐が有る いきがいがある worthwhile living

生ける屍 いけるしかばね living corpse, living dead

生き字引き いきじびき walking dictionary

長生き ながいき long life, longevity

人はパンのみにて生くるに非ず ひとはぱんのみにていくるにあらず Man does not live by bread alone

② [formerly also 活きる] **be enlivened**

生き生きと いきいきと lively, vividly

その一語で文章が生きる そのいちごでぶんしょうがいきる That single word gives life to the style

③ *baseball* **be safe**

一塁に生きる いちるいにいきる be safe on first base

活きる

Ⓚ0345

[now usu. 生きる] **be enlivened**

その一語で文章が活きる そのいちごでぶんしょうがいきる That single word gives life to the style

056　　いく

行く

Ⓚ0187

① **go, proceed, leave for; attend; visit**

行き いき(=ゆき) going

行き着く いきつく arrive at, get to

行き先 いきさき(=ゆきさき) one's destination

行き過ぎる いきすぎる go too far, go to extremes

行き過ぎ いきすぎ going too far

行き渡る ゆきわたる(=いきわたる) spread all over, pervade

行き来 いきき comings and goings, traffic

行き違い いきちがい crossing, missing each other; misunderstanding

余所行きの よそゆき(=よそいき)の formal (language); best (clothes)

② ⓐ **go [fare] (well), turn out**

　ⓑ **go well, turn out well, proceed satisfactorily**

　ⓒ *slang* **ejaculate, come**

旨く行かない うまくいかない go badly, be unsuccessful

満足が行く まんぞくがいく be satisfied

③ [following the TE-form of verbs]

　ⓐ auxiliary indicating change in progress: **turn, grow**

　ⓑ auxiliary indicating continuation of action: **go on, continue**

段段夜が明けて行った だんだんよがあけていった Night melted into day

どうにか食って行く どうにかくっていく manage to keep body and soul together

逝く ⓚ2673

depart this life, pass away, die

057　いける

生ける ⓚ2933

① [mainly in compounds] **keep alive**
　生け捕る いけどる catch [capture] alive
　生け贄 いけにえ victims, sacrifice
② [formerly also 活ける] **arrange (flowers)**
　生け花 いけばな flower arrangement

活ける ⓚ0345

[now usu. 生ける] **arrange (flowers)**
　活け花 いけばな flower arrangement

埋ける ⓚ0364

bury; bury coals in ashes

058　いさお

勲 ⓚ2500

[also 功] *elegant* **meritorious service, merit**

功 ⓚ0165

[also 勲] *elegant* **meritorious service, merit**

059　いたずら

悪戯 ⓚ2393

mischief, prank, practical joke

徒 ⓚ0377

uselessness, idleness
　徒に いたずらに in vain, uselessly, aimlessly, idly

060　いただく

頂く ⓚ0125

① [humble]
　ⓐ **receive humbly, accept with thanks, be given, be favored with**
　ⓑ **eat, drink**
　ⓒ **trouble someone to do something, have something done**
　頂き いただき windfall, unexpected gain; unauthorized borrowing
　頂けない いただけない unapprovable, unsatisfactory
　頂き物 いただきもの gift, present
　有り難く頂く ありがたくいただく accept (a thing) with thanks
　この本を頂いても良いですか このほんをいただいてもいいですか Can I have this book?
　酒も煙草も頂きます さけもたばこもいただきます I both drink and smoke
　十分頂きました じゅうぶんいただきました I have had enough
　今晩来て頂きたい こんばんきていただきたい I hope you will come this evening

お茶を入れて頂けませんか おちゃを
いれていただけませんか May I
trouble you for a cup of tea?

② **have over, be presided over by,
live under (a ruler)**

指導者として頂く しどうしゃとして
いただく have (a person) as one's
leader

彼らは女王を頂く かれらはじょうお
うをいただく They have a queen
over them

③ **wear (a crown); be crowned (with
snow)**

雪を頂いた山 ゆきをいただいたやま
snow-crowned mountain

戴く
®2815

① ⓐ **receive humbly, accept with
thanks, be given, be favored
with**
ⓑ **eat, drink**
ⓒ **trouble someone to do something, have something done**

② **have over, be presided over by,
live under (a ruler)**

③ **wear (a crown); be crowned (with
snow)**

061　　　　　いたむ

痛む
®2799

① **feel pain, hurt, ache**

痛み いたみ (physical or mental
suffering) pain, ache

痛み止め いたみどめ painkiller,
analgesic

② **be pained, be grieved at heart**

痛み入る いたみいる be greatly
obliged; be very sorry

懐が痛む ふところがいたむ suffer in
one's pocket [purse]

胸が痛む様な出来事 むねがいたむよ
うなできごと painful incident

傷む
®0137

① **be damaged, be spoiled, wear out**

傷み いたみ damage, injury, bruise;
wear; rot

傷んだ家 いたんだいえ damaged
house

② **rot, spoil**

傷んだトマト いたんだとまと rotten
tomatoes

悼む
®0443

mourn, grieve over, be grieved at

死を悼む しをいたむ mourn over the
death of

062　　　　　いためる

痛める
®2799

① **inflict pain, hurt, injure**

腹を痛める はらをいためる have a
stomachache; give birth to

心を痛める こころをいためる be
grieved at heart

② **pain, bother, worry, afflict**

痛め付ける いためつける rebuke,
taunt; give a good shaking, knock
about

傷める
®0137

damage, spoil

花を傷める はなをいためる spoil a
flower

063 いたる

至る Ⓚ1869

① [sometimes also 到る] **come to, arrive at, reach; lead (to)**

至り いたり extremity, utmost limit; result

至る処 いたるところ everywhere, all over

箱根に至る道 はこねにいたるみち road leading to Hakone

② **come to (do something), get to, result in**

信じるに至る しんじるにいたる come to believe

大事に至る だいじにいたる develop into a serious affair

到る Ⓚ1163

[usu. 至る] **arrive at, reach, come to**

目的地に到る もくてきちにいたる arrive at one's destination

064 いつわる

偽る Ⓚ0114

ⓐ (state untruthfully) **falsify, misrepresent, lie**

ⓑ [formerly also 詐る] (cause to believe a falsehood) **falsify, deceive, cheat**

ⓒ **feign, pretend**

偽り いつわり lie, falsehood, fabrication

大学生と身分を偽る だいがくせいとみぶんをいつわる misrepresent oneself as a university student

詐る Ⓚ1362

[now usu. 偽る] (cause to believe a falsehood) **falsify, deceive, cheat**

詐って金を取る いつわってかねをとる obtain money by fraud

065 いとぐち

緒 Ⓚ1260

[now usu. 糸口] **beginning, first step; clue**

緒を開く いとぐちをひらく make a beginning; find a clue

糸口 Ⓚ1866

[formerly also 緒] **beginning, first step; clue**

066 いぬ

犬 Ⓚ2912

① **dog, hound, puppy**

飼い犬 かいいぬ house dog

小犬 こいぬ little dog, puppy

② **spy**

警察の犬 けいさつのいぬ police spy

狗

① **dog (esp. of small variety)**

喪家の狗 そうかのいぬ feeling lost like a stray dog

② **spy**

警察の狗 けいさつのいぬ police spy

戌

11th sign of the Oriental zodiac: **the Dog**—(time) 7-9 p.m., (direction) WNW, (season) September (of the lunar calendar)

戌年 いぬどし Year of the Dog

戌亥(=乾) いぬい one of the four supplementary signs of the Oriental zodiac: **northwest**

067 いのり

祈り ⓀK0779

[formerly also 祷り] **prayer**

祷り ⓀK0885

[now usu. 祈り] **prayer**

068 いのる

祈る ⓀK0779

[formerly also 祷る] **pray, wish for**

祈り いのり prayer
祈り求める いのりもとめる pray for

祷る ⓀK0885

[now usu. 祈る] **pray, wish for**

祷り いのり prayer

069 いましめ

戒め ⓀK2760

① [sometimes also 警め]
  ⓐ **caution, admonition, warning**
  ⓑ **caution, guard**
  ⓒ **commandment, precept**
② **binding, bondage**

警め ⓀK2512

[usu. 戒め]
ⓐ **caution, admonition, warning**
ⓑ **caution, guard**
ⓒ **commandment, precept**

070 いましめる

戒める ⓀK2760

① [sometimes also 警める]
  ⓐ [sometimes also 誡める] **caution against, admonish, warn**
  ⓑ **take caution (against), take precautions, guard against**
  戒め いましめ caution, admonition, warning; caution, guard; commandment, precept; binding, bondage
  不心得を戒める ふこころえをいましめる caution a person against misconduct
  自ら戒める みずからいましめる take precautions, guard against
② **bind, restrict**
  後ろ手に戒める うしろでにいましめる bind a person's hands behind his back

誡める

[usu. 戒める, sometimes also 警める] **caution against, admonish, warn**

警める ⓀK2512

ⓐ [sometimes also 誡める] **caution against, admonish, warn**
ⓑ **take caution (against), take precautions, guard against**

警め いましめ caution, admonition, warning; caution, guard; commandment, precept
自ら警める みずからいましめる take precautions, guard against

071 いや

嫌な
®0583

[formerly also 厭な] **disagreeable, repulsive**

厭な

[now usu. 嫌な] **disagreeable, repulsive**

否
®2130

ⓐ **no**
ⓑ **being unwilling, wanting to say no**
否でも応でも いやでもおうでも whether one likes it or not, willy-nilly
否応無しに いやおうなしに whether one likes it or not, willy-nilly
否否 いやいや definitely [absolutely] not

072 いやしい

卑しい
®2295

① [formerly also 賤しい] (low in social status) **mean, lowly, humble, inferior in position**
卑しさ いやしさ meanness, vulgarity
卑しい生まれの いやしいうまれの lowborn
② [formerly also 賤しい]
ⓐ (of poor appearance) **mean, shabby, seedy**

ⓑ (lacking elevating human qualities) **mean, base, vulgar, despicable**
卑しい身形 いやしいみなり shabby appearance
卑しからぬ いやしからぬ decent, respectable
卑しい根性 いやしいこんじょう mean spirit
卑しい笑い いやしいわらい mean smirk
③ **greedy, gluttonous**
卑しん坊 いやしんぼう greedy person, glutton

賤しい

① (low in social status) **mean, lowly, humble, inferior in position**
賤しい稼業 いやしいかぎょう mean occupation
② ⓐ (of poor appearance) **mean, shabby, seedy**
ⓑ (lacking elevating human qualities) **mean, base, vulgar, despicable**
賤しい身形 いやしいみなり shabby appearance
賤しい笑い いやしいわらい mean smirk

073 いやしむ

卑しむ
®2295

[formerly also 賤しむ] **despise, disdain, look down on, regard with contempt**
卑しみ いやしみ contempt
卑しむべき いやしむべき despicable
労働を卑しむ ろうどうをいやしむ despise labor

賤しむ

[now usu. 卑しむ] **despise, disdain, look down on, regard with contempt**
賤しむべき いやしむべき despicable
労働を賤しむ ろうどうをいやしむ despise labor

074　　いやしめる

卑しめる
⑥2295

[formerly also 賤しめる] **same as** 卑しむ いやしむ

賤しめる

[now usu. 卑しめる] **same as** 賤しむ いやしむ

075　　いり

要り
⑥2290

[also 入り] **expense(s)**

入り
⑥2859

①ⓐ **entering**
　ⓑ **be encased, be placed in**
　出入り でいり going in and out; frequentation, usual visit (as by a merchant); indentations; incomings and outgoings; trouble, fight
　立ち入り たちいり entering
　箱入りの はこいりの cased, boxed
② (be accepted as a member) **enter, join, enroll**
　プロ入り ぷろいり turning professional
　仲間入り なかまいり joining the ranks of
③ⓐ **including, accompanied by**

ⓑ **containing, having a capacity of**
　蜂蜜入りの はちみついりの containing honey
　鳴り物入りで なりものいりで with a flourish of trumpets
　一リットル入りの瓶 いちりっとるいりのびん bottle holding a liter

076　　いる

要る
⑥2290

ⓐ **need, want, require**
ⓑ **be necessary [required]; cost, take**
　金が要る かねがいる I need [want] money/It takes money
　要り いり expense(s)

入る
⑥2859

①ⓐ **enter, go in, come in**
　ⓑ (of the sun) **set**
　入り いり setting (of the sun); attendance; beginning; income
　入り口 いりぐち entrance
　押し入る おしいる enter by force, break into
　入り日 いりひ setting sun
② **attain**
　老境に入る ろうきょうにいる be advanced in age
③ [usu. 要る]
　ⓐ **need, want, require**
　ⓑ **be necessary [required]; cost, take**
　入り いり expense(s)
　入り用 いりよう need, want

入れる　　　Ⓚ2859

①ⓐ **put in, enter, insert, fit; add to**
　ⓑ **let in, admit, show in**
　入れ替え いれかえ replacement,
　　shifting; switching
　ポケットに入れる ぽけっとにいれる
　　put (a thing) in one's pocket
②ⓐ (cause to enter) **send, deliver,**
　extend
　ⓑ (permit to enter or join) **take in,**
　admit; hire, employ
　ⓒ (put into action or use) **exercise**
　(care), exert
　申し入れる もうしいれる propose;
　　make representations to
　患者を入れる かんじゃをいれる
　　admit a patient
　手入れ ていれ care, repairs, trimming;
　　(police) raid
③ **accommodate, hold, contain**
　入れ物 いれもの receptacle, con-
　　tainer
　受け入れ うけいれ reception; accep-
　　tance
　乗り入れ のりいれ extension (of a
　　railway line) into
　取り入れる とりいれる take in;
　　harvest; accept, adopt, introduce
　押し入れ おしいれ closet; wall-
　　cupboard
④ **include, count in**
　数に入れる かずにいれる include in
　　the number
⑤ **make (tea), brew (coffee)**
⑥ [sometimes also 容れる] **accept, toler-**
　ate, be compatible
　受け入れる うけいれる accept,
　　consent to; receive, accommodate

相入れない あいいれない incompat-
　ible
聞き入れる ききいれる comply with,
　accept

容れる　　　Ⓚ1968

[usu. 入れる] **accept, tolerate, be**
compatible
　相容れない あいいれない incompat-
　ible

岩　　　Ⓚ1921

[formerly also 巌 or 磐] **rock, crag**
　岩山 いわやま rocky mountain
　岩屋 いわや [also 窟] cave, cavern,
　　hole

磐　　　Ⓚ2482

[now usu. 岩] **rock, crag**
　磐座 いわくら dwelling place of a god

巌　　　Ⓚ2804

[usu. 岩] **same as** 岩

飢える　　　Ⓚ1490

ⓐ **starve, be hungry, famish**
ⓑ **hunger [starve] for (love), thirst for**
(knowledge)
　飢え うえ hunger, starvation
　飢え死に うえじに (death by) star-
　　vation
　愛に飢える あいにうえる hunger
　　[starve] for love

餓える ®1546

ⓐ **starve, be hungry, famish**
ⓑ **hunger [starve] for (love), thirst for (knowledge)**

餓え死に うえじに (death by) starvation

080 うける

受ける ®2146

①ⓐ **receive, accept, get, take, catch**
ⓑ **accept (an offer)**
ⓒ **receive (an insult), suffer, be subjected to**
ⓓ [sometimes also 享ける] **enjoy, be granted**

受け取る うけとる receive, accept; understand
受取 うけとり receipt
受け付ける うけつける receive; accept
受付 うけつけ receipt, reception, acceptance; receptionist, information clerk; information office [desk]
受け身 うけみ passiveness; passive voice
お受けしましょう おうけしましょう I will accept it
受け入れる うけいれる accept, consent to; receive, accommodate
受け持ちの うけもちの in charge of, in one's care
引き受ける ひきうける undertake; answer for, guarantee
被害を受ける ひがいをうける be damaged
恩寵を受ける おんちょうをうける enjoy (a person's) favor

② [sometimes also 承ける] **inherit, get**

受け継ぐ うけつぐ inherit, succeed to

③ **parry (a blow), defend (in chess, etc.)**

受けを誤る うけをあやまる make a faulty defense
受け流す うけながす ward off, elude; turn aside (a joke)

④ **take, interpret**

真に受ける まにうける take seriously, believe

⑤ **appeal to the public, be popular**

受けが良い うけがよい be popular (with)
馬鹿受け ばかうけ great hit

⑥ **face, front on**

南を受ける みなみをうける face the south

⑦ **be modified**

享ける ®1765

[usu. 受ける] **enjoy, be granted**

生を享ける せいをうける be born, live
恩寵を享ける おんちょうをうける enjoy (a person's) favor

承ける ®0007

[usu. 受ける] **inherit, get**

親の気質を承ける おやのきしつをうける inherit one's parent's disposition

請ける ®1426

① **undertake, take upon oneself**

請け合う うけあう assure, guarantee; undertake
請け負う うけおう contract for, undertake
下請け したうけ subcontract

② **redeem (pawned goods), ransom**
請け出す うけだす redeem, pay off, take out of pawn

081 うし

牛 Ⓚ2903

[also suffix] **cattle, cow, bull, ox**
小牛 こうし calf
去勢牛 きょせいうし bullock

丑 Ⓚ2889

second sign of the Oriental zodiac: **the Ox**—(time) 1-3 a.m., (direction) NNE, (season) December (of the lunar calendar)
丑の刻 うしのこく two o'clock in the morning
丑の年 うしのとし Year of the Ox
丑三つ時 うしみつどき in the dead of night
丑寅 うしとら [also 艮] one of the four supplementary signs of the Oriental zodiac: **northeast**

082 うす

臼 Ⓚ2957

[sometimes also 碓] **mortar; hand mill**
石臼 いしうす stone mortar [mill]
碾き臼 ひきうす hand mill, quern
茶臼 ちゃうす tea-grinding mill

碓 Ⓚ1109

[usu. 臼] **mortar; trip-hammer mill**
碓氷峠 うすいとうげ Usui Pass

083 うた

歌 Ⓚ1621

① [sometimes also 唄] **song, ballad**
歌声 うたごえ singing (voice)
歌合戦 うたがっせん singing matches
替え歌 かえうた parody on a song
子守歌 こもりうた lullaby
② **Japanese poem, waka, tanka, ode, verse**
歌詠み うたよみ tanka composer
召し歌 めしうた tanka dedicated to the emperor in response to His Majesty's public invitation

唄 Ⓚ0358

[usu. 歌] [also suffix] **ditty, song, ballad**—used esp. in reference to traditional Japanese songs
小唄 こうた ditty, ballad
子守唄 こもりうた lullaby
鼻唄 はなうた humming

084 うたう

歌う Ⓚ1621

① [sometimes also 唄う] **sing, recite**
歌い手 うたいて singer
歌い上げる うたいあげる sing at the top of one's voice; express one's feelings fully in a poem
② **express in a poem**
神の徳を歌った歌 かみのとくをうたったうた poem in praise of God

謡う Ⓚ1445

recite, chant (esp. from a noh drama text)

謡を謡う うたいをうたう recite an *utai*

唄う
Ⓚ0358

[usu. 歌う] **recite, sing**—used esp. in reference to traditional Japanese songs

謳う

ⓐ (sing the joys of) **extol, eulogize**
ⓑ **declare, state, express**
謳われる うたわれる be famous for
謳い文句 うたいもんく catchphrase, promotional line

085　　　　　うち

内
Ⓚ2914

① [sometimes also 中] [also prefix and suffix] **inside, interior**
内側 うちがわ inside, interior
内幕 うちまく inside facts, inner workings; [original meaning] inner curtain
内訳 うちわけ items (of an account), details, breakdown
内ポケット うちぽけっと inside pocket
内気な うちきな shy, bashful
仲間内の なかまうちの private, informal, among one's people [group]
② [sometimes also 中] **within (a given period), in the course of, while, during**
一週間の内に いっしゅうかんのうちに within a week
若い内 わかいうち while young
その内 そのうち before long, one of these days, sooner or later; in the meantime

③ [sometimes also 中] **among, between**
両者の内 りょうしゃのうち between the two
④ [also 家]
　ⓐ **house, one's home**
　ⓑ **one's family, household**
内を建てる うちをたてる build one's house
内の人 うちのひと my husband; one's family
内中 うちじゅう whole family; all over the house
内弟子 うちでし pupil boarding in his master's home, apprentice
⑤ (group or organization one belongs to) **we; ourselves; our group, our company**
内の会社 うちのかいしゃ our company
内内で うちうちで among ourselves
身内 みうち relations, relative

中
Ⓚ2902

① **inside, interior**
心の中で こころのうちで in one's mind
② **within (a given period), in the course of, while, during**
一週間の中に いっしゅうかんのうちに within a week
③ **among, between**
両者の中 りょうしゃのうち between the two

家
Ⓚ1963

ⓐ **house, one's home**
ⓑ **one's family, household**
家を建てる うちをたてる build one's house

うち

家の人 うちのひと my husband; one's family

打つ ®0170

① ⓐ **strike, hit, beat, give a blow, thrash**
　ⓑ (of a clock) **strike (the hour)**
　ⓒ (impress upon) **strike, move, impress**
　打ち込む うちこむ strike [drive] into, ram down; devote oneself to, be absorbed in
　打ち上げる うちあげる launch, shoot up; (of waves) dash, wash up [ashore]; finish, close
　鞭打つ むちうつ whip, lash, give the rod; spur on
　三時を打つ さんじをうつ strike three
　心を打つ こころをうつ impress (a person), touch (a person's) heart
② perform an action by striking, as:
　ⓐ **drive in (a nail), affix**
　ⓑ **cut off (a person's head)**
　ⓒ **water, sprinkle**
　ⓓ **play (as a game of go)**
　ⓔ **till (the soil)**
　ⓕ **make something by striking**
　銘打つ めいうつ engrave an inscription; call [designate] itself
　打ち首 うちくび decapitation, beheading
　打ち水 うちみず watering, sprinkling
　碁を打つ ごをうつ play (a game of) go
　田を打つ たをうつ till [plow] a rice paddy
　刀を打つ かたなをうつ temper [forge] a sword
③ perform an action (as if by striking), as:

　ⓐ **send (a telegram)**
　ⓑ **pay (money on a contract)**
　ⓒ **perform, run**
　電報を打つ でんぽうをうつ send a telegram
　手付けを打つ てつけをうつ advance money (on a contract)
　芝居を打つ しばいをうつ give [present] a play; play a trick, put up a false show
　仕打ち しうち (unfavorable) treatment, (cool) attitude
　投げ打つ なげうつ [also 抛つ] fling away, abandon
④ [usu. 撃つ, sometimes also 討つ] **attack, strike, assault**
　不意を打つ ふいをうつ make a surprise attack, take (a person) unawares
　挟み打ち はさみうち attack on both sides [flanks], pincer attack
　追い打ち おいうち attacking the routed enemy, pursuit

撃つ ®2492

① **fire, shoot, discharge**
　撃ち落とす うちおとす shoot down
　早撃ち はやうち quick [snap] shooting; quick [snap] shot [draw]
② [sometimes also 打つ or 討つ] **attack, strike, assault**
　撃ち破る うちやぶる defeat, crush
　迎え撃つ むかえうつ fight the attack of an enemy

討つ ®1324

① **kill (with a sword or spear)**
　敵討ち かたきうち vendetta, revenge

②ⓐ **suppress by armed force, put down [attack] the enemy, send a punitive expedition**
ⓑ [usu. 撃つ, sometimes also 打つ] **attack, strike, assault**
敵を討つ てきをうつ quell the enemy
討ち入る うちいる break into (a house to kill the master), raid
手討ち てうち capital punishment given personally by a feudal lord
不意討ち ふいうち surprise attack
夜討ち ようち night attack

087　　うつす

写す　　　　　　　　Ⓚ1726

① **copy, make a copy, transcribe, reproduce, imitate**
写し うつし copy, transcript, duplicate, imitation
生き写し いきうつし close resemblance
② **portray, picture, depict, describe, express**
山水を写した絵 さんすいをうつしたえ picture representing a landscape
③ **take a picture, photograph, shoot**
写真を写す しゃしんをうつす take a picture, photograph

映す　　　　　　　　Ⓚ0793

① **reflect, mirror**
鏡に自分の姿を映す かがみにじぶんのすがたをうつす reflect oneself in a mirror
② **project (a motion picture)**
映画をスクリーンに映す えいがをすくりーんにうつす project a motion picture on a screen

障子に影を映す しょうじにかげをうつす project a shadow on a *shoji* (paper sliding door)

移す　　　　　　　　Ⓚ1087

①ⓐ **shift, move, transfer**
ⓑ **transfuse (liquids or colors)**
ⓒ **divert, turn, direct**
移し替える うつしかえる shift [move] (an object) to [into]
都会に移す とかいにうつす move (an object or person) to the city
口移し くちうつし mouth-to-mouth feeding; conveying by word of mouth
計画を実行に移す けいかくをじっこうにうつす carry a plan into practice
② **transmit (a disease)**
風邪を移す かぜをうつす give [transmit] a cold (to someone)

088　　うつり

映り　　　　　　　　Ⓚ0793

①ⓐ **reflection**
ⓑ **quality of a picture [film]**
② **match, harmony**

写り　　　　　　　　Ⓚ1726

print, impression

移り　　　　　　　　Ⓚ1087

① **change, transition**
② **return present**

089　うつる

写る　Ⓚ1726

① (of pictures) **be taken, come out**
写り うつり print, impression
この写真に写っている人 このしゃしんにうつっているひと the man in this photograph

② **be seen through**
透けて写る すけてうつる be seen through

③ **appear upon, be impressed upon (a surface in the original form)**
紙の裏に写った字 かみのうらにうつったじ letter imprinted from the next page (by chance)

映る　Ⓚ0793

① ⓐ **be reflected, be imaged, be mirrored**
ⓑ **be projected, be on (TV)**
映り うつり reflection; quality of a picture [film]; match, harmony
鏡に映る かがみにうつる be reflected in a mirror

② **match, suit, be becoming**
この色は良く映る このいろはよくうつる The colors match well

移る　Ⓚ1087

① **move (to a new house)**
移り うつり change, transition; return present
東京に移る とうきょうにうつる move to Tokyo

② **shift, change, pass**
移り変わり うつりかわり change, transition

③ **be infected with; be contagious**
燃え移る もえうつる (of fire) spread, extend itself
下痢が移った げりがうつった be infected with diarrhea

④ (of odors) **soak in**
移り香 うつりが lingering [absorbed] scent

090　うば

姥　Ⓚ0314

① **old woman**
姥捨て うばすて practice of abandoning old women
姥桜 うばざくら woman past her prime who is still attractive; cherry trees that blossom before putting forth leaves
姥貝 うばがい Sakhalin surf clam
山姥 やまんば(=やまうば) mountain witch

② **noh mask of an old woman**

姆

[now always 乳母] **wet nurse**

091　うま

馬　Ⓚ2809

① ⓐ **horse, pony**
ⓑ **vaulting horse**
馬が合う うまがあう get on well (with a person)
馬屋 うまや [also 厩] horse stable, horse barn
勝馬 かちうま winning horse
竹馬 たけうま(=ちくば) stilts

② (name of chess piece in shogi) (Japanese chess) *keima*, **knight**

桂馬 けいま *keima*, knight

③ **stepping ladder**

④ **person who accompanies a reveler home to collect payment**

付け馬 つけうま person who accompanies a reveler home to collect payment

午
®1720

seventh sign of the Oriental zodiac: **the Horse**—(time) 11 a.m.-1 p.m., (direction) south, (season) May (of the lunar calendar)

092　　うまい

旨い
®1744

① [also 甘い] **delicious, tasty; sweet**

旨い料理 うまいりょうり tasty dish

② **successful, satisfactory; profitable**

旨い仕事 うまいしごと profitable business

③ [also 巧い or 上手い] **skillful, clever; splendid, excellent**

旨く うまく skillfully, cleverly; successfully; luckily

旨い絵 うまいえ excellent picture [painting]

英語が旨い えいごがうまい speak English well

甘い
®2930

[also 旨い] **delicious, tasty; sweet**

甘さ うまさ deliciousness, relish

甘い料理 うまいりょうり tasty dish

巧い
®0166

[also 上手い or 旨い] **skillful, clever; splendid, excellent**

巧さ うまさ skillfulness, ingenuity

巧い絵 うまいえ excellent picture [painting]

英語が巧い えいごがうまい speak English well

上手い
®2876

[also 巧い or 旨い] **skillful, clever; splendid, excellent**

093　　うまれる

産まれる
®2812

(undergo the physical act of birth) **be born**

男の子が産まれた おとこのこがうまれた A boy was born

赤ん坊が産まれた あかんぼうがうまれた The baby was born

生まれる
®2933

ⓐ (of persons) (come into being) **be born, come into existence**

ⓑ (of things in general) **appear, see the light, be a result (of)**

彼はアメリカで生まれた かれはあめりかでうまれた He was born in America

生まれ付き うまれつき one's nature; by nature

生まれて初めて うまれてはじめて for the first time in one's life

生まれ乍らの詩人 うまれながらのしじん born poet

貧乏に生まれる びんぼうにうまれる be born poor

持って生まれた もってうまれた natural, inborn, innate

同情から愛が生まれた どうじょうからあいがうまれた Sympathy engendered love

★ 産まれる is used in the narrow sense of being born, referring to the physical act of birth. 生まれる is used in the broader sense of a person coming into the world.

094　うみ

産み　Ⓚ2812

(physical) **birth**

生み　Ⓚ2933

production, bringing into the world

095　うむ

産む　Ⓚ2812

(produce offspring) **give birth to, bear offspring, beget, breed; spawn**

彼女は子供を五人産んだ かのじょはこどもをごにんうんだ She gave birth to five children

産み うみ (physical) birth

産み出す うみだす begin to give birth to

産み月 うみづき last month of pregnancy

生む　Ⓚ2933

① **have children**

彼女は子供を五人生んだ かのじょはこどもをごにんうんだ She has five children

生み うみ production, bringing into the world

生みの親 うみのおや one's real parent; creator

② **produce, bring forth, give rise to, yield**

生み出す うみだす bring forth, produce, yield

★ These verbs share the meaning of giving birth. 産む, the more common form, refers to the physical act of bearing offspring, while 生む is used in the more abstract sense of having children. The principal use of 生む is in the sense of producing or giving rise to.

096　うらない

占い　Ⓚ1729

[formerly also 卜] **divination, fortune-telling**

卜　Ⓚ2856

[now usu. 占い] **divination, fortunetelling**

097　うらなう

占う　Ⓚ1729

[formerly also 卜う] **divine, tell (a person's) fortune, augur**

占い うらない divination, fortunetelling

占い師 うらないし diviner, fortuneteller

星占い ほしうらない astrology

トう
Ⓚ2856

[now usu. 占う] **divine, tell (a person's) fortune, augur**

098　うらみ

恨み
Ⓚ0328

[formerly also 怨み] **grudge, hatred, malice**

怨み
Ⓚ2227

[now usu. 恨み] **grudge, hatred, malice**

憾み
Ⓚ0690

regret, matter for regret

099　うらむ

恨む
Ⓚ0328

ⓐ [formerly also 怨む] **hold a grudge, feel resentment, feel bitter against**
ⓑ **blame, reproach**

恨み うらみ grudge, hatred, malice
逆恨み さかうらみ unjustified resentment through misunderstanding
恨み言 うらみごと grudge; reproach
我が身を恨む わがみをうらむ blame oneself

怨む
Ⓚ2227

[now usu. 恨む] **hold a grudge, feel resentment, feel bitter against**

怨み うらみ grudge, hatred, malice
怨み言 うらみごと grudge, reproach
人を怨むより身を怨め ひとをうらむよりみをうらめ Everyone is the son of his own works

憾む
Ⓚ0690

be sorry for, regret

憾み うらみ regret, matter for regret
それは片手落ちの憾みが有る それはかたておちのうらみがある I'm sorry to say so, but it may not be quite fair

100　うらめしい

恨めしい
Ⓚ0328

ⓐ [formerly also 怨めしい] **resentful, reproachful, indignant**
ⓑ **regrettable**

恨めし気に うらめしげに reproachfully
彼が金を貸してくれないのが恨めしかった かれがかねをかしてくれないのがうらめしかった I thought it cruelly unkind of him not to lend me money

怨めしい
Ⓚ2227

[now usu. 恨めしい] **resentful, reproachful, indignant**

怨めしや うらめしや You shall feel my wrath!

101　うれい

憂い
Ⓚ1842

anxiety, trouble, worry; danger

後顧の憂い こうこのうれい anxiety about the future

愁い
Ⓚ2463

melancholy, grief, sorrow, sadness

愁い顔 うれいがお sad face

102 うれえる

憂える ⓚ1842

be anxious, fear, be apprehensive
国の将来を憂える くにのしょうらい
をうれえる be anxious about the
future of one's country

愁える ⓚ2463

grieve, lament, feel sorrow
友の死を愁える とものしをうれえる
grieve for the death of a friend

103 え

絵 ⓚ1233

ⓐ [sometimes also 画] **picture, painting,
drawing, sketch, illustration, cut,
(woodcut) print**
ⓑ [usu. 画] **television field**

画 ⓚ2586

ⓐ [usu. 絵] [also suffix] **picture, painting,
drawing, sketch, illustration, cut,
(woodcut) print**
ⓑ [sometimes also 絵] **television field**
本に画を入れる ほんにえをいれる
illustrate a book with pictures
似顔画 にがおえ likeness, portrait

104 えがく

描く ⓚ0445

① [sometimes also 画く] (represent in a
picture) **depict, draw, paint**
油絵を描く あぶらえをえがく paint
in oil
② (represent in words) **depict, describe**

描き出す えがきだす delineate,
depict, portray
思い描く おもいえがく imagine,
figure, see

画く ⓚ2586

[usu. 描く] **draw, paint**
油絵を画く あぶらえをえがく paint
in oil

105 えらい

偉い ⓚ0128

①ⓐ **great, grand; famous, eminent**
ⓑ [sometimes also 豪い] **remarkable,
extraordinary**
偉さ えらさ greatness; remarkableness
偉い人 えらいひと great man, extraordinary character
偉がる えらがる be self-important, be
conceited
お偉方 おえらがた dignitary, exalted
personalities
偉物 えらぶつ extraordinary [able]
character
② [sometimes also 豪い] **awful, serious**
ど偉い どえらい terrible, very serious

豪い ⓚ1838

① **remarkable, extraordinary**
豪さ えらさ remarkableness
豪物 えらぶつ extraordinary [able]
character
② **awful, serious**
ど豪い どえらい terrible, very serious

選ぶ Ⓚ2734

①ⓐ **choose, prefer, select**
　ⓑ **elect**
　選び出す えらびだす select, pick out
　上手に選ぶ じょうずにえらぶ make a
　　good choice
　選ばれる えらばれる be chosen; be
　　elected
②[usu. 撰ぶ] **compile, edit**

撰ぶ Ⓚ0672

[sometimes also 選ぶ] **compile, edit**

襟 Ⓚ1156

ⓐ **collar, lapel, neck**
ⓑ **nape**
　襟巻き えりまき scarf, muffler
　襟を正す えりをただす straighten
　　oneself
　詰め襟 つめえり stand-up collar
　襟首 えりくび neck, back of neck

衿 Ⓚ1055

ⓐ [original meaning] **collar, lapel, neck**
ⓑ **nape**
　衿裏 えりうら lining of the collar
　半衿 はんえり neckpiece (on a
　　kimono)

得る Ⓚ0435

①[sometimes also 獲る] **acquire, get,
gain, obtain, win**
　得難い えがたい hard to get, rare
　見得 みえ [sometimes also 見え] pose,
　　posture
　勝ち得る かちえる achieve, win, gain
　心得る こころえる know, understand,
　　give consent
②**can, be able to**
　止むを得ない やむをえない unavoid-
　　able, cannot be helped
　...せざるを得ない …せざるをえな
　　い cannot help (doing)

獲る Ⓚ0699

① **catch game, hunt, fish**
　獲物 えもの game, spoils, catch,
　　capture; good luck, prize
②[usu. 得る] **acquire, get, gain, obtain, win**
　地位を獲る ちいをえる acquire a
　　position

雄- Ⓚ0920

ⓐ (of plants) **male**
ⓑ **manly, masculine**
ⓒ [sometimes also 牡-] (of animals) **male**
ⓓ [also 男] **the larger or stronger of
two**
　雄花 おばな male flower
　雄雄しい おおしい manly, brave,
　　heroic
　雄牛 おうし bull, steer

雄滝 おだき the greater waterfall (of the two)

牡-   Ⓚ0743

[usu. 雄] (of animals) **male**

牡牛 おうし bull, steer
牡羊座 おひつじざ Aries, the Ram (constellation)

男   Ⓚ2199

① *elegant* **man, male**
男の子 おのこ man

② [in compounds] **the larger or stronger of two**
男滝(=雄滝) おだき the greater waterfall (of the two)
益荒男(=丈夫) ますらお manly [brave] man

110   **お²**

御-   Ⓚ0529

① ⓐ **general honorific prefix for conveying respect or politeness**
ⓑ **general honorific prefix for conveying humility**
御顔 おかお your (honorable) face
御日様 おひさま sun
御美しい事 おうつくしいこと How nice!
御玉 おたま ladle; egg
御会い出来て嬉しゅう御座います おあいできてうれしゅうございます I'm delighted to have the honor of seeing you

② [also 阿-] **prefix for conveying intimacy, esp. before names of women**
御花さん おはなさん Ohana

阿-   Ⓚ0305

[also 御-] **prefix for conveying intimacy, esp. before names of women**
阿父様 おとうさま Father
阿国 おくに Okuni (female name)

111   **おいて**

措いて   Ⓚ0463

except, no other

於て   Ⓚ0755

① **at, in, on**—in reference to time or place
東京に於て とうきょうにおいて in Tokyo

② **as for, on one's part**
その点に於て そのてんにおいて on that point, in that respect

112   **おおう**

覆う   Ⓚ2376

ⓐ **cover, veil**
ⓑ **hide, conceal, screen**
ⓒ **enfold, envelop**
覆い おおい cover, mantle
顔を覆う かおをおおう cover one's face
事実を覆う じじつをおおう disguise a fact
日覆い ひおおい sunscreen
霧に覆われる きりにおおわれる be enveloped in mist

被う   Ⓚ1077

[usu. 覆う] **cover, veil**
被い おおい cover, mantle

雪で被われる ゆきでおおわれる be covered with snow

蓋う   Ⓚ2040

- ⓐ **cover, veil**
- ⓑ **hide, conceal, screen**
- ⓒ **enfold, envelop**

　空を蓋う そらをおおう cover up the sky

蔽う   Ⓚ2084

[now usu. 覆う] **screen, shield, hide**

　蔽い おおい cover, covering
　事実を蔽う じじつをおおう disguise a fact

掩う

- ⓐ **cover, veil**
- ⓑ **hide, conceal, screen**

　棺を掩う かんをおおう cover the coffin
　顔を掩う かおをおおう cover one's face

鳳   Ⓚ2601

① [also 大鳥 or 鴻] **large wild bird such as a crane or white stork**
② [also 大鳥 or 鵬] **huge bird such as a mythical Chinese phoenix**

鵬   Ⓚ1021

[also 大鳥 or 鳳] **huge bird such as a mythical Chinese phoenix**

鴻   Ⓚ0710

[also 大鳥 or 鳳] **large wild bird such as a crane or white stork**

丘   Ⓚ2931

[sometimes also 岡] **hill, hillock, mound**

　丘辺 おかべ vicinity of a hill

岡   Ⓚ2584

① [usu. 丘] **hill, hillock, mound**—used chiefly in proper names

　岡山県 おかやまけん Okayama Prefecture
　岡野 おかの surname
　静岡県 しずおかけん Shizuoka Prefecture
　福岡県 ふくおかけん Fukuoka Prefecture

② [sometimes also 傍-] [in compounds] **outsider, third party, bystander**

　岡っ引き おかっぴき detective, secret policeman (in Edo Japan)
　岡惚れ おかぼれ illicit love

陸   Ⓚ0496

land, shore

　陸釣り おかづり angling from the shore
　陸稲 おかぼ(=りくとう) rice grown in a dry field

傍-   Ⓚ0127

[usu. 岡] **outsider, third party, bystander**

傍目八目 おかめはちもく Onlookers can see [read] the game far better than the players themselves

★ 丘 and 岡 have the same meaning. The former is used in both common nouns and place names, while the latter is used chiefly in the writing of proper names.

115 おかす

侵す Ⓚ0085

ⓐ (enter by force) **invade, raid**
ⓑ (intrude upon) **invade, infringe on, violate**
国境を侵す こっきょうをおかす invade the frontier district, violate the border
権利を侵す けんりをおかす infringe upon someone's right

犯す Ⓚ0175

① **offend against, violate, infringe upon, commit (a crime), sin against**
犯し難い おかしがたい dignified
法を犯す ほうをおかす violate the law
罪を犯す つみをおかす commit a crime
② **rape, violate, deflower**
女を犯す おんなをおかす rape a girl

冒す Ⓚ2155

①ⓐ **risk, brave, defy**
ⓑ (risk the danger of using a great person's name) **assume (another's name); bear**

危険を冒す きけんをおかす brave [defy] a danger
源の姓を冒す みなもとのせいをおかす assume the clan name of Minamoto
② **affect, attack, afflict**
病に冒される やまいにおかされる be attacked by a disease

116 おく

置く Ⓚ2262

①ⓐ **put, place, set**
ⓑ **assign; post, station**
置き場 おきば storehouse, place to put something in [on]
置き時計 おきどけい table clock
置き換える おきかえる replace, rearrange, interchange
置き物 おきもの ornament
歩哨を置く ほしょうをおく post a sentinel
②ⓐ **leave, leave behind, leave with**
ⓑ **leave (undone), let (alone)**
ⓒ **leave (a day or space) open**
置き忘れる おきわすれる leave behind, forget
書き置き かきおき note [letter] left behind
据え置く すえおく leave as it is; defer (payment)
一軒置いて隣 いっけんおいてとなり next door but one
③ [following the TE-form of verbs] (perform an action and leave it in the state of having been done) **do beforehand, do anyhow**
調べて置く しらべておく examine beforehand

一応聞いて置く いちおうきいておく
hear someone out anyway

④ **establish, set up, organize**
委員会を置く いいんかいをおく form
a committee

⑤ **engage, employ; lodge, keep**
下宿人を置く げしゅくにんをおく
keep boarders

⑥ (of frost or dew) **be formed**
霜を置いた しもをおいた frosted;
gray, hoary

措く ⓀⓀ0463

① **desist from, discontinue**
賞賛して措かない しょうさんしておか
ない extol, applaud highly

② **except, set apart, lay aside**
措いて おいて except, no other
ここを措いて道は無い ここをおい
てみちはない There is no other
alternative

擱く

lay down (one's pen)
筆を擱く ふでをおく lay down one's
pen, stop writing

送る Ⓚ2664

① **send, ship, dispatch, mail; transmit**
送り先 おくりさき destination; receiv-
er, consignee
送り込む おくりこむ send into
申し送る もうしおくる send word
to, hand over (one's business to
another)

②ⓐ **see off, send off**

ⓑ **escort, take a person (home)**
送り おくり seeing off; funeral; send-
ing
見送る みおくる see off
送り届ける おくりとどける send to,
deliver; escort (a person) home

③ **spend (time), lead (one's life)**
空しく日を送る むなしくひをおくる
spend days in vain

④ **add kana affixes to Chinese characters**
送り仮名 おくりがな *okurigana*, kana
affixes

贈る Ⓚ1472

① **present (a gift), give (a present)**
贈り物 おくりもの present, gift
花を贈る はなをおくる give flowers
as a gift

② **bestow on, confer upon**
死後に位を贈る しごにくらいをおくる
confer a posthumous rank

後れ Ⓚ0321

① **backwardness, lag**
② **failure, defeat**

遅れ Ⓚ2700

ⓐ **being late**
ⓑ (of clocks) **going slow**

後れる Ⓚ0321

ⓐ **fall behind, fall back, be out-
stripped, be backwards**

ⓑ **outlive**

後れ **おくれ** backwardness, lag; failure, defeat

後れを取る **おくれをとる** be beaten, be defeated

後れ毛 **おくれげ** straggling hair

手後れ **ておくれ** being too late

死に後れる **しにおくれる** outlive, survive

遅れる ⓚ2700

ⓐ **be late, be tardy, be delayed**
ⓑ (of clocks) **go slow, lose**

遅れ **おくれ** being late; (of clocks) going slow

遅れ馳せの **おくればせの** belated, eleventh-hour

知恵遅れ **ちえおくれ** mental retardation

乗り遅れる **のりおくれる** miss [fail to catch] (a train)

---

120 おこす

起こす ⓚ2818

① **raise up, set upright**

抱き起こす **だきおこす** lift (a person) in one's arms, help (a person) sit up

② **wake up, awake, arouse**

揺り起こす **ゆりおこす** shake up, wake by shaking

③ **give rise to, bring about, raise**

引き起こす **ひきおこす** bring about, cause, provoke; pull up

④ⓐ **start, begin, launch, inaugurate**
ⓑ **establish, set up**

書き起こす **かきおこす** begin [start] writing

会社を起こす **かいしゃをおこす** set up a company

⑤ (of heat or electricity) **produce, generate**

水力で電気を起こす **すいりょくででんきをおこす** generate electricity by hydraulic power

⑥ **plow**

畑を起こす **はたけをおこす** plow a field

興す ⓚ2525

cause to rise (to prosperity), promote, further, advance, develop

工業を興す **こうぎょうをおこす** promote industry

廃れた家を興す **すたれたいえをおこす** restore a family to its former prosperity

---

121 おこる

起こる ⓚ2818

① **happen, occur, take place**

沸き起こる **わきおこる** arise

② [also 興る] (come into existence) **rise, spring up, be established**

新たに起こった国 **あらたにおこったくに** newly established country

③ **arise from, originate in, result from**

起こり **おこり** origin, source, beginning; cause, genesis

不眠から起こる疲労 **ふみんからおこるひろう** fatigue resulting from insomnia

④ (of heat or electricity) **be generated, be produced**

摩擦で起こった熱 **まさつでおこったねつ** heat generated from friction

⑤ (of diseases) **develop, have an attack of**

喘息が起こる ぜんそくがおこる have an attack of asthma

⑥ **be kindled**

赤赤と起こった火 あかあかとおこった ひ blazing fire

興る ®2525

① **rise to prosperity, prosper, thrive, flourish**

国が興る くにがおこる The country prospers

② [also 起こる] (come into existence) **rise, spring up, be established**

新しい産業が興った あたらしいさんぎょうがおこった A new industry has sprung up

122	おさえ

押さえ ®0278

① **weight, paperweight**
② **rear guard**

抑え ®0229

ⓐ **check, defense, suppression**
ⓑ **control**

123	おさえる

押さえる ®0278

① **press down, hold down, force down**

押さえ おさえ weight, paperweight; rear guard

押さえ込む おさえこむ immobilize, pin down

② **stop up, cover**

耳を押さえる みみをおさえる hold one's ears

③ⓐ **seize (goods), distrain, levy distress on**

ⓑ **seize, secure**

差し押さえ さしおさえ attachment, seizure, distraint

証拠を押さえる しょうこをおさえる seize [secure] evidence

抑える ®0229

①ⓐ (hold down) **suppress, repress, restrain, control, hold down; check, curb, stop; keep back, withhold**

ⓑ (put down forcibly) **suppress, subdue, bring under control**

抑え おさえ check, defense, suppression; control

抑え難い おさえがたい irrepressible, uncontrollable

反乱を抑える はんらんをおさえる stifle a rebellion

② **catch, arrest**

警官に抑えられる けいかんにおさえられる be caught by a policeman

124	おさまる

納まる ®1195

①ⓐ **be paid**

ⓑ **be delivered**

国庫に納まった金 こっこにおさまったかね money paid to the (National) Treasury

品物が納まった しなものがおさまった Commodities have been delivered

② ⓐ **be placed (in a position or post), be installed**

　 ⓑ **stay (in the stomach)**

　 学長に納まる がくちょうにおさまる take one's position as rector

　 食べ物が胃に納まらない たべものがいにおさまらない No food I eat stays in my stomach

③ **be satisfied**

　 納まらない おさまらない be unsatisfied, feel grieved

収まる　　　　　　Ⓚ0016

① **be put (back) in place, be restored**

　 箱に収まる はこにおさまる be stored in a box

② ⓐ **be settled, be brought to a settlement**

　 ⓑ **calm down (as of the wind)**

　 収まり おさまり conclusion, end, settlement

　 争いが収まる あらそいがおさまる be settled

　 台風が収まった たいふうがおさまった The typhoon spent itself out

治まる　　　　　　Ⓚ0297

① **be in peace, be governed well**

　 国が治まる くにがおさまる Peace reigns in the country

② **be cured, be relieved (of pain)**

　 痛みが治まる いたみがおさまる A pain is cured

修まる　　　　　　Ⓚ0105

govern oneself, conduct oneself well

　 素行が修まらない そこうがおさまらない conduct oneself loosely, be dissolute

納める　　　　　　Ⓚ1195

① hand over payment or goods:

　 ⓐ **pay to the authorities, make payment**

　 ⓑ **deliver to a customer, supply goods**

　 月謝を納める げっしゃをおさめる pay a school fee

　 品物を納める しなものをおさめる deliver goods

② **offer (as to a god), dedicate, present**

　 絵馬を納める えまをおさめる offer a votive picture (of a horse) to a shrine

③ ⓐ **put away, store, consign**

　 ⓑ [also 収める] **put (back) in place, replace**

　 倉庫に納める そうこにおさめる store in a warehouse

　 元の所に納める もとのところにおさめる put (a thing) back in its place

④ [also 収める] **accept**

　 どうぞお納め下さい どうぞおおさめください Please accept it

収める　　　　　　Ⓚ0016

① ⓐ **gain, obtain, reap**

　 ⓑ **achieve, attain**

　 勝利を収める しょうりをおさめる win, gain a victory

　 成果を収める せいかをおさめる achieve success

② **collect materials and record [write down]**

　 情報を収めた本 じょうほうをおさめたほん book containing the information

③ [also 納める] **put (back) in place, replace**

元の所へ収める もとのところへおさめる put (a thing) back in its place

④ [also 納める] **accept**

どうぞお収め下さい どうぞおおさめください Please accept it

治める ⓚ0297

ⓐ **govern, rule over, reign over, manage**

ⓑ **bring under control, put down, suppress, pacify, quell**

国を治める くにをおさめる govern a country, manage a state

暴動を治める ぼうどうをおさめる quell a disturbance

修める ⓚ0105

① **cultivate, pursue, practice, study; master, complete**

学を修める がくをおさめる pursue knowledge [one's studies]

② **order (one's life)**

身を修める みをおさめる order one's life

126 おし

押し ⓚ0278

① **push (oneself or others) to perform an action**

押し付ける おしつける press against; force, compel

押し通す おしとおす push through, carry it through, hold out to the end

押し切る おしきる have one's own way, push one's way through

押し掛ける おしかける force oneself upon (a person), go uninvited

② **emphatic verbal prefix**

押し並べて おしなべて generally

押し隠す おしかくす conceal, cover up

押し黙る おしだまる keep silent, clam up

押し寄せる おしよせる advance on, rush for, push to one side

圧し ⓚ2563

① **pressing down**

② **weight**

③ **authority, commanding presence**

127 おす¹

押す ⓚ0278

① ⓐ (force to move) **push, press, thrust, shove**

ⓑ [formerly also 圧す] **press down, press; compress, squash**

押し おし pushing, push; self-confidence, impudence; fall (in prices)

押す PUSH (marking on doors)

押し上げる おしあげる push up, boost

押し返す おしかえす push back, force back

押し釦 おしぼたん push-button

押し屋 おしや commuter train packer

押しも押されもせぬ おしもおされもせぬ of established reputation

後押し あとおし pushing; support, backing

押し潰す おしつぶす squash, crush, flatten

② (force to act) **push [force] oneself; push a person (to do something)**

押して おして forcibly, by compulsion; importunately

押し売り おしうり coercive touting, importunate peddling [peddler]

押し問答 おしもんどう bandying words, haggling, argument

中押し ちゅうおし one-sided game, victory by a wide margin (in go)

病気を押して行く びょうきをおしていく go in spite of illness

③ [sometimes also 捺す] **fix a seal, stamp**

スタンプを押す すたんぷをおす stamp

④ **overwhelm, have an edge over**

⑤ **perform an action though it is not necessary, make doubly sure**

念を押す ねんをおす call attention to, make sure of, emphasize

駄目を押す だめをおす make sure

⑥ **put (gold) leaf over, gild**

手押し ておし hand gilding

⑦ (of prices) **sag, drop, fall**

押し目 おしめ weakness, relapse, scale-down

推す ⓚ0465

① **infer, deduce, conjecture, surmise, guess**

推して おして by conjecture [deduction]

推し量る おしはかる conjecture, surmise, guess

② **recommend, propose, nominate**

会長に推す かいちょうにおす recommend (a person) for the post of president

圧す ⓚ2563

[now usu. 押す] **press down, press; compress, squash**

圧し おし pressing down; weight; authority, commanding presence

気圧される けおされる be overawed [overpowered]

捺す ⓚ0456

[usu. 押す] **affix a seal, stamp**

判を捺す はんをおす affix a seal

雄 ⓚ0920

[sometimes also 牡] (of animals) **male**

雄犬 おすいぬ male dog

牡 ⓚ0743

[usu. 雄] (of animals) **male**

牡猫 おすねこ tomcat

牡馬 おすうま stallion, male horse

恐れ ⓚ2306

① **fear, dread, terror**

② [also 虞] **fears (of undesirable event), danger, risk, signs, adverse chance, possibility**

虞 ⓚ2783

[also 恐れ] **fears (of undesirable event), danger, risk, signs, adverse chance, possibility**

失敗の虞 しっぱいのおそれ risk of failure

雨の虞が有る あめのおそれがある
There is some fear of rain
感染の虞を無くす かんせんのおそれ
をなくす preclude the possibility
of infection

130 おそれる

恐れる ⓚ2306

ⓐ **fear, dread, be afraid of**
ⓑ **apprehend, be anxious about**
ⓒ [formerly also 畏れる] **be overawed, stand in awe, fear**

恐れ おそれ fear, dread, terror; [also 虞] fears (of undesirable event), danger, risk, signs, adverse chance, possibility
恐れていた通り おそれていたとおり as apprehended
恐れ多い おそれおおい gracious, august
恐れ入る おそれいる be over-whelmed [dumbfounded] (as with gratitude, shame, regret or astonishment)

畏れる ⓚ2218

[now usu. 恐れる] **be overawed, stand in awe, fear**

畏れ おそれ fear, anxiety, awe
畏れ多くも おそれおおくも graciously
畏れ入る おそれいる be sorry, feel small; be grateful; be amazed, be stunned
神を畏れる かみをおそれる fear God

131 おどかす

脅かす ⓚ1811

ⓐ **threaten, menace, intimidate**
ⓑ **startle**

脅かして金を取る おどかしてかねをとる scare money out of (a person)
脅かすなよ おどかすなよ What a start you gave me!

威かす ⓚ2993

ⓐ [now usu. 脅かす] **threaten, menace, intimidate**
ⓑ **startle**

威かして金を取る おどかしてかねをとる scare money out of (a person)

嚇かす ⓚ0702

ⓐ **threaten, menace, intimidate**
ⓑ **startle**

嚇かして金を取る おどかしてかねをとる scare money out of (a person)

132 おどし

脅し ⓚ1811

[formerly also 威し] **threat, menace, intimidation**

威し ⓚ2993

①ⓐ [now usu. 脅し] **threat, menace, intimidation**
ⓑ [in compounds] **something that scares or startles**

鳥威し とりおどし scarecrow
②[usu. 縅し] **braid or thread of Japanese armor**

縅し

[sometimes also 威し] **braid or thread of Japanese armor**

緋縅し鎧 ひおどしよろい scarlet-threaded suit of armor

133 おどす

脅す Ⓚ1811

[formerly also 威す] **threaten, menace, intimidate**

脅し おどし threat, menace, intimidation

脅し文句 おどしもんく threatening language, bluff

威す Ⓚ2993

[now usu. 脅す] **threaten, menace, intimidate**

敵を威す てきをおどす threaten the enemy

134 おどり

踊り Ⓚ1410

[also suffix] **dance, dancing**

盆踊り ぼんおどり Bon Festival dance

躍り Ⓚ1484

leaping, jumping

135 おどる

踊る Ⓚ1410

dance (energetically)

踊り手 おどりて dancer

躍る Ⓚ1484

ⓐ **leap, jump, bound**
ⓑ (of one's heart) **throb, leap**

躍り おどり leaping, jumping

躍り上がる おどりあがる spring up, leap to one's feet

躍り込む おどりこむ jump into; rush into

136 おびやかす

脅かす Ⓚ1811

[rarely also 劫かす] **threaten, menace, endanger; intimidate, scare; coerce**

平和が脅かされている へいわがおびやかされている Peace is at stake

劫かす Ⓚ1033

[now always 脅かす] **threaten, menace, endanger; intimidate, scare; coerce**

137 おも

主な Ⓚ1696

[sometimes also 重な] **chief, principal, main, foremost**

主に おもに mainly, chiefly; mostly

主立った おもだった principal, leading, chief, main

重な Ⓚ2991

[usu. 主な] **chief, principal, main, foremost**

重んじる(=重んずる) おもんじる(=おもんずる) hold in high regard; think much of

重立った おもだった principal, leading, chief, main

138 おもう

思う ⓀK2221

① ⓐ **think, consider; regard**
　ⓑ (believe) **think, believe, hold**
　ⓒ (consider likely) **think, expect, hope; guess**

思い おもい thought, idea; feelings; desire, wish; heart

思い付く おもいつく think of, hit upon

思い付き おもいつき idea, plan

思い上がる おもいあがる get conceited, get stuck-up

思い込む おもいこむ be under the impression that, be convinced that

私は彼が間違っていると思います わたしはかれがまちがっているとおもいます I believe that he is wrong

思わず おもわず unintentionally; unconsciously; unexpectedly

思い掛けない おもいがけない unexpected; accidental

② **wish, desire, want**

思惑 おもわく thought, intention, purpose

思い切る おもいきる resign oneself to, give up; resolve, determine

思い切って おもいきって boldly, decisively, daringly

思い切り おもいきり decisiveness; resignation; to one's heart content; with all one's might

思い止まる おもいとどまる abandon (an idea), refrain from (doing)

思う存分 おもうぞんぶん to one's heart's content

したいと思う したいとおもう want to do something

③ [sometimes also 想う] (recall a thought) **think, recollect, recall, remember**

思い出 おもいで recollections, memory, reminiscences

思い出す おもいだす recollect, recall, remember

④ **think of, care for, love**

思い遣り おもいやり sympathy, compassion; thoughtfulness

⑤ **wonder**

想う ⓀK2462

[usu. 思う] (recall a thought) **think, recollect, recall, remember**

昔を想う むかしをおもう recall the old days

139 おもて

表 ⓀK2151

① ⓐ [also prefix] (front or outer side) **front side, face, outside, right side; the obverse, the head**
　ⓑ **the front (of a house)**
　ⓒ **superficial [outward] appearance, outside**

表門 おもてもん front gate

表通り おもてどおり main street, street

表日本 おもてにほん Pacific side of Japan

葉書の表 はがきのおもて front of a post card

裏表に着る うらおもてにきる wear (a coat) wrong side out

表の戸 おもてのと street [front] door

表向きの理由 おもてむきのりゆう ostensible [surface] reason

② **outdoors, outside**

表で遊ぶ おもてであそぶ play outside [out of doors]

③ **matting**

表替え おもてがえ refacing mats

④ *baseball* **first half of an inning, top**

五回の表 ごかいのおもて top of the fifth inning

⑤ **formal, official, public**

表立つ おもてだつ become public [open]

面 Ⓚ1796

①ⓐ (front of head) **face**

　ⓑ (outer surface) **face, surface (as of water)**

細面 ほそおもて slender face

水の面 みずのおもて face of the water

② **mask**

赴く Ⓚ2816

① **proceed to, go to, head for**

死地に赴く しちにおもむく ride into the jaws of death

② **become, tend towards**

快方に赴く かいほうにおもむく get better, improve, convalesce

趣く Ⓚ2827

① **proceed to, go to, head for**

死地に趣く しちにおもむく ride into the jaws of death

② **become, tend towards**

盛大に趣く せいだいにおもむく grow in prosperity

重り Ⓚ2991

[also 錘] **weight, plumb, sinker, plummet**

糸に重りを付ける いとにおもりをつける weight a line

錘 Ⓚ1559

[also 重り] **weight, plumb, sinker, plummet**

糸に錘を付ける いとにおもりをつける weight a line

泳ぐ Ⓚ0289

[sometimes also 游ぐ] **swim;** (figuratively) **swim, get along**

泳ぎ およぎ swimming

平泳ぎ ひらおよぎ breast stroke

人波を泳ぐ ひとなみをおよぐ wade through a crowd

時流に乗って泳ぐ じりゅうにのっておよぐ swim with the current

游ぐ

[usu. 泳ぐ] **swim;** (figuratively) **swim, get along**

游ぎ およぎ swimming

下りる Ⓚ2862

① (move downward) **go down, come down(stairs), descend (from a mountain)**

駆け下りる かけおりる run down

坂を下りる さかをおりる go down a slope, go downhill

幕が下りる まくがおりる The curtain falls

② **be discharged; abort**

下り物 おりもの discharge from the womb

③ **be granted, be issued**

免許が下りた めんきょがおりた The license was granted

④ **be locked**

錠が下りている じょうがおりている be locked

降りる Ⓚ0414

①ⓐ (dismount) **alight, get off, disembark**

ⓑ (come down from a high place) **alight, land, swoop**

ⓒ (of frost or rain) **fall, come down**

乗り降り のりおり boarding and alighting

飛び降りる(=飛び下りる) とびおりる jump off (a moving vehicle), jump down

舞い降りる まいおりる fly down, alight

② **retire (from a position), withdraw, drop out (of a program), quit**

折る Ⓚ0225

① (separate through the application of a sudden bending force) **break off (as a branch), break (a bone), snap (in two), split**

歯を一本折る はをいっぽんおる break a tooth

へし折る へしおる smash, shatter

② **fold**

折り重ねる おりかさねる fold back [up]

折り紙 おりがみ folded paper; the art of paper folding

③ **bend, turn back**

折り曲げる おりまげる bend, double, turn up [down]

折り返す おりかえす turn back; turn up

折り返し おりかえし turn, turning point; return (trip), shuttle (service); lapel

④ **yield, give in**

折り合い おりあい mutual relations; compromise

⑤ **break off, quit**

枝折り しおり [usu. 栞] bookmark; guidebook

筆を折る ふでをおる break off writing

織る Ⓚ1295

weave

織り込む おりこむ interweave

織物 おりもの cloth, textile, fabric

機織り はたおり weaving; weaver; grasshopper

卸 　Ⓚ1315

[also prefix and suffix] **wholesale, whole-sale trade; wholesaler**

卸商 おろししょう wholesaler

卸売り おろしうり wholesale

卸値 おろしね wholesale price

卸相場 おろしそうば wholesale price [market]

野菜を卸しで買う やさいをおろしでかう buy vegetables wholesale

貴金属卸 ききんぞくおろし wholesale [wholesaler] in precious metals

棚卸し(=店卸し) たなおろし inventory

卸し 　Ⓚ1315

see comment below

下ろし 　Ⓚ2862

grated radish; vegetable grater

★ 卸し is a verbal gerund while 卸 is a noun. Both these forms are used in the sense of wholesaling. In the sense of grating vegetables, only 下ろし should be used. In the latter sense, おろし is sometimes mistakenly written 卸し.

下ろす 　Ⓚ2862

① **bring down, take down, let down, lower, pull down**

振り下ろす ふりおろす swing down-ward

雪下ろし ゆきおろし removing snow from the roof of a house

ボートを下ろす ぼーとをおろす lower a boat

根を下ろす ねをおろす take root

② **wear for the first time**

仕立て下ろし したておろし brand-new clothes

③ **have an abortion performed**

下ろし薬 おろしぐすり aborticide

④ **withdraw (one's savings)**

貯金を下ろす ちょきんをおろす with-draw one's savings

⑤ **lock up**

錠を下ろす じょうをおろす fasten a lock, lock

⑥ **grate (vegetables)**

下ろし おろし grated radish; vegeta-ble grater

下ろし金 おろしがね vegetable grater

降ろす 　Ⓚ0414

① **set (a passenger) down, discharge, unload**

乗客を降ろす じょうきゃくをおろす discharge passengers

② **demote, deprive (someone) of (his) role**

主役から降ろす しゅやくからおろす relieve someone of the leading role

卸す 　Ⓚ1315

wholesale, sell wholesale

小売りに卸す こうりにおろす sell wholesale to a retailer

★ In the sense of grating vegetables, おろす is sometimes mistakenly written 卸す.

147 おわる

終わる   Ⓚ1223
[rarely also 畢る] *vi* **end, come to an end, finish, terminate; end one's life, die**
終わり おわり end(ing), conclusion
終わり頃 おわりごろ toward the end

畢る   Ⓚ2240
[now always 終わる] **end, come to an end, finish, terminate; end one's life, die**

148 おん

雄   Ⓚ0920
[sometimes also 牡] (of animals) **male**
雄鳥(=雄鶏) おんどり rooster

牡   Ⓚ0743
[usu. 雄] (of animals) **male**
牡鳥(=牡鶏) おんどり rooster

149 か

耶   Ⓚ1179
[formerly also 乎; now always か] **interrogative particle**
女子有り問うて曰く誰耶と じょしありとうていわくたれかと A woman asked, "Who art thou?"

乎   Ⓚ2939
[formerly also 耶; now always か] **interrogative particle**
管仲は倹なる乎 かんちゅうはけんなるか Is Guan Zhong thrifty?

150 かえ

変え   Ⓚ1782
change, changing

代え   Ⓚ0018
substitute, proxy

換え   Ⓚ0537
rate of exchange

替え–   Ⓚ2424
substitute, spare, extra
替え玉 かえだま substitute, double
替え刃 かえば extra blades
替え着 かえぎ spare (change of) clothes

★ The above words are easily confused. Study the examples above in addition to the examples under each entry. Note that the distinction between these words as independent *kun* words does not necessarily apply to their meanings in the formation of compounds. For example, though 両替 りょうがえ 'changing money, exchange of money' is written with 替, かえる in the sense of changing money is written 換える.

151 かえす

返す   Ⓚ2633
①ⓐ **return, send back, put back, give back, repay**
  ⓑ **return (a kindness), repay**

お返し おかえし return present;
answer, reply; revenge; change
(for money)
恩返し おんがえし repaying another's
kindness
② **dismiss, discharge, divorce**

−返す ⓀＫ2633

① **do over, redo, re-**
繰り返す くりかえす repeat, do over
again
読み返す よみかえす reread, read
again
②ⓐ **do back, do in return**
ⓑ **take back, recover**
仕返し しかえし doing over, tit for tat,
revenge
言い返す いいかえす talk back, retort
取り返す とりかえす take back, regain
引き返す ひきかえす turn back,
retrace one's steps
③ **turn over, overturn, reverse**
ひっくり返す ひっくりかえす turn
over, upset
裏返す うらがえす turn over, turn
inside out

帰す ⓀＫ0113

**let (someone) return, see out, send
(someone) home, dismiss**
生徒を帰す せいとをかえす dismiss
the pupils

反す ⓀＫ2549

vt **turn over, overturn, upset, reverse**
干し草を反す ほしくさをかえす turn
over hay

★ In the sense of overturn, かえす
should be written 反す, though this
reading is not approved. However, as
a verbal suffix meaning to overturn,
かえす is written 返す, as in 裏返す うら
がえす 'turn over, turn inside out'.

152　かえりみる

顧みる ⓀＫ1677

①ⓐ **look back, turn around**
ⓑ **look back upon the past, review,
retrospect**
顧みて他を言う かえりみてたをいう
give an evasive answer
昔を顧みる むかしをかえりみる look
back upon the past
② **have regard for, consider**
家庭を顧みない かていをかえりみな
い think little of one's family

省みる ⓀＫ2164

**introspect, examine oneself, reflect
upon oneself**
自分の行いを省みる じぶんのおこな
いをかえりみる reflect upon one's
deeds

153　かえる¹

帰る ⓀＫ0113

ⓐ **return (to one's original position),
come back, come home**
ⓑ **go back [home], take one's leave**
帰り道 かえりみち the way back,
return trip
お帰りなさい おかえりなさい Hello!/
Welcome back

日帰りする ひがえりする return on
the same day, make a day's trip
家に帰る いえにかえる come back
home
帰り かえり return, coming back;
going home
帰れ かえれ Get out!/Go home!

還る   Ⓚ2743

ⓐ **return (to one's original position),
come back, come home**
ⓑ **go back [home], take one's leave**
家に還る いえにかえる go back home

返る   Ⓚ2633

① **be restored to, return to (the
original state)**
返り咲き かえりざき second bloom; a
comeback (in business)
振り返る ふりかえる turn one's head,
turn round
生き返る いきかえる revive, come to
oneself; be restored to life
② **be given back**

反る   Ⓚ2549

vi **turn over, become overturned**
スカートの裾が反る すかーとのす
そがかえる The hem of the skirt
turns over

154	かえる²

変える   Ⓚ1782

ⓐ **change, alter, convert, transform,
turn into**
ⓑ **change to a different time or place**
ⓒ **reform, revise, amend**

馬を牛に変える うまをうしにかえ
る Change a horse into a cow (by
magic)
変え かえ change, changing
形と色を変える かたちといろをかえる
change the shape and color of
鉛を金に変える なまりをきんにかえる
convert lead into gold
観点を変える かんてんをかえる
change one's point of view
予定を変える よていをかえる change
the schedule
位置を変える いちをかえる change
the position of
法律を変える ほうりつをかえる revise
[amend] the law

代える   Ⓚ0018

**substitute, use in place of, replace
(something) with (another)**
馬を牛に代える うまをうしにかえる
Substitute a horse for a cow/Use a
horse in place of a cow
代え かえ substitute, proxy
. . . に代えて …にかえて instead of…,
in place of…
BさんをAさんに代える びーさんを
えーさんにかえる substitute Mr. A
for Mr. B

換える   Ⓚ0537

[sometimes also 替える] **exchange,
interchange, trade, barter, change
(money), convert**
換え かえ rate of exchange
本を金に換える ほんをかねにかえる
exchange a book for money
ドルを円に換える どるをえんにかえ
る convert dollars into yen

十ドル札を換える じゅうどるさつを
かえる get change for a ten-dollar
bill

馬を牛と換える うまをうしとかえる
Exchange a horse for a cow

本と時計を換える ほんととけいをか
える swap a watch for a book

引き換える ひきかえる exchange,
change, convert

一リットル百円換えで買う いちりっと
るひゃくえんがえでかう purchase
at 100 yen per liter

替える   Ⓚ2424

① ⓐ **replace (one thing or person by another), renew, change**
   ⓑ **change to something new (as a job or set of clothes), change over to**

馬を替える うまをかえる Replace an
old horse with a new one

替え かえ replacement, spare

畳の表を替える たたみのおもてを
かえる replace the covers of old
mats with new ones

塗り替える ぬりかえる repaint

取り替える とりかえる change, renew,
replace, substitute

両替 りょうがえ money changing,
exchange of money

商売を替える しょうばいをかえる
change to a new business

着替える きがえる change clothes

② [usu. 換える] **exchange, interchange, trade, barter, change (money), convert**

引き替える ひきかえる exchange,
change, convert

---

155   かえる³

-返る   Ⓚ2633

[also –反る] [emphatic verbal suffix] **utterly, completely**

静まり返る しずまりかえる become
still as death

呆れ返る あきれかえる be utterly
amazed

-反る   Ⓚ2549

[also –返る] [emphatic verbal suffix] **utterly, completely**

呆れ反る あきれかえる be utterly
amazed

156   かおり

香り   Ⓚ2225

sweet smell, perfume, fragrance, scent

桃の花の香り もものはなのかおり
fragrance of peach blossom

薫り   Ⓚ2094

fragrance, aroma

157   かおる

香る   Ⓚ2225

smell sweet, be fragrant

薫る   Ⓚ2094

look sweet-smelling [balmy], look fragrant

薫り かおり fragrance, aroma

若葉が薫る わかばがかおる The fresh verdure looks sweet-smelling

★ 香 and 薫 are practically indistinguishable. Strictly speaking, 香 refers to physical perception by the olfactory organ, while 薫 is used figuratively or poetically.

158 　　かかり

掛かり
Ⓚ0449

① **expenses**
掛かりが嵩む かかりがかさむ Expenses get heavy

② **scale, scope**
大掛かりな おおがかりな large-scale, extensive

③ **engagement, catching on**
歯車の掛かりが悪い はぐるまのかかりがわるい The gears are improperly engaged

④ **attack**

掛
Ⓚ0449

ⓐ **person in charge (of a post, esp. in a government agency or railway company)**

ⓑ **charge, duty, post**
掛長 かかりちょう chief clerk
掛の人 かかりのひと official in charge

係り
Ⓚ0078

relation, connection (esp. in grammar)

★ Note that 係り, *not* 係かり or 係, is the correct form here.

係
Ⓚ0078

ⓐ **person in charge, official in charge, clerk**

ⓑ **charge, duty, post**
係員 かかりいん clerk in charge
係長 かかりちょう chief clerk
係官 かかりかん official in charge
係の人 かかりのひと person in charge
係をする かかりをする be in charge

159 　　かかる

掛かる
Ⓚ0449

① **hang, be suspended**
壁に掛かる かべにかかる hang on the wall

② **be set over, cover**
そこに布団が掛かっている そこにふとんがかかっている The quilt is spread over there
霧が地面に掛かっている きりがじめんにかかっている Fog covers the ground

③ **splash**
掛かり湯 かかりゆ fresh bathwater to pour over oneself
私のズボンに水が掛かった わたくしのずぼんにみずがかかった My trousers were splashed with water

④ **lean against**
伸し掛かる のしかかる lean on (a person), bear down on
寄り掛かる よりかかる lean against something
梯子が壁に掛かっている はしごがかべにかかっている The ladder is leaning against the wall

⑤ⓐ **be caught, be trapped**

(b) **be caught (on one's mind), weigh**

罠に掛かる わなにかかる caught in a trap

引っ掛かる ひっかかる be caught, catch on; get entangled; be trapped

心に掛かる こころにかかる weigh on one's mind

気掛かり きがかり anxiety, concern, worry

⑥ **set about, apply oneself to, be engaged in**

仕事に掛かる しごとにかかる get to work

用意に掛かる よういにかかる set about preparations

取り掛かる とりかかる commence, undertake

仕事に掛かり切りになる しごとにかかりきりになる give one's whole time to the job

⑦ⓐ **depend upon, hinge upon**
　ⓑ **involve, concern**

責任は彼に掛かる せきにんはかれにかかる Responsibility rests with him

金が有るか無いかに掛かる かねがあるかないかにかかる depend on whether or not there is money

子供に掛かる こどもにかかる depend on one's children

掛かり合い かかりあい involvement

手掛かり てがかり something to rely on, clue

⑧ **consult (a doctor)**

掛かり付けの医者 かかりつけのいしゃ family physician [doctor]

⑨ **start, start operating, work**

エンジンが掛かる えんじんがかかる The engine starts

電話が掛かって来る でんわがかかってくる get a phone call

⑩ **appear (at a theater)**

今映画が掛かっている いまえいががかかっている A film is now being shown

⑪ **require, cost; weigh**

時間が掛かる じかんがかかる take time

余り金が掛からない あまりかねがかからない It doesn't cost very much

目方はどの位掛かりますか めかたはどのくらいかかりますか How much does it weigh?

⑫ **attack, fall upon**

襲い掛かる おそいかかる assault, pounce upon, sweep down on (a person)

飛び掛かる とびかかる spring upon

敵に掛かる てきにかかる assail the enemy

⑬ **approach, come near**

山道に掛かる やまみちにかかる come to a mountain path

⑭ [formerly 繋る] **anchor, moor**

懸かる

Ⓚ2532

① **be suspended in midair (as of the moon), hang**

月が空に懸かる つきがそらにかかる The moon hangs in the sky

② **have a prize offered, have a reward (set on one's head)**

犯人の首に賞金が懸かっている はんにんのくびにしょうきんがかかっている There is a reward on the criminal's head

架かる Ⓚ2226

span, (of cables) be laid across, be built across
川に架かる橋 かわにかかるはし
bridge spanning a river

係る Ⓚ0078

① **affect, concern, involve**
面目に係る問題 めんぼくにかかるもんだい problem concerning one's honor

② *gram* **modify**
係り かかり relation, connection (esp. in grammar)
係り結び かかりむすび relation, connection (esp. in grammar)
副詞は動詞に係る ふくしはどうしにかかる Adverbs modify verbs

③ **is the work of, is done by**
これは浅田氏に係る小説だ これはあさだしにかかるしょうせつだ This novel is the work of Mr. Asada

繋る Ⓚ2521

[now usu. 掛かる] **anchor, moor**
沖に繋る船 おきにかかるふね ship mooring off the coast

罹る

fall ill, contract (a disease)
病気に罹る びょうきにかかる contract a disease

★ 掛かる is the intransitive form of 掛ける and shares most of its meanings. Study the equivalents and examples under かかる above. Note that 掛かる is to hang in the sense of being snagged or caught on something,

whereas 懸かる means to be suspended in midair.

160　　かかわる

係わる Ⓚ0078

① **be concerned in, be involved**
係わり かかわり relation, connection
事件に係わる じけんにかかわる be involved in a case

② **influence (adversely), affect**
命に係わる いのちにかかわる be threatening to one's life, be a matter of life and death

関わる Ⓚ2842

① **be concerned in, be involved**
関わり かかわり relation, connection
事件に関わる じけんにかかわる be involved in a case

② **influence (adversely), affect**
命に関わる いのちにかかわる be threatening to one's life, be a matter of life and death, fatal

拘わる Ⓚ0274

adhere to, stick to
. . . にも拘わらず …にもかかわらず in spite of…, regardless of…

161　　かがみ

鏡 Ⓚ1576

① **mirror**
鏡板 かがみいた panel, scene-panel
手鏡 てかがみ hand glass

② **round mirror-shaped rice cake**

鏡開き かがみびらき cutting of New Year's rice cakes

③ **barrelhead**
鏡を抜く かがみをぬく open a barrel

鑑
Ⓚ1580

(something worthy of being copied) **mirror, model, paragon**
武士の鑑 ぶしのかがみ paragon of knighthood

162　　かがやく

輝く
Ⓚ1280

[sometimes also 耀く or 赫く] **shine brilliantly, glitter, gleam, sparkle, light up, brighten**
輝き かがやき brilliancy
輝かしい かがやかしい bright (future), brilliant (achievement)
輝き渡る かがやきわたる shine out far and wide
輝かしい業績 かがやかしいぎょうせき brilliant achievements, bright future
喜びに輝く目 よろこびにかがやくめ eyes sparkling with joy

耀く
Ⓚ1301

[usu. 輝く, sometimes also 赫く] **shine brilliantly, glitter, gleam, sparkle, light up, brighten**
耀く太陽 かがやくたいよう the shining sun
目が耀く めがかがやく one's eyes sparkle
栄誉に耀く えいよにかがやく shine in the glory

赫く

[usu. 輝く, sometimes also 耀く] **shine brilliantly, glitter, gleam, sparkle, light up, brighten**

163　　かき

垣
Ⓚ0311

[formerly also 牆] [also suffix] **fence, wall, hedge; barrier**
垣根 かきね fence, hedge
生け垣 いけがき hedge, quickset
石垣 いしがき stone wall
四つ目垣 よつめがき lattice fence

牆

[now replaced by 垣] [also suffix] **fence, wall**

164　　かく

書く
Ⓚ2314

ⓐ **write, pen**
ⓑ (compose written texts) **write, compose**
書き換える かきかえる rewrite, renew (a bill), transfer
書き順 かきじゅん stroke order (in writing Chinese characters)
書き方 かきかた how to write, way [style] of writing
書き言葉 かきことば written language
書き取り かきとり dictation
書留 かきとめ registered mail
読み書き よみかき reading and writing

小説を書く しょうせつをかく write
a novel

描く Ⓚ0445

draw, paint

絵描き えかき painter, artist

165 かけ

掛け Ⓚ0449

① **noodles in broth**
掛けうどん かけうどん thick noodles
in broth
② **credit, installment**
掛けにする かけにする give credit
掛け買い かけがい credit purchase
掛け売り かけうり credit sale

賭け Ⓚ1451

bet, wager

166 かける

掛ける Ⓚ0449

① ⓐ **set, put on, put over, spread**
ⓑ **set against, put up against,
fasten**
ⓒ **set on a scale, weigh**
ⓓ (set on one's head or shoulders) **wear,
put on**
掛け布団 かけぶとん covering quilt
薦を掛ける こもをかける spread a
mat
掛け小屋 かけごや lean-to; tempo-
rary theater
薬缶を掛ける やかんをかける put a
kettle on (the stove)

梯子を掛ける はしごをかける set a
ladder up against
計りに掛ける はかりにかける weigh
on a scale
眼鏡を掛ける めがねをかける wear
glasses
ショールを掛ける しょーるをかける
put a shawl on
② **set one's body down, sit, sit down**
掛け心地 かけごこち feel of a chair
腰掛け こしかけ chair, seat, bench,
stool
腰を掛ける こしをかける sit down
③ **pour, sprinkle**
掛け汁 かけじる dressing, gravy
振り掛ける ふりかける sprinkle,
spatter
水を掛ける みずをかける sprinkle
water on (something)
④ **set going, set in motion, turn on,
start, operate; phone**
火を掛ける ひをかける set fire
レコードを掛ける れこーどをかける
play a record
仕掛け しかけ device, mechanism
電話を掛ける でんわをかける make a
phone call, telephone
⑤ ⓐ **set before, present, pose**
ⓑ **set (a tax) on, lay, impose**
お目に掛ける おめにかける show to
someone, present
舞台に掛ける ぶたいにかける put on
stage
謎を掛ける なぞをかける pose a
riddle
持ち掛ける もちかける propose, offer
(a suggestion)
見せ掛け みせかけ outward appear-
ance

掛け金 かけきん installment; premium

掛け値 かけね overcharge, inflated price; exaggeration

税金を掛ける ぜいきんをかける place a tax on

保険を掛ける ほけんをかける insure (something)

⑥ **exert influence on, impose**

迷惑を掛ける めいわくをかける impose trouble

心配を掛ける しんぱいをかける cause someone to worry

面倒を掛ける めんどうをかける put someone to trouble

⑦ **hang, hang up, suspend**

掛け物 かけもの hanging scroll

掛け看板 かけかんばん hanging sign

カーテンを掛ける かーてんをかける hang up a curtain

⑧ **fasten onto, affix**

掛け時計 かけどけい wall clock

引っ掛ける ひっかける hang on, hook; throw on; trap, cheat; have a drink

フックに掛ける ふっくにかける hang on a hook

⑨ **fasten (one's mind) upon**

気に掛ける きにかける have one's mind upon, take to heart

願を掛ける がんをかける make a wish (to a god)

⑩ **lock, close**

掛け金 かけがね (window) latch

錠を掛ける じょうをかける fasten a lock

⑪ **speak, call out**

掛け声 かけごえ shout to mark time, shout of encouragement

掛け合い かけあい dialogue, duet; bargaining

気合いを掛ける きあいをかける raise a shout, cheer on

話し掛ける はなしかける call out to someone, accost

⑫ **entrust someone to (a physician), put under medical treatment**

医者に掛ける いしゃにかける entrust to a doctor (for treatment)

⑬ **spend (time or money)**

時間を掛ける じかんをかける spend time (on doing something)

お金を掛ける おかねをかける spend money (on something)

⑭ **raise**

帆を掛ける ほをかける raise a sail

⑮ **multiply**

掛け算 かけざん multiplication

八掛ける二 はちかけるに 2 times 8

⑯ **mate (animals), cross (plants or animals)**

二つの植物を掛け合わせて新種を作る ふたつのしょくぶつをかけあわせてしんしゅをつくる Make a new plant by crossing two others

⑰ **pun, play on words**

掛け詞 かけことば play on words (as a poetic device)

これは書名に掛けた謳い文句だ これはしょめいにかけたうたいもんくだ This slogan plays on the name [title] of the book

架ける ⓚ2226

lay (a bridge or wire) across, build across, span (a river) with (a bridge), bridge

電線を架ける でんせんをかける lay a wire

★ かける in the sense of span or bridge is correctly written 架ける, not 掛ける. This is in spite of the fact that かけはし 'suspension bridge' is normally written 掛け橋.

懸ける ⓚ2532

① [sometimes also 賭ける] **stake (one's life), risk**
命懸けで いのちがけで at the risk of one's life

② **offer [set] a prize**
賞金を懸ける しょうきんをかける offer a prize

③ [in compounds] **be (greatly) different from, be far apart**
懸け離れる かけはなれる be far apart; be greatly different from

賭ける ⓚ1451

ⓐ **wager, bet money**
ⓑ [usu. 懸ける] **stake (one's life), risk**
賭け かけ bet, wager
賭け金 かけきん stakes, bet
賭け事 かけごと betting, gambling
賭け碁 かけご playing go for stakes
金を賭ける かねをかける bet money
命を賭ける いのちをかける risk one's life

駆ける ⓚ1619

gallop, run quickly, dash
駆けっこ かけっこ race, foot race, running match
駆け回る かけまわる bustle about, run about
駆け落ち かけおち elopement
駆け引き かけひき bargaining; tactics

駆け足 かけあし gallop, run
先駆け さきがけ [sometimes also 魁] the first to charge; lead, pioneer

翔る ⓚ1241

soar, fly
天翔る あまがける ride the skies
飛び翔る とびかける soar, fly

★ 掛ける is a complicated word with many meanings. Make a careful study of the equivalents and examples. In the sense of hang or suspend, 掛ける, *not* 懸ける, is correct. This is in spite of the fact that 懸 means to suspend or hang when used in compounds, as for example in 懸垂 けんすい 'suspension, etc.'.

167 かげ

影 ⓚ1671

①ⓐ (partial darkness) **shadow, silhouette**
ⓑ (reflected image) **shadow, image, reflection**
淡い影 あわいかげ light shadow
影武者 かげむしゃ dummy general, general's double
影を映す かげをうつす mirror the image (of)

②ⓐ (faint indication) **shadow (of), traces (of), signs (of)**
ⓑ [in compounds] **figure, appearance**
影も形も無い かげもかたちもない nowhere to be seen
面影 おもかげ face; traces
人影 ひとかげ human figure; shadow of a person

③ [in compounds] **light**

日影 ひかげ sunshine; shadow
火影(=灯影) ほかげ shadows from firelight
月影 つきかげ moonlight; moonshine

陰 ⓚ0494

① [formerly also 蔭] **shade**
日陰 ひかげ the shade
② [formerly also 蔭]
  ⓐ **back side, reverse side**
  ⓑ **behind the scenes**
  戸の陰に隠れる とのかげにかくれる hide behind a door
  陰で かげで behind one's back
  陰口 かげぐち backbiting
③ [also 蔭] [in the form of お陰 おかげ] **grace, favor**
  お陰で おかげで indebtedness; favor; help
  お陰様で おかげさまで [polite] thanks to, due to

蔭 ⓚ2073

① [also 陰] [in the form of お蔭 おかげ] **grace, favor**
  お蔭で おかげで thanks to; due to
  お蔭様で皆元気です おかげさまでみなげんきです We are all well and fine, thank you
② [now usu. 陰] **shade**
  木蔭 こかげ shade of a tree, bower
  日蔭 ひかげ the shade
③ [now usu. 陰]
  ⓐ **back side, reverse side**
  ⓑ **behind the scenes**
  カーテンの蔭に隠れる かーてんのかげにかくれる hide behind a curtain
  蔭口 かげぐち backbiting

★ Though 影 has the basic meaning of shadow, in compounds it is used in the more or less the opposite sense, i.e., light. 陰 specifically refers to shade; it also signifies the reverse side of something, or, figuratively, behind the scenes.

168 かげり

陰り ⓚ0494

[formerly also 翳り] **shade; gloom**

翳り

[now usu. 陰り] **shade; gloom**

169 かげる

陰る ⓚ0494

[also 翳る] **darken, be clouded**
  陰り かげり shade; gloom

翳る

[also 陰る] **darken, be clouded**
  翳り かげり shade; gloom
  翳りの有る顔 かげりのあるかお face shaded with pensiveness

170 かさ

傘 ⓚ1829

ⓐ **umbrella, parasol**
ⓑ **something that protects like an umbrella**
  傘を差す かさをさす hold an umbrella
  雨傘 あまがさ umbrella
  日傘 ひがさ parasol

洋傘 ようがさ umbrella, parasol
核の傘 かくのかさ nuclear umbrella

笠 ⓚ2320

① ⓐ **sedge hat, bamboo hat, conical hat**
   ⓑ **something that protects like a hat**
   笠雲 かさぐも cap cloud
   笠の台が飛ぶ かさのだいがとぶ be decapitated; be fired
   編み笠 あみがさ braided hat
   陣笠 じんがさ ancient soldier's hat; party rank and file
   父親の威光を笠に着る ちちおやのいこうをかさにきる shelter oneself under one's father's influence

② **shade (of a lamp), hood, something shaped like a sedge hat**
   煙突の笠 えんとつのかさ chimney cap
   松笠 まつかさ pine cone

171 かじ

舵 ⓚ1226

ⓐ **rudder**
ⓑ **helm, tiller, wheel**
   舵板 かじいた rudder blade
   舵取り かじとり helmsman, coxswain; steering, guidance
   舵を取る かじをとる steer; manage
   面舵 おもかじ starboarding the helm
   取り舵 とりかじ porting the helm

梶 ⓚ0866

① **paper mulberry**
   梶の木 かじのき paper mulberry

② steering device:
   ⓐ [usu. 舵] **rudder**
   ⓑ [usu. 舵] **helm, tiller, wheel**
   ⓒ **oar**
   ⓓ **shafts (of a rickshaw)**
   梶木(=梶木鮪) かじき(=かじきまぐろ) marlin, swordfish
   梶棒 かじぼう shafts (of a rickshaw or similar vehicle), thills

172 かすむ

霞む ⓚ2450

ⓐ **haze, be hazy, mist**
ⓑ [formerly 翳む] **have dim sight**
   遠くに霞む とおくにかすむ loom in the distance
   年で霞んだ目 としでかすんだめ eyes dimmed with age

翳む

[now usu. 霞む] **have dim sight**

173 かする

掠る ⓚ0458

ⓐ **graze**
ⓑ **squeeze, exploit**
   掠り傷 かすりきず scratch, graze, slight wound

擦る ⓚ0707

ⓐ **graze**
ⓑ **squeeze, exploit**

174 かすれる

掠れる   Ⓚ0458
ⓐ **become blurred**
ⓑ **become hoarse [husky]**
  声が掠れる こえがかすれる become hoarse

擦れる   Ⓚ0707
ⓐ **become blurred**
ⓑ **become hoarse [husky]**

175 かずら

葛   Ⓚ2017
[sometimes also 蔓] **vine, creeper**
  風船葛 ふうせんかずら balloon vine

蔓   Ⓚ2074
[usu. 葛] **vine, creeper**
  靫蔓 うつぼかずら pitcher plant
  日陰の蔓 ひかげのかずら running ground pine

176 かた

型   Ⓚ2292
① (general form characterizing a class) **type, kind, pattern, form**
  型に嵌める かたにはめる squeeze into a pattern, regiment
  大型 おおがた large size; large pattern
  新型 しんがた new style, new model
  痩せ型 やせがた slender figure
② (pattern from which something is made) **type, mold, model**

  型紙 かたがみ paper pattern (for a dress)
  鋳型 いがた mold, cast, matrix, die
  歯型 はがた impression of the teeth, tooth-mark
③ **set [traditional] form, *kata* (in martial arts and plays)**
  空手の型 からてのかた *kata* (in karate)

形   Ⓚ0749
①ⓐ **shape, form; pattern, design**
  ⓑ **marks, traces**
  形どる かたどる [usu. 象る] model after, represent
  形が崩れる かたがくずれる lose shape, get out of shape
  花形 はながた floral pattern; star, lion; leading, popular, favorite
  形見 かたみ keepsake, memento
② **security, pledge**
  借金の形 しゃっきんのかた security for a loan
  手形 てがた promissory note; hand print

177 かたい

固い   Ⓚ2658
①ⓐ (glutinous or not flexible) **stiff, firm, thick**
  ⓑ (not easily moved) **stiff, tight, fast**
  固さ かたさ stiffness
  固練りコンクリート かたねりこんくりーと stiff-consistency concrete
  固いカラー かたいからー stiff collar
  ドアが固い どあがかたい The door sticks [has stiff hinges]

固い結び目 かたいむすびめ tight knot

固い握り かたいにぎり tight grip

②ⓐ (unshakable) **stiff, firm, resolute, strong**

ⓑ (unyielding) **stiff (stand), obstinate, stubborn, inflexible**

固い約束 かたいやくそく solemn promise

決意が固い けついがかたい be firmly determined

団結が固い だんけつがかたい be strongly united

固苦しい かたくるしい formal, stiff, strained; strict; rigid

頭が固い あたまがかたい obstinate, thickheaded, inflexible

③ **rigid, strict, stern**

固く戒める かたくいましめる admonish sternly

④ **certain, sure**

合格は固い ごうかくはかたい He is certain to pass the exam

硬い ®1095

① (resisting pressure) **hard, tough, strong (esp. metals or stone)**

硬さ かたさ hardness

硬い石 かたいいし hard stone

②ⓐ **stiff (style), uninteresting**

ⓑ **stiff (facial expression)**

硬い文章 かたいぶんしょう stiff style

硬い表情 かたいひょうじょう stiff expression

堅い ®2457

① (resisting deformation) **firm, hard (lumber)**

② **steady (market or business), sound (investment)**

③ⓐ **steadfast, reliable, trustworthy**

ⓑ **honest, honorable, upright, serious, chaste**

④ **stiff, formal, bookish**

難い ®1632

difficult, hard

言うは易く行うは難し いうはやすくおこなうはかたし Easier said than done

★ かたい is a source of confusion to all users of Japanese, with many dictionaries disagreeing with each other. Though the information here is lexically "correct," it is not always reliable for determining meaning in actual occurrences, esp. in reference to physical hardness. Study the equivalents and examples under each entry. In the ordinary sense of hard, 硬い is used, esp. in reference to metals or stone. In reference to wood, 堅い is the correct choice, though the two are often used interchangeably. 固い implies stickiness, as in pasty substances, resistance to motion (stiff hinges) or tightness (tight knot or grip). It does *not* mean solid, despite the fact that it has that meaning in *on* compounds. In figurative uses, 堅い is basically positive (steadfast, trustworthy, upright, chaste), while 固い has negative overtones (stiff, obstinate). However, 固い is also used positively (solemn promise, firm determination). In reference to speech or writing, 硬い means uninteresting or unpolished, while 堅い means formal (style) or bookish. The verbs かためる and か

たまる are always written 固める and 固まる. 難い is a literary expression for difficult or a verbal suffix meaning hard to do. It is never interchangeable with the above three.

178　かたき

敵　　　　　　　　　Ⓚ1648
ⓐ [also 仇] **enemy, foe**
ⓑ **opponent, rival**
ⓒ [also 仇] **revenge, retaliation**
　　商売敵 しょうばいがたき business rival
　　敵討ち かたきうち vendetta, revenge

仇
ⓐ **enemy, foe**
ⓑ **revenge, retaliation**
　　仇同士 かたきどうし mutual enemies
　　父の仇を討つ ちちのかたきをうつ avenge one's father

179　かたち

形　　　　　　　　　Ⓚ0749
① **shape, form**
　　形作る かたちづくる form, shape, make, mold
② [formerly also 貌] **appearance, looks, figure**
　　顔形 かおかたち features, looks

貌　　　　　　　　　Ⓚ1408
ⓐ **appearance, looks, figure**
ⓑ **aspect, condition**
　　顔貌 かおかたち features, looks

180　かたどる

象る　　　　　　　　Ⓚ1831
[sometimes also 形どる] **model after, represent**
　　手を象った字 てをかたどったじ character representing a hand

形どる　　　　　　　Ⓚ0749
[usu. 象る] **model after, represent**

181　かたまり

固まり　　　　　　　Ⓚ2658
① [sometimes also 塊] **lump, mass, clod; ingot**
　　鉄の固まり てつのかたまり iron ingot
② [usu. 塊] **group, crowd, cluster**
③ [sometimes also 塊] **devotee, worshiper; incarnation (of selfishness), personification**
　　欲の固まり よくのかたまり incarnation of selfishness
　　拝金主義の固まり はいきんしゅぎのかたまり money worshiper

塊　　　　　　　　　Ⓚ0579
① [usu. 固まり] **lump, mass, clod; ingot**
　　血の塊 ちのかたまり clot of blood
② [sometimes also 固まり] **group, crowd, cluster**
③ [usu. 固まり] **devotee, worshiper; incarnation (of selfishness), personification**
　　欲の塊 よくのかたまり lump of avarice, incarnation of selfishness
　　拝金主義の塊 はいきんしゅぎのかたまり money worshiper

182 かたよる

偏る   Ⓚ0116

- ⓐ be one-sided, be prejudiced, be partial, be unfair
- ⓑ deviate

偏った考え かたよったかんがえ partial [one-sided] view, prejudice

偏り かたより deviation, offset; polarization

偏りシリンダー かたよりしりんだー offset cylinder

片寄る   Ⓚ2910

concentrate on one side [place], go aside

183 かたり

語り   Ⓚ1402

narrative

騙り

fraud, swindle

184 かたる

語る   Ⓚ1402

- ①ⓐ (express in words) tell, talk, speak
- ⓑ tell (a story), narrate, relate

真実を語る しんじつをかたる speak the truth

語り手 かたりて narrator, storyteller

語り伝える かたりつたえる pass on (a story or tradition)

語り合う かたりあう talk together, have a chat with

語り かたり narrative

語り草(=語り種) かたりぐさ story, topic

物語 ものがたり story, tale, legend

- ② recite, chant

義太夫語り ぎだゆうかたり *gidayu* reciter

騙る

- ① swindle, defraud

騙り かたり fraud, swindle

- ② assume (another's) name

他人の名を騙って たにんのなをかたって under a false name

185 かつ

勝つ   Ⓚ0918

- ①ⓐ win, defeat, triumph
- ⓑ [formerly 克つ] control (oneself), overcome

勝ち かち win, victory

勝ち取る かちとる gain, win

赤が勝っている あかがかっている predominated by red

- ② unclassified compounds

勝手 かって one's own way; convenience; circumstances; kitchen

克つ   Ⓚ1760

[now usu. 勝つ] control (oneself), overcome

己に克つ おのれにかつ control oneself

186 かつて

嘗て   Ⓚ2268

- ⓐ previously, formerly, once, before

ⓑ [in negative constructions] (not) **ever**
嘗ての友 かつてのとも former friend
未だ嘗て いまだかつて [in negative
constructions] (not) until now, (not)
ever before, (not) yet

曽て
®1823

ⓐ **previously, formerly, once, before**
ⓑ [in negative constructions] (not) **ever**
未だ曽て いまだかつて [in negative
constructions] (not) until now, (not)
ever before, (not) yet

187　　かなう

適う
®2726

ⓐ **suit, serve (the purpose)**
ⓑ **agree with, be consistent with**
道理に適う どうりにかなう stand to
reason

敵う
®1648

① **be a match for, compare with**
君には敵わない きみにはかなわない I
am no match for you
② **stand, bear**
こう暑くては敵わない こうあつくては
かなわない I can't stand the heat

叶う
®0161

① (of a wish) **be fulfilled, be realized,
be granted**
叶わない かなわない be unable, be
beyond one's power
叶わぬ時の神頼み かなわぬときの
かみだのみ Man turns to God in
times of trouble

望みが叶う のぞみがかなう have
one's wish realized
② **be able to, can (do)**

188　　かなしい

悲しい
®2416

ⓐ (low in spirit) **sad, unhappy, sorrowful**
ⓑ [sometimes also 哀しい] (causing sorrow)
sad, sorrowful, pathetic
悲しさ かなしさ sadness, sorrow, grief
悲しげに かなしげに sadly, with a sad
look
悲しがる かなしがる be sad, feel
sorrow

哀しい
®1781

[now usu. 悲しい] (causing sorrow) **sad,
sorrowful, pathetic**
哀しい歌 かなしいうた sad song,
doleful song
哀しい出来事 かなしいできごと sad
event

189　　かば

樺
®0961

① **birch**
白樺 しらかば white birch, Betula
tauschii
② **reddish yellow**
樺色 かばいろ reddish yellow

椛
®0869

birch

190　かま

窯　⊛2081

kiln, oven, furnace, stove; pottery

窯元 かまもと pottery
窯印 かまじるし potter's mark

釜　⊛1808

① ⓐ **iron pot, kettle, cauldron**
　 ⓑ **boiler**

釜茹で かまゆで boiling in a cauldron
電気釜 でんきがま electric rice-
　　cooker
鍋釜 なべかま pots and pans; kitchen
　　utensils
後釜 あとがま successor, replacement
風呂釜 ふろがま bath heater

② *slang* **buttocks**

お釜 おかま (male) homosexual

罐

boiler

191　かみ

上　⊛2876

① ⓐ **upper part, top, head**
　 ⓑ **upper stream**
　 ⓒ [also prefix before place names] **Up-
　　per, Northern**

上手 かみて upper part, upper
　　reaches; left stage
川上 かわかみ upstream, upriver
上カプアス山脈 かみかぷあすさん
　　みゃく Upper Kapuas Mountains

② **first (in a series of two or three)**

上の句 かみのく first half of a tanka
　　poem

上半期 かみはんき first half of the
　　(fiscal) year

③ **persons of superior rank:**
　 ⓐ **superiors, high rank**
　 ⓑ **government, authorities**
　 ⓒ **emperor, sovereign**

上下 かみしも superiors and inferiors
お上 おかみ government, authorities;
　　emperor; wife, madam, landlady

守　⊛1861

feudal governor, lord, baron

豊後の守 ぶんごのかみ Lord of
　　Bungo

192　かや

茅　⊛1922

[also 萱] **thatch grass such as cogongrass, eulalias and other gramine-
ous plants**

茅葺き かやぶき roofing with thatch
　　grass
茅戸 かやと hilly place with a thick
　　cogongrass bush

萱　⊛2016

[also 茅] **thatch grass such as cogongrass, eulalias and other gramine-
ous plants**

萱葺き かやぶき roofing with thatch
　　grass
萱鼠 かやねずみ harvest mouse
茅萱 ちがや cogongrass

空 Ⓚ1913

① **emptiness, vacancy, hollow**
空の からの empty, vacant, hollow
空っぽ からっぽ empty, hollow
空手 からて karate; empty hand

② [prefix]
ⓐ (void of content) **empty**
ⓑ (lacking substance) **empty, vain, bogus, false**
空瓶 からびん empty bottle
空梅雨 からつゆ dry rainy season, rainless *tsuyu*
空約束 からやくそく empty promise
空手形 からてがた bad [fictitious] bill; empty promise

殻 Ⓚ1354

① ⓐ **shell, crust**
ⓑ **husk, hull**
殻を閉ざす からをとざす retire into one's shell, close up like an oyster
卵の殻 たまごのから eggshell
貝殻 かいがら shell
豆殻 まめがら bean husk

② **castoff skin, refuse**
抜け殻 ぬけがら castoff skin; mere shadow of one's true self

唐 Ⓚ2685

ⓐ **elegant term for China, Cathay**
ⓑ [also 韓] **foreign countries**
唐様 からよう Chinese style [design]
唐草模様 からくさもよう arabesque design

唐獅子 からじし imaginary animal similar to a lion

韓 Ⓚ1575

ⓐ **elegant term for Korea**
ⓑ [also 唐] **foreign countries**
韓人 からびと Korean

辛い Ⓚ1755

① ⓐ **pungent, hot**
ⓑ [formerly also 鹹い] **salty, briny, saline**
ⓒ **dry (wine)**
辛い味 からいあじ pungent taste
辛子(=芥子) からし mustard
唐辛子 とうがらし red pepper
塩辛い しおからい salty
辛口の からくちの salty; hot; dry (sake)

② **strict, severe**
点が辛い てんがからい be severe in marking
世知辛い せちがらい hard to live, exigent

③ [in compounds] **bare, narrow**
辛うじて かろうじて barely, narrowly
辛くも からくも barely, narrowly, with difficulty

鹹い

[now usu. 辛い] **salty, briny, saline**
海の水は鹹い うみのみずはからい Seawater tastes salty

196 からす

枯らす   Ⓚ0801

  ① **let wither, blight, kill**
    木枯らし こがらし cold wintry wind
  ② **season**

涸らす

  dry up, exhaust
    出涸らし でがらし used and insipid
    (as of tea or coffee)

197 かる

刈る   Ⓚ0017

  ⓐ (cut grass, hair or the like by sharp instrument) **clip, crop, cut, shear, mow, prune, trim**
  ⓑ **reap, crop, harvest**
    刈り込む かりこむ prune
    刈り取る かりとる mow, cut down, reap, harvest
    刈り立ての かりたての newly mown, newly cropped (head), just clipped
    草刈り くさかり mowing, mower
    羊毛を刈る ようもうをかる shear sheep
    刈り入れ かりいれ harvest, reap
    稲刈り いねかり rice reaping

狩る   Ⓚ0356

  hunt
    狩人 かりゅうど hunter
    狩り込み かりこみ roundup
    狩り出す かりだす hunt out, round up
    狩り集める かりあつめる muster, gather

駆る   Ⓚ1619

  ① **drive (a car), urge (a horse) on, spur on**
    駆り立てる かりたてる drive, spur on; stir up
    駆り集める かりあつめる mobilize, round up
  ② **prompt, inspire**
    駆られる からられる be driven by (one's feelings), succumb to

198 かれる

枯れる   Ⓚ0801

  ① **wither, die**
    枯れ葉 かれは dead [withered] leaf
    枯れ木 かれき dead [withered] tree
    枯れ野 かれの desolate [dreary] field
    立ち枯れの たちがれの blighted, withered
    夏枯れ なつがれ summer inactivity, summer slump
  ② **be seasoned**
    枯れた演技 かれたえんぎ well-seasoned acting

涸れる

  dry up, run dry, be exhausted

199 かわ¹

川   Ⓚ0001

  ⓐ **river, stream, brook**
  ⓑ **suffix after names of (esp. Japanese) rivers**
    川上 かわかみ upstream, upriver
    川瀬 かわせ rapids, shallows of a river
    小川 おがわ brook, streamlet

江戸川 えどがわ Edo River

河 ⓚ0298

ⓐ **river, stream**
ⓑ **suffix after names of (esp. foreign) rivers**
河底 かわぞこ riverbed
アマゾン河 あまぞんがわ Amazon River

皮 ⓚ2615

①ⓐ **skin, hide, pelt; fur; leather**
　ⓑ **skin, bark, peel, husk, shell**
皮財布 かわざいふ leather wallet
牛皮 ぎゅうかわ cowhide, oxhide
毛皮 けがわ fur
鰐皮 わにがわ crocodile skin [hide]
バナナの皮 ばななのかわ banana peel
②ⓐ **outer covering of articles**
　ⓑ **outward appearance, veneer**
薄皮 うすかわ thin skin film
布団皮(=蒲団皮) ふとんがわ ticking, quilting
皮切り かわきり beginning, start
化けの皮を現わす ばけのかわをあらわす expose one's true colors [character]

革 ⓚ2163

[also prefix and suffix] **leather**
革靴 かわぐつ leather shoes
革手袋 かわてぶくろ leather gloves
牛革 ぎゅうかわ cowhide, oxhide
エナメル革 えなめるがわ enameled [patent] leather

乾き ⓚ1500

drying, dryness

渇き ⓚ0473

thirst

乾く ⓚ1500

vi **dry (up), run dry**
乾き かわき drying, dryness
乾きの早い かわきのはやい fast drying (clothes)

渇く ⓚ0473

be thirsty, thirst
渇き かわき thirst
喉が渇く のどがかわく be thirsty

変わり ⓚ1782

① **change**
変わり無く かわりなく without change, uniformly; peacefully, well
② **difference**
どっちでも変わりは無い どっちでもかわりはない Whichever you choose, it makes no difference
③ **something wrong, accident**
④ **eccentricity**
風変わり ふうがわり eccentricity, extraordinariness

代わり

Ⓚ0018

① ⓐ **substitution, substitute**
  ⓑ **substitute, deputy, proxy**
  父の代わりとして ちちのかわりとして
  in place of one's father
  身代わり みがわり substitution; substitute, stand-in; scapegoat

② **compensation, exchange**
  お代わり おかわり second helping
  歩く代わりに走る あるくかわりにはしる run instead of walk

③ **though...on the other hand**
  高価な代わりに持ちが良い こうかなかわりにもちがよい Though it is expensive, on the other hand it will last a long time

換わり

Ⓚ0537

exchange

替わり

Ⓚ2424

① **turn, shift**
② **replacement (for a maid)**
③ **substitute program (of a kabuki play)**

204　　　かわる

変わる

Ⓚ1782

① ⓐ **change, undergo change, be altered, be transformed**
  ⓑ **change addresses, move, be transferred**
  機械の機構が変わった きかいのきこうがかわった The machine's mechanism has undergone changes.
  変わり目 かわりめ turning point

移り変わる うつりかわる change, shift
生まれ変わる うまれかわる be born again; start one's life afresh
天気が変わった てんきがかわった The weather changed
相変わらず あいかわらず as usual, as before
新しい家に変わる あたらしいいえにかわる move to a new house

② **be different, differ; be extraordinary, be odd**
  変わり者 かわりもの eccentric person, queer fish
  変わった かわった different; unusual, extraordinary, odd

代わる

Ⓚ0018

substitute, be substituted for (a person), take the place of
  機械が人力に代わる きかいがじんりょくにかわる Machines take the place of human labor
  代わる代わる かわるがわる by turns, alternately
  父親に代わって言う ちちおやにかわっていう speak for one's father
  ...に代わって …にかわって for..., in place of..., instead of...

換わる

Ⓚ0537

be exchanged, become interchanged, be converted, change
  この機械は金に換わる このきかいはかねにかわる This machine can be traded in for money
  換わり かわり exchange
  段ボールがお金に換わる だんぼーるがおかねにかわる Cardboard can be traded in for money

替わる Ⓚ2424

be replaced, change places with, replace, take turns, relieve, change

機械が替わった きかいがかわった The (old) machine was replaced (by a new one)

替わり かわり turn, shift; replacement (for a maid); substitute program (of a kabuki play)

替わってくれないか かわってくれないか Could you take over, please?

立ち替わる たちかわる take turns, alternate

入れ替わり いれかわり replacement, substitution, change, shifting

校長が替わった こうちょうがかわった A new school principal took over the job

205　　がかり

-掛かり Ⓚ0449

① [suffix] **combined, in a group of**

一家掛かりで いっかがかりで with the whole family

五人掛かりで運ぶ ごにんがかりではこぶ be carried by five people

② [suffix] **requiring (a period of time)**

三年掛かりの仕事 さんねんがかりのしごと job requiring three years

③ [also suffix] **resembling**

能掛かり のうがかり resembling a noh performance

④ **be entrusted to, depend on**

親掛かりの おやがかりの dependent on one's parents

-掛 Ⓚ0449

[usu. -係] [suffix] **person in charge (of a post, esp. in a government agency or railway company)**

出札掛 しゅっさつがかり ticket agent

-係 Ⓚ0078

[sometimes also -掛] [suffix] **person in charge, official in charge, clerk**

案内係 あんないがかり clerk at the information desk

会計係 かいけいがかり accountant, treasurer

受付係 うけつけがかり reception clerk

★ Note how the meanings of かかり and -がかり vary in accordance with the different *okurigana* inflections.

206　　がた

-型 Ⓚ2292

[also suffix] **type, model**

O型 おーがた model O; blood type O

血液型 けつえきがた blood type

千九百五十四年型 せんきゅうひゃくごじゅうよねんがた 1954 model

-形 Ⓚ0749

[also suffix] **-shaped**

卵形の たまごがたの egg-shaped

弓形の ゆみがたの arched, crescent-shaped

木 ⓚ2901

① [sometimes also 樹] **tree**

木登り **きのぼり** tree climbing

植木 **うえき** garden plant, shrub, pot plant

苗木 **なえぎ** sapling, young tree

並木 **なみき** row of trees, roadside trees

正木 **まさき** [also 柾] spindle tree

② **wood, timber, lumber**

木切れ **きぎれ** piece of wood, splinter

木彫り **きぼり** woodcarving

白木 **しらき** plain wood

頸木 **くびき** [also 軛] yoke

③ **wooden clappers**

樹 ⓚ0987

[usu. 木] **standing tree, tree**

効き ⓚ1164

effectiveness (esp. of drugs)

利き ⓚ1029

function, efficacy

効く ⓚ1164

be effective, have an effect, produce a desired effect

効き **きき** effectiveness (esp. of drugs)

効き目 **ききめ** effect, efficacy

良く効く薬 **よくきくくすり** very efficacious medicine

利く ⓚ1029

① **work (well), function (properly)**

利き **きき** function, efficacy

耳が利く **みみがきく** have a sharp ear

左利き **ひだりきき** left-handedness; left-hander; drinker, wine lover

② **speak (esp. as a mediator)**

口利き **くちきき** mediation; mediator, mouthpiece

聞く ⓚ2840

① ⓐ **hear**

ⓑ **hear of, be informed**

聞き苦しい **ききぐるしい** disagreeable to hear, offensive to the ear

聞き手 **ききて** listener, audience

聞き取る **ききとる** catch, follow, understand

聞き取り **ききとり** aural comprehension

盗み聞き **ぬすみぎき** eavesdropping, tapping

聞かせる(=聞かす) **きかせる(=きかす)** inform, tell; read to, play for, sing for

② **obey, follow**

親の言う事を聞く **おやのいうことをきく** obey one's parents

③ [formerly also 訊く] **ask, inquire**

聞き返す **ききかえす** inquire again

道を聞く **みちをきく** ask the way

聴く ⓚ1292

listen (to), give an ear to
民の声を聴く たみのこえをきく listen to the voice of the people

訊く ⓚ1320

[now usu. 聞く] **ask, inquire**
訊き返す ききかえす ask again; ask in return
道を訊く みちをきく ask the way

211 きざし

兆し ⓚ0199

omen, sign, symptom
凶事の兆し きょうじのきざし omen of disaster

萌し ⓚ1995

germination, sprouting; dawning

212 きざす

兆す ⓚ0199

show signs [symptoms] of

萌す ⓚ1995

germinate, sprout; spring up, dawn
萌し きざし germination, sprouting; dawning

213 きず

傷 ⓚ0137

① **wound, injury, bruise, scar**
傷口 きずぐち wound

傷跡 (=傷痕) きずあと scar, cicatrix
傷付ける きずつける wound, injure, damage; hurt (a person's feelings), disgrace (one's family name)
傷付く きずつく get injured, be wounded [bruised]; be (emotionally) hurt
掠り傷 かすりきず scratch, graze, slight wound
古傷 ふるきず old wound, scar; past misdeed
② [formerly also 疵] **defect, flaw, crack, fault, weak point**
傷物 きずもの defective article; deflowered girl

疵

[now usu. 傷] **defect, flaw, crack, fault, weak point**
疵物 きずもの defective article; deflowered girl
玉に疵 (=玉に瑕) たまにきず flaw in the crystal, fly in the ointment
脛に疵持つ すねにきずもつ have a guilty conscience

214 きぬ

絹 ⓚ1243

silk, silk fabrics
絹織物 きぬおりもの silk fabrics [goods]
絹地 きぬじ silk fabrics
絹糸 きぬいと silk thread
薄絹 うすぎぬ sheer silk

衣 ⓚ1736

elegant **garment**
衣擦れ きぬずれ rustling (of clothes)

濡れ衣 ぬれぎぬ false charge, un-founded suspicion

歯に衣を着せない はにきぬをきせない not mince matters

215 きまる

決まる ⓀK0233

① **be decided [fixed], be settled, be arranged**

決まり きまり settlement, conclusion; rule, regulation; custom

十五日と決まっている じゅうごにちときまっている The date is fixed for the 15th of the month

② **be certain [sure], be a matter of course**

雨が降るに決まっている あめがふるにきまっている It is sure to rain

行かないに決まっている いかないにきまっている Of course I won't go

極まる ⓀK0900

① **be decided [fixed], be settled, be arranged**

② **be certain [sure], be a matter of course**

216 きめる

決める ⓀK0233

① **decide, determine, fix**

自分で決める じぶんできめる decide by oneself

② **agree upon, arrange**

取り決め とりきめ decision, agreement

③ (bring to a conclusion) **settle, conclude**

決め付ける きめつける scold, take (a person) to task

決め手 きめて decisive factor, clincher; trump card, winning move

極める ⓀK0900

① **decide, determine, fix**

② **agree upon, arrange**

③ (bring to a conclusion) **settle, conclude**

217 きよめる

清める ⓀK0479

①ⓐ [sometimes also 浄める] (rid of dirt or impurities) **cleanse, purify**

ⓑ [usu. 浄める] (rid of moral taint) **purify, purge**

清め きよめ purification, ablution

② [sometimes also 浄める] **exorcise**

身を清める みをきよめる cleanse oneself

浄める ⓀK0342

①ⓐ [usu. 清める] (rid of dirt or impurities) **cleanse, purify**

ⓑ [sometimes also 清める] (rid of moral taint) **purify, purge**

② [usu. 清める] **exorcise**

218 きる

切る ⓀK0015

①ⓐ **cut, slice, carve**

ⓑ [sometimes also 伐る] **cut down (trees), fell, chop down**

ⓒ [formerly also 剪る] **prune, trim, shear**

ⓓ [formerly also 截る] **cut (flat things such as cloth or paper)**

切り離す きりはなす cut [chop] off, sever, detach

切り捨てる きりすてる cut down, cut away; omit

切手 きって postage stamp

切符 きっぷ ticket

切っ先 きっさき [sometimes also 鋒] point of a blade [sword]; tone of argument, force of an attack

切り倒す きりたおす fell (a tree)

② [also 斬る] **cut (a person) with a sword, cut down, kill**

試し切り ためしぎり trying out a new sword (on someone)

裏切る うらぎる betray, turn traitor, double-cross

③ (separate from the main body) **cut off, break away**

切符を切る きっぷをきる punch a ticket, rip off a coupon

封切り ふうきり release, first run, premiere

④ **perform an action as if by cutting**

波を切る なみをきる cut one's way through the waves

踏切 ふみきり railroad crossing

皮切り かわきり beginning, start

⑤ⓐ (discontinue an action) **cut off, pause, break off, turn off, hang up**

ⓑ **cut [sever] connection with**

切り替える きりかえる switch, change, renew

思い切る おもいきる resign oneself to, give up; resolve, determine

打ち切る うちきる put an end to, break off, finish

縁切り えんきり severing off connections

⑥ **cut off [divide] by or as if by a partition**

締切(=〆切) しめきり closing day, deadline; Closed, No Entrance

仕切る しきる partition, divide, mark off; settle accounts; *sumo* toe the mark

⑦ **fall short of, be below**

千円を切る せんえんをきる be less than 1000 yen

⑧ **perform an action boldly**

切り札 きりふだ trump (card), last resort

踏み切る ふみきる make a bold start, take a plunge; take off; *sumo* step out of the ring

見得を切る みえをきる pose, assume a posture; make a defiant [proud] gesture

⑨ **drain (water)**

水切り みずきり drainer; cutwater, forefoot; ducks and drakes

伐る　　　　　　　　Ⓚ0027

[now usu. 切る] **cut down (trees), fell, chop down**

木を伐る きをきる fell a tree

剪る

[now usu. 切る] **prune, trim, shear**

枝を剪る えだをきる prune a tree

截る

[now usu. 切る] **cut (flat things such as cloth or paper)**

布を截る ぬのをきる cut cloth

斬る　　　　　　　　Ⓚ1347

① [also 切る] **cut (a person) with a sword, cut down, kill**

斬り死に きりじに fighting (with a sword) to death

斬り掛かる きりかかる slash at, assault with a sword

斬り捨てる きりすてる cut down, slay; truncate, round down; discard, cast away

首斬り くびきり decapitation; firing, layoff; *hist* small sword for decapitation

② **criticize severely, attack**

219 きわまり

極まり ⓚ0900

[sometimes also 窮まり] **extremity, limit**

極まり無い きわまりない extremely, in the extreme

痛快極まり無い つうかいきわまりない be extremely thrilling

窮まり ⓚ2078

[now usu. 極まり] **extremity, limit**

窮まり無い きわまりない extremely, in the extreme

220 きわまる

極まる ⓚ0900

[also suffix] **reach an extreme (state or point), be extremely (dangerous)**

感極まる かんきわまる be overcome with emotion

危険極まる きけんきわまる extremely dangerous

窮まる ⓚ2078

ⓐ **come to an end, terminate**

ⓑ **come to the end of one's tether, be at a loss**

道が窮まる みちがきわまる come to a dead end

進退窮まる しんたいきわまる be at a loss

谷まる ⓚ1758

ⓐ **come to an end, terminate**

ⓑ **come to the end of one's tether, be at a loss**

221 きわみ

極み ⓚ0900

height, apex, utmost

栄華の極み えいがのきわみ apex of prosperity

窮み ⓚ2078

extremity, end, limit

窮み無き きわみなき endless, without limit

222 きわめる

極める ⓚ0900

ⓐ **carry to extremity, go to extremes, be extremely (cruel)**

ⓑ **go to the extreme [end], reach an extreme, go to the highest point**

極めて きわめて extremely, very

口を極めて誉める くちをきわめてほめる be lavish in another's praise

暴虐を極める ぼうぎゃくをきわめる act with extreme violence

惨状を極める さんじょうをきわめる present a very terrible [miserable] sight

貧困を極める ひんこんをきわめる be reduced to extreme poverty, be extremely poor

極め付きの品 きわめつきのしな article of certified genuineness

見極める みきわめる see through, discern; ascertain, grasp

山頂を極める さんちょうをきわめる reach the summit

窮める　　　　　Ⓚ2078

① [also 極める]
- ⓐ **carry to extremity, go to extremes, be extremely (cruel)**
- ⓑ **go to the extreme [end], reach an extreme, go to the highest point**

口を窮めて誉める くちをきわめてほめる be lavish in another's praise

貧困を窮める ひんこんをきわめる be reduced to extreme poverty, be extremely poor

② [usu. 究める] **investigate thoroughly, study exhaustively, master**

学を窮める がくをきわめる study exhaustively

究める　　　　　Ⓚ1885

[sometimes also 窮める] **investigate thoroughly, study exhaustively, master**

奥義を究める おうぎをきわめる master the secrets of an art

223　　　　ぎ

-着　　　　　　Ⓚ2826

[sometimes also -衣] [also suffix] **wear, clothes, dress, suit**

晴れ着 はれぎ one's best (clothes), gala [holiday] dress

肌着 はだぎ underwear

上着 うわぎ outer garment, coat, jacket

水着 みずぎ bathing [swimming] suit

不断着(=普段着) ふだんぎ everyday wear [clothes], home wear

訪問着 ほうもんぎ visiting [gala] dress

-衣　　　　　　Ⓚ1736

[usu. -着] **outer garment, clothes, wear**

上衣 うわぎ outer garment, coat, jacket

224　　　　ぎめ

-決め　　　　　Ⓚ0233

[usu. -極め] **indicates periods of time (esp. months)**

-極め　　　　　Ⓚ0900

[sometimes also -決め] **indicates periods of time (esp. months)**

月極め駐車場 つきぎめちゅうしゃじょう parking lot rented on a monthly basis

-切れ Ⓚ0015

① **expiration of, depletion of**

品切れ しなぎれ absence [exhaustion] of stock

時間切れ じかんぎれ expiration of the allotted time

② **fragments from writings by famous historical figures**

高野切れ こうやぎれ fragments from the old literary work kept at Koyasan

-裂れ Ⓚ2347

[also suffix] **fragment (of old textile), strip**

縁裂れ ふちぎれ border strip

古代裂れ こだいぎれ ancient cloth fragment

226 くう

食う Ⓚ1787

① ⓐ **eat, have a meal**
  ⓑ **live on, subsist on, feed on**

食い物 くいもの food; victim

食い違う くいちがう cross; be in discord (with)

飯を食う めしをくう have a meal

食い詰める くいつめる go broke

翻訳で食って行く ほんやくでくっていく live on translation

② **hold on to (in one's mouth), not let go**

食い下がる くいさがる hang on (to one's opponent); persist

食い込む くいこむ eat (one's way) into, encroach; cause a deficit

食い止める くいとめる check, hold back

③ **consume, spend**

ガソリンを食う車 がそりんをくうくるま gas-guzzling car

④ **beat, excel**

横綱を食う よこづなをくう beat a grand champion

⑤ [formerly also 喰う] **get (as a slap in the face)**

喰う Ⓚ0507

① ⓐ **eat (greedily), devour**
  ⓑ [now usu. 食う] **get (as a slap in the face)**

虫喰い むしくい worm-eaten; vermiculation, wormhole, moth hole; leaf warbler

一口喰う ひとくちくう take a bite, have a munch

飯を喰う めしをくう devour a meal

びんたを喰う びんたをくう get slapped in the face

② **unclassified compounds**

漆喰 しっくい plaster, stucco

227 くす

楠 Ⓚ0930

[sometimes also 樟] **camphor tree**

楠の木 くすのき camphor tree

樟 Ⓚ0980

[usu. 楠] **camphor tree**

樟の木 くすのき camphor tree

228 くすのき

楠 Ⓚ0930

[sometimes also 樟] **camphor tree**

樟 Ⓚ0980

[usu. 楠] **camphor tree**

229 くすり

薬 Ⓚ2100

drug, medicine, remedy; powdered medicine, pill; chemical; enamel, glaze; benefit
- 薬屋 くすりや drugstore
- 薬指 くすりゆび third finger, ring finger
- 薬になる くすりになる be beneficial (to), do (a person) good
- 飲み薬 のみぐすり medicine, internal medicine
- 風邪薬 かぜぐすり remedy for a cold
- 上薬 うわぐすり [also 釉 or 釉薬] glaze, enamel

釉 Ⓚ1374

glaze, enamel
- 釉掛け(=薬掛け) くすりがけ glazing, enameling
- 灰釉 はいぐすり ash glaze

230 くだく

砕く Ⓚ1048

[formerly also 摧く] *vt* **crush, smash, break into pieces, shatter; rack (one's brains); explain plainly**
- 打ち砕く うちくだく break to pieces, smash, crush; baffle, frustrate
- 噛み砕く かみくだく crunch; simplify, explain plainly

摧く

[now replaced by 砕く] *vt* **crush, smash, break into pieces, shatter; rack (one's brains); explain plainly**

231 くだける

砕ける Ⓚ1048

[formerly also 摧ける] *vi* **be crushed, be broken, be smashed; break down, buckle, give way; become softened, become complaisant, get friendly; be easy [plain]**
- 砕け散る くだけちる be smashed up
- 砕けた態度 くだけたたいど friendly attitude
- 砕けた文章 くだけたぶんしょう plain [informal] writing
- 腰砕け こしくだけ breaking down in the middle of a bout; weakening of one's attitude

摧ける

[now replaced by 砕ける] *vi* **be crushed, be broken, be smashed; break down, buckle, give way; become softened, become complaisant, get friendly; be easy [plain]**

232 くだす

下す Ⓚ2862

① **bring down, lower**

位を下す くらいをくだす lower in rank, degrade

見下す みくだす look down upon, think lightly of

② ⓐ **give to an inferior, grant, bestow**
ⓑ **give a command, issue orders**

神の下し給うた物 かみのくだしたもうたもの heavenly gift, godsend

進軍の命令を下す しんぐんのめいれいをくだす give a marching order

③ **pass (judgment), hand down (a decision)**

結論を下す けつろんをくだす draw a conclusion

④ [sometimes also 降す] **subjugate, subdue; defeat, beat**

⑤ **have loose bowels**

腹下し はらくだし diarrhea, laxity; purgative (medicine), evacuant

降す
®0414

[usu. 下す] **subjugate, subdue; defeat, beat**

くだる

下る
®2862

① ⓐ **go down, descend, step down from; go downstream**
ⓑ **go down or away from a central place (as the capital)**
ⓒ (decline in level or grade) **fall, drop, be inferior**

丘を下る おかをくだる go down a hill
川を下る かわをくだる descend a river
駆け下る かけくだる run down
九州へ下る きゅうしゅうへくだる go down to Kyushu
野に下る やにくだる leave the government service

下らない くだらない be no less than; trifling, worthless; absurd

② **be given (orders), be issued**

判決が下る はんけつがくだる Sentence is passed

③ **have loose bowels**

腹が下る はらがくだる have loose bowels

④ **elapse, pass**

時代が更に下って じだいがさらにくだって later in the period

降る
®0414

surrender, submit to

軍門に降る ぐんもんにくだる surrender, capitulate

くつ

靴
®1586

[sometimes also 沓] [also suffix] **shoes, boots**

靴下 くつした socks, stockings
靴墨 くつずみ shoe polish
靴音 くつおと sound of a person's footsteps
靴直し くつなおし shoe mending
靴ブラシ くつぶらし shoe brush
皮靴 かわぐつ leather shoes
長靴 ながぐつ boots, top boots
運動靴 うんどうぐつ sneakers
紳士靴 しんしぐつ men's shoes
スケート靴 すけーとぐつ skates

沓
®2144

[usu. 靴] **footwear, sandals, clogs**

沓脱ぎ くつぬぎ stepstone, doorstone

沓下 くつした socks
沓摺り くつずり doorsill
雪沓 ゆきぐつ straw snow boots
[shoes]

235 くび

首 ®1956

① [formerly also 頸]
  ⓐ **neck**
  ⓑ **narrow part, neck (of a bottle)**
  首飾り くびかざり necklace
  手首 てくび wrist
  バイオリンの首 ばいおりんのくび
    neck of a violin
② **head**
  首を傾げる くびをかしげる put one's
    head on one side
③ **firing, discharge**
  首切り くびきり firing, dismissal;
    decapitation
  首になる くびになる be fired, be
    dismissed

頸

  ⓐ [original meaning] **neck**
  ⓑ **narrow part, neck (of a bottle)**
  頸飾り くびかざり necklace
  頸木 くびき [also 軛] yoke
  手頸 てくび wrist
  バイオリンの頸 ばいおりんのくび
    neck of a violin

236 くぼむ

凹む ®2924

[in compounds] (of things) **become hollow, become depressed**

凹目 くぼめ sunken [deep-set] eyes

窪む ®2063

(of the ground) **become hollow, become depressed, cave in**
  窪み くぼみ hollow, cavity, dent,
    depression
  落ち窪む おちくぼむ sink in, cave in

237 くむ

酌む ®1331

drink, have a drink
  酒を酌み交わす さけをくみかわす
    drink together, help one another
    to sake

汲む ®0235

① ⓐ **draw water, ladle, scoop up,
    pump**
  ⓑ **pour (a drink) into a cup [glass]**
  汲み取る くみとる draw [dip] up,
    drain; take into consideration
  汲み立ての くみたての freshly drawn
  汲み干す くみほす drain out, pump
    dry
  水汲み みずくみ drawing water
  茶汲み ちゃくみ serving tea (to
    guests); someone who serves tea
② **consider, sympathize with**
  意を汲む いをくむ enter into a
    person's feelings

238 くやしい

悔しい ®0324

[also 口惜しい] **vexing, mortifying,
regrettable**

悔しさ くやしさ vexation, chagrin, regret
悔し泣き くやしなき crying from vexation, tears of regret

口惜しい Ⓚ2865

[also 悔しい] **vexing, mortifying, regrettable**

239 くら

倉 Ⓚ1807

[also 蔵, sometimes also 庫] **storehouse (esp. for grains or goods), warehouse, granary**
倉荷 くらに warehouse goods
倉渡し くらわたし ex warehouse

蔵 Ⓚ2088

[also 倉, sometimes also 庫] **storehouse (for temporary preservation), storeroom, godown**
蔵出し くらだし delivery of goods from a storehouse
米蔵 こめぐら rice granary
大蔵省 おおくらしょう Ministry of Finance

庫 Ⓚ2682

[usu. 倉, sometimes also 蔵] **warehouse (for merchandise), storeroom**
庫入れ くらいれ warehousing

240 くらい

暗い Ⓚ0921

ⓐ [sometimes also 昏い, 闇い, or 冥い] **dark, dim;** (of colors) **dark;** (producing gloom) **dark, dreary, dismal;** (concealed) **dark, shadowy, shady**
ⓑ **be ignorant, be a stranger to**
暗さ くらさ darkness; gloom
暗闇 くらやみ in darkness
暗い色 くらいいろ dark color
暗い過去 くらいかこ shadowy past
暗い気持になる くらいきもちになる feel gloomy
薄暗い うすぐらい gloomy, dim
世事に暗い せじにくらい know little of the world

冥い Ⓚ1810

[usu. 暗い, sometimes also 昏い or 闇い] **dark, dim;** (of colors) **dark;** (producing gloom) **dark, dreary, dismal;** (concealed) **dark, shadowy, shady**

昏い Ⓚ2143

[usu. 暗い, sometimes also 闇い or 冥い] **dark, dim;** (of colors) **dark;** (producing gloom) **dark, dreary, dismal;** (concealed) **dark, shadowy, shady**

闇い Ⓚ2846

[usu. 暗い, sometimes also 昏い or 冥い] **dark, dim;** (of colors) **dark;** (producing gloom) **dark, dreary, dismal;** (concealed) **dark, shadowy, shady**

241 くらう

食らう ⓀＫ1787
① **eat, drink**
大食らい おおぐらい glutton
② [formerly also 喰らう] **get (as a slap in the face)**
食らい込む くらいこむ be sent up, be imprisoned

喰らう Ⓚ0507
ⓐ **eat (greedily), devour**
ⓑ [now usu. 食らう] **get (as a slap in the face)**
面喰らう めんくらう be confused, be bewildered
一発喰らわす いっぱつくらわす give a blow

242 くらべる

比べる Ⓚ0014
[sometimes also 較べる] **compare, contrast**
比べ物にならない くらべものにならない be no match for
背比べ せいくらべ comparison of statures

較べる Ⓚ1397
[usu. 比べる] **compare, contrast**
大きさを較べる おおきさをくらべる compare the size

243 くらます

暗ます Ⓚ0921
① **abscond, conceal oneself**
② **deceive, fool, dissemble**

晦ます Ⓚ0864
① **abscond, conceal oneself**
② **deceive, fool, dissemble**

244 くるわ

郭 Ⓚ1499
① **red-light district**
郭通いをする くるわがよいをする frequent a house of ill fame
② **area enclosed by earthwork**

廓
① **red-light district**
② **area enclosed by earthwork**

245 ぐさ

-草 Ⓚ1953
① [sometimes also -種] **material, stuff**
質草 しちぐさ article for pawning
笑い草 わらいぐさ laughingstock
② [suffix] **writing**
徒然草 つれづれぐさ Random Thoughts from My Leisure Hours

-種 Ⓚ1128
[usu. -草] **material, stuff**
質種 しちぐさ article for pawning
笑い種 わらいぐさ laughingstock

険しい
Ⓚ0495

[sometimes also 嶮しい] (sharply inclined and difficult to climb) **steep, precipitous; craggy; severe, grim, fierce, angry**

険しさ けわしさ steepness; severity, grimness

険しい山 けわしいやま steep [craggy] mountain

険しい顔 けわしいかお grim face

嶮しい

[usu. 険しい] (sharply inclined and difficult to climb) **steep, precipitous; craggy; severe, grim, fierce, angry**

247　　こ[1]

子
Ⓚ2872

① offspring of humans or animals:
　ⓐ **child, son, daughter**
　ⓑ [formerly also 仔] **offspring, youngling; puppy; cub; roe**
　ⓒ [sometimes also 児] (boy or girl) **child, kid, youngster**

子供 こども child, kid; son, daughter

親子 おやこ(=しんし) parent and child

息子 むすこ son

子犬 こいぬ puppy

男の子 おとこのこ boy, baby boy

迷子 まいご lost child

② [also 娘 or コ] **girl, gal**

あいつは行ける子だ あいつはいけるこだ She's a nice gal [good-looking broad]

③ **interest**

児
Ⓚ2203

[now usu. 子] (boy or girl) **child, kid, youngster**

良い児 いいこ good boy (or girl)

男の児 おとこのこ boy, baby boy

娘
Ⓚ0367

[also 子 or コ] **girl, gal**

良い娘だ いいこだ She's a nice [good-looking] girl [gal]

仔
Ⓚ0022

[now usu. 子] **animal offspring such as a puppy, cub or roe**

仔牛 こうし calf

仔犬 こいぬ puppy

小−
Ⓚ0002

①ⓐ (less in size or quantity) **small, little, short**
　ⓑ (less in intensity) **small, light, slight**

小型(=小形)の こがたの small-sized, small; pocket (dictionary)

小物 こもの small articles, gadget

小鳥 ことり small [little] bird

小麦 こむぎ wheat

小唄 こうた ditty, ballad

小屋 こや cottage, hut, cabin; playhouse

小切手 こぎって check

小口 こぐち small lot, small sum [amount]; end, edge

小幅 こはば single breadth, narrow range

小指 こゆび little finger, pinkie; little toe

小文字 こもじ lowercase letter

小雪 こゆき light snowfall

小声 こごえ low voice, whisper
② ⓐ (of secondary importance) **secondary, sub-**
　　ⓑ [belittling] **small, petty, little**
小売り こうり retail, sale in small quantities
小売店 こうりてん retail store
小分け こわけ subdivision
小僧 こぞう priestling; servant boy; kid, brat
小役人 こやくにん petty official
③ [emphatic preceding adjectives or verbs] **a little, slightly, very**
小戻す こもどす (of the market) rally a little
小恥ずかしい こはずかしい a little shameful
小高い こだかい slightly elevated
④ **nearly, almost**
小一時間 こいちじかん nearly one hour

248　　　こ²

-子　　　　　　　　　Ⓚ2872
① [also suffix] **child, kid, boy, girl**
継子 ままこ stepchild
悪戯っ子 いたずらっこ mischievous kid
② [also -っこ] [sometimes also 児]
　　ⓐ **person, performer of an action**
　　ⓑ [suffix] **native of a specific place**
売り子 うりこ shopgirl, sales clerk
踊り子 おどりこ dancer, dancing girl
売れっ子歌手 うれっこかしゅ popular singer
江戸っ子 えどっこ Edoite, Tokyoite
神戸っ子 こうべっこ native of Kobe
③ [also -っこ] **noun forming suffix, esp. for small objects**

振り子 ふりこ pendulum
玉子 たまご [also 卵] egg
根っ子 ねっこ root; stump, stub
梯子 はしご ladder
④ **element for forming female names**
恵子 けいこ Keiko
典子 のりこ Noriko

-児　　　　　　　　　Ⓚ2203
ⓐ **person, performer of an action**
ⓑ [suffix] **native of a specific place**
売り児 うりこ shopgirl, sales clerk

249　　　こう

請う　　　　　　　　Ⓚ1426
ⓐ **ask, request, solicit**
ⓑ [also 乞う] **beg**
寄付を請う きふをこう solicit donations

乞う　　　　　　　　Ⓚ1707
ⓐ [also 請う] **beg**
ⓑ [in compounds] **solicit, pray for**
物乞い ものごい beggar; begging
命乞い いのちごい begging for one's life
乞い願わくは(=希くは) こいねがわくは I pray in earnest that, I beg that, I yearn that
雨乞い あまごい ritual prayer for rain
暇乞い いとまごい leave-taking, farewell visit

250 こうむる

被る   Ⓚ1077

[also 蒙る] **be subjected to, undergo, receive, sustain**

損害を被る そんがいをこうむる suffer a loss

恩恵を被る おんけいをこうむる share in the benefit

蒙る   Ⓚ2045

[also 被る] **be subjected to, undergo, receive, sustain**

損害を蒙る そんがいをこうむる suffer a loss

251 こえる

越える   Ⓚ2825

go over, go across, go beyond, jump over

乗り越える のりこえる get over, climb over; surmount, overcome

川を越える かわをこえる cross a river

超える   Ⓚ2824

ⓐ (go beyond in quantity or degree) **exceed, surpass, be over**

ⓑ (go beyond the limit) **surpass, excel, be above, transcend**

限度を超える げんどをこえる pass the limit, go beyond the limit

観客は百人を超えた かんきゃくは ひゃくにんをこえた The audience exceeded 100

人知を超えた じんちをこえた beyond human understanding

★ The differences between the above verbs are subtle, and they are easily confused. Make a careful study of the equivalents and examples under each entry. There is no consensus among lexicographers as to their correct usage.

252 こおる

凍る   Ⓚ0111

[formerly also 氷る] **freeze, congeal**

凍り付く こおりつく freeze

氷る   Ⓚ0025

[now usu. 凍る] **freeze**

253 こす

越す   Ⓚ2825

①ⓐ **go over, cross over, pass, go across**

  ⓑ **surmount, pass through, overcome**

通り越す とおりこす go beyond, pass through

乗り越す のりこす ride past

山を越す やまをこす go across a mountain; surmount a difficulty

②ⓐ **be better than, surpass**

  ⓑ **outstrip, outrun**

それに越した事は無い それにこし たことはない Nothing could be better

勝ち越す かちこす have more wins than losses; lead (someone) by (three) matches

追い越す おいこす outrun, pass; overtake

③ **pass, spend (time)**
年越し としこし welcoming the new year

④ **move, change quarters**
引っ越す ひっこす move, change quarters

⑤ **go, come**
斎藤さんがお越しです さいとうさんがおこしです Mr. Saito has come

超す Ⓚ 2824

(go beyond in quantity or degree) **surpass, exceed, rise above, be over**
一万人を超す人人 いちまんにんをこすひとびと more than 10,000 people

254 こたえる

答える Ⓚ2340

ⓐ **answer (a question), reply, respond**
ⓑ **answer (a problem), solve**
質問に答える しつもんにこたえる answer a question

応える Ⓚ2640

① **come home to (one), strike home, have effect on; be a great strain**
暑さが応える あつさがこたえる feel the heat very much

② **repay, reward**
親切に応える しんせつにこたえる repay a kindness

255 こと¹

殊 Ⓚ0850

[in compounds] **specialness, distinctiveness**
殊に ことに especially, distinctly, exceptionally, above all
殊の外 ことのほか exceedingly, beyond measure; unexpectedly
殊更に ことさらに especially; intentionally, deliberately

異 Ⓚ2241

difference
異にする ことにする differ, be different

256 こと²

琴 Ⓚ2422

[sometimes also 箏] [also suffix] **koto, (Japanese) zither, harp, lute**
琴爪 ことづめ artificial fingernail [plectrum] of ivory used in playing the koto
竪琴 たてごと harp
大正琴 たいしょうごと taishogoto, Nagoya harp

箏

[usu. 琴] **koto, (Japanese) zither**

257 この

此の Ⓚ0728

[sometimes also 斯の] demonstrative **this**
此の世界 このせかい this world

此度 このたび this occasion, now
此の頃 このごろ recently; these days
此の手 このて this way (of doing); this sort
此の方 このかた since; [polite] this person

斯の ⓀK1521

[usu. 此の] *demonstrative* **this**

258 こぼす

零す ⓀK2433

① **spill, drop; shed (tears)**
② **let out (a smile)**
③ **complain, grumble**

溢す ⓀK0601

①ⓐ **spill**
　ⓑ **shed (tears)**
　目溢し めこぼし connivance, overlook
② **grumble**

259 こぼれる

零れる ⓀK2433

① **spill, drop, fall; overflow**
② (issue involuntarily from) **escape, find vent, break out**

溢れる ⓀK0601

①ⓐ **spill, fall out**
　ⓑ **overflow**
　咲き溢れる さきこぼれる bloom all over
②ⓐ **leak out (as of light)**
　ⓑ **show (as of a smile)**

込む ⓀK2608

①ⓐ [original meaning] **move inward, get in, come in**
　ⓑ **cause to move inward, put in, bring in**—used as a verbal suffix to indicate action directed inward
　乗り込む のりこむ board, go on board; march into
　迷い込む まよいこむ stray [wander] into
　割り込み わりこみ breaking into a queue, wedging oneself in
　払い込む はらいこむ pay in, pay up
　吸い込む すいこむ inhale, breathe in; suck in
　持ち込む もちこむ carry [bring] in; propose, refer to; bring (a matter) to
②ⓐ **emphatic verbal suffix indicating intense involvement in an activity** (similar to *up* in *polish up*)
　ⓑ **verbal suffix indicating continuation of present state**
　眠り込む ねむりこむ fall asleep
　黙り込む だまりこむ sink into silence
　住み込みの すみこみの live-in
　泊まり込み とまりこみ staying in (to do one's job)

混む ⓀK0475

[usu. 込む] **be crowded, be congested, be packed**
　混み合う こみあう be crowded, be packed, be jammed
　人混み ひとごみ crowd [throng] (of people)

込める　　Ⓚ2608

① [also verbal suffix] **put in, coop in, shut up**

閉じ込める とじこめる shut in [up], lock in [up]

引っ込める ひっこめる put [pull, move] back

② **load (a gun), charge**

元込め銃 もとごめじゅう breechloading rifle, breechloader

③ⓐ **include, count in**
　ⓑ [formerly also 籠める] **impregnate with, imply**

一切を込めた宿泊料 いっさいをこめたしゅくはくりょう all-inclusive hotel charges

警告の意味を込めて けいこくのいみをこめて with an implication of warning

④ [formerly also 籠める] **concentrate on, devote oneself to**

心を込めて こころをこめて with all one's heart, wholeheartedly

⑤ [formerly also 籠める] **hang over, envelop, shroud**

霧が立ち込めた港 きりがたちこめたみなと harbor wrapped in a mist

籠める　　Ⓚ2383

① **concentrate on, devote oneself to**

心を籠めて こころをこめて with all one's heart, wholeheartedly

② **impregnate with, imply**

警告の意味を籠めて けいこくのいみをこめて with an implication of warning

③ **hang over, envelop, shroud**

霧が立ち籠めた港 きりがたちこめたみなと harbor wrapped in a mist

是　　Ⓚ2157

[also 之] pronoun **this**

之　　Ⓚ2886

[also 是] pronoun **this**

之は何ですか これはなんですか What is this?

此れ　　Ⓚ0728

[also 是 or 之] pronoun **this**

此れから これから after this, from now on; the future

此れ位 これくらい (=これぐらい) (about) this much [amount]

此れ見よがしに これみよがしに ostentatiously

此れと言って これといって [in negative constructions] in particular, to speak of

彼此 あれこれ one thing or another, this and that

惟　　Ⓚ0438

[archaic] **emphatic adverb**

弁明惟努めたい べんめいこれつとめたい Well, I shall explain myself

怖い　　Ⓚ0263

[also 恐い] **fearful, scary, uncanny; be afraid**

怖さ こわさ fear, dreadfulness
怖怖 こわごわ timidly, gingerly
怖い顔 こわいかお angry look, grim face
犬が怖い いぬがこわい be afraid of dogs

恐い ⓚ2306

[also 怖い] **fearful, scary, uncanny; be afraid**
　恐さ こわさ fear, dreadfulness
　犬が恐い いぬがこわい be afraid of dogs

強い ⓚ0432

tough, hard, stiff
　情が強い じょうがこわい be hard-headed, be stubborn

264　　こわがる

怖がる ⓚ0263

[also 恐がる] **be afraid of, be frightened**
　怖がり こわがり timidity; coward

恐がる ⓚ2306

[also 怖がる] **be afraid of, be frightened**
　恐がり こわがり timidity; coward

265　　こわす

壊す ⓚ0684

[sometimes also 毀す] *vt* **break (down), destroy, smash, take apart; spoil, mar, upset**

取り壊し とりこわし demolition, pulling down
ぶち壊す ぶちこわす destroy, demolish, smash; spoil, upset

毀す ⓚ1592

[usu. 壊す] *vt* **break (down), destroy, smash, take apart; spoil, mar, upset**
　取り毀す とりこわす demolish, pull down

266　　こわれる

壊れる ⓚ0684

[sometimes also 毀れる] *vi* **break (down), be broken; get out of order; be broken off, fall through, be upset**
　壊れ物 こわれもの fragile article, breakables; broken article
　壊れた時計 こわれたとけい broken clock
　縁談が壊れた えんだんがこわれた The match was broken off

毀れる ⓚ1592

ⓐ **break (down), be broken; get out of order**
ⓑ **be broken off, fall through, be upset**

267　　ごみ

塵

[sometimes also 芥] **trash, garbage, rubbish, litter; dirt, dust**
　塵箱 ごみばこ trash can [bin], garbage can

塵溜め ごみため garbage dump, trash heap

粗大塵 そだいごみ bulk trash, over-sized garbage

芥   Ⓚ1895

[usu. 塵] **trash, garbage, rubbish, litter; dirt, dust**

芥箱 ごみばこ trash can [bin], garbage can

芥溜め ごみため garbage dump, trash heap

268   さ

小–   Ⓚ0002

[also prefix] *elegant* **little, nice**

小百合 さゆり lily

小夜曲 さよきょく serenade

早–   Ⓚ2120

young, supple

早乙女 さおとめ rice-planting girl; girl

早苗 さなえ rice sprouts

269   さか

坂   Ⓚ0206

slope, incline, hill

坂道 さかみち slope

上り坂 のぼりざか ascent, upward slope

阪   Ⓚ0243

slope, incline, hill—now used almost exclusively in the writing of names

大阪府 おおさかふ Osaka Prefecture

★ Both forms have the same meaning, but the latter is now used almost exclusively in the writing of names.

270   さかい

境   Ⓚ0618

boundary, border; place, region

境目 さかいめ border, boundary line; crisis

境を異にする さかいをことにする live in different worlds

国境 くにざかい (national, state or provincial) boundary [border]

見境 みさかい distinction, discrimination

生死の境 せいしのさかい between life and death

堺   Ⓚ0513

Sakai

堺市 さかいし Sakai city (in Osaka Prefecture)

271   さかな

魚   Ⓚ1825

[also suffix] **fish**

魚屋 さかなや fish shop; fish dealer

小魚 こざかな small fish, fry

干し魚 ほしざかな dried fish, stockfish

焼き魚 やきざかな broiled fish

肴   Ⓚ1780

ⓐ **side dish to go with drinks**

ⓑ **entertainment [conversation] to liven up a drinking party**

肴舞 さかなまい dance performed at a feast

272 さかのぼる

逆上る ⓚ2662

[usu. 遡る]
ⓐ **go upstream**
ⓑ **go back (to the past); retroact**

遡る ⓚ2785

ⓐ **go upstream, go back (to the past)**
ⓑ **retroact**
鮭は川を遡る さけはかわをさかのぼる Salmon swim up the river
キリスト教の伝来は十六世紀に遡る きりすときょうのでんらいはじゅうろくせいきにさかのぼる The introduction of Christianity goes back to the sixteenth century
五月一日に遡って ごがつついたちにさかのぼって retroactive to May 1

273 さかんな

盛んな ⓚ2332

[also 旺んな] **prosperous, flourishing; vigorous, energetic, active; hearty, cordial, enthusiastic, furious; keen; extensive, large; popular**
盛んに さかんに vigorously, energetically, actively; heartily, enthusiastically
盛んな商売 さかんなしょうばい thriving business
盛んになる さかんになる prosper, grow prosperous, thrive
盛んな歓迎 さかんなかんげい cordial reception

旺んな ⓚ0757

[also 盛んな] **vigorous, energetic, lively**
精力が旺んだ せいりょくがさかんだ be full of energy [vigor]

274 さがす

捜す ⓚ0389

[also 探す] **look for (a lost object), search for, hunt for**
捜し物 さがしもの looking for something lost; thing to look for
宝捜し たからさがし treasure hunt
本を捜す ほんをさがす look for a book

探す ⓚ0466

[also 捜す] **search for (something desired), search about, look for**
探し回る さがしまわる search about for
職探し しょくさがし job hunting

275 さき

崎 ⓚ0428

ⓐ [formerly also 埼] **promontory, cape**
ⓑ **suffix after names of promontories or capes**
州崎 すさき sandbar
御前崎 おまえざき Cape Omaezaki

埼 ⓚ0422

ⓐ [now usu. 崎] **promontory, cape**
ⓑ **suffix after names of promontories or capes**

犬吠埼 いぬぼうさき Cape Inubo

276　さく

裂く　Ⓚ2347

① **split, tear, rend, rip**
引き裂く **ひきさく** tear off, tear to pieces, split; separate, estrange, sever
八つ裂きにする **やつざきにする** tear (a person) limb from limb, tear to pieces

② (sever relations) **split up, separate, break off**
夫婦の仲を裂く **ふうふのなかをさく** bring about marital separation

割く　Ⓚ1611

① **spare (time), set [put] aside**
時間を割く **じかんをさく** spare time (for)

② **cede, alienate**
領土を割く **りょうどをさく** cede a territory

277　さげる

下げる　Ⓚ2862

①ⓐ (move downward) **lower, bring down, drop**
　ⓑ (lower the level of) **lower (the price), bring down, cut**
　ⓒ **reduce to lower rank, demote**
頭を下げる **あたまをさげる** bow one's head
掘り下げる **ほりさげる** dig down; investigate, probe, delve into
値下げ **ねさげ** reduction in price

引き下げる **ひきさげる** lower, reduce, put back; pull down
格下げ **かくさげ** degradation

② **hang (down), suspend**
お下げ **おさげ** hair hanging down the back, pigtail
ぶら下げる **ぶらさげる** hang, suspend, dangle

③ⓐ **move back [backwards]**
　ⓑ **let (a person) go away, dismiss**
お膳を下げる **おぜんをさげる** clear the table
下げ渡す **さげわたす** grant, release
取り下げる **とりさげる** withdraw, dismiss

④ **withdraw (one's deposit from the bank)**
貯金を下げる **ちょきんをさげる** withdraw one's savings

⑤ (of tides) **ebb**
下げ潮 **さげしお** ebb tide

提げる　Ⓚ0540

carry in hand, take (a thing) with (a person)
手提げ袋 **てさげぶくろ** handbag

278　ささ

笹　Ⓚ2321

[sometimes also 篠] **bamboo grass**
笹原 **ささはら** field of bamboo grass
笹舟 **ささぶね** toy bamboo-leaf boat
熊笹 **くまざさ** *Sasa albo-marginata*, low and striped bamboo

篠　Ⓚ2372

[usu. 笹] **bamboo grass**

105　　　　　　　　さき

差し ®2821

① ⓐ [emphatic or polite prefix] **do, exe-cute**
   ⓑ [verbal prefix] **send, present**
   差し当たり(=差し当たって) さしあたり (=さしあたって) for the time being, for the present, at present
   差し上げる さしあげる give (to superior)
   差し控える さしひかえる be moderate in; withhold, desist from, refrain from
   差し止める さしとめる prohibit, forbid; suspend (a paper)
   差し掛かる さしかかる come near, approach
   差し引き さしひき balance (of an account); ebb and flow
   差し支え さしつかえ hindrance, complications; objections
   差し回す さしまわす send (a car) around
   差し出す さしだす present, submit, send; stretch, reach
   差し出し先 さしだしさき address
② [in compounds] **measure, measuring**
   物差し ものさし ruler
③ [in compounds] **vessel for pouring**
   水差し みずさし pitcher, jug
④ **counter for dances**
⑤ **sumo move**
⑥ **tête-à-tête**
   差しで さしで between two persons, face to face
⑦ **unclassified compounds**
   眼差し まなざし look, expression

刺し ®1171

① **stabbing, piercing, pricking**
② **stitch**
   刺し子 さしこ quilting
③ *sashimi*, **sliced raw flesh (esp. of fish)**
   刺身 さしみ *sashimi*, sliced raw flesh (esp. of fish)
   牛刺 ぎゅうさし sliced raw beef

-指し ®0337

[suffix] **player (of shogi)**
   将棋指し しょうぎさし shogi player

-止し ®2545

[verbal suffix] **leaving something unfinished**
   読み止しの本 よみさしのほん unfinished book

差す ®2821

① **offer, present, provide**
   杯を差す さかずきをさす offer a cup (of sake)
② **hold up, spread (over one's hand)**
   傘を差す かさをさす hold an umbrella
③ **wear in one's belt or hair**
   刀を差す かたなをさす wear a sword
④ **become tinged with**
   赤味が差している あかみがさしている tinged red
⑤ (of water) **rise, flow**
   潮が差す しおがさす The tide comes in

⑥ **be struck by**
魔が差す まがさす be tempted by an evil spirit
⑦ [sometimes also 注す] **pour (into), fill up**
器に水を差す うつわにみずをさす fill a pitcher with water
⑧ [sometimes also 注す] **color**
⑨ [also 射す] **shine on**
障子に影が差す しょうじにかげがさす A shadow is cast on the *shoji* (paper sliding door)

指す
Ⓚ0337

① ⓐ **point to, point at, indicate**
ⓑ **aim at, have in view**
指し図 さしず directions
方向を指す ほうこうをさす point to a direction
目指す (=目差す) めざす aim for, have an eye on
頂上を目指す ちょうじょうをめざす set out for the summit
② **appoint, nominate; finger, accuse**
名指し なざし nomination, calling names
③ **play board games (esp. shogi)**
指し手 さして shogi move, shogi player
早指しチェス はやざしちぇす blitz chess

刺す
Ⓚ1171

① ⓐ **stab, pierce, prick, thrust**
ⓑ **sting, bite**
突き刺す つきさす stab, pierce, thrust
蜂に刺される はちにさされる be stung by a bee
② **sew, stitch**

雑巾を刺す ぞうきんをさす quilt a dustcloth
③ *baseball* **catch (a runner) out**
三塁で刺される さんるいでさされる be put [thrown] out at third base

挿す
Ⓚ0390

ⓐ **insert, put into, stick between**
ⓑ **insert seedlings, plant**
挿し絵 さしえ illustration (in a book)
挿し木 さしき cutting; cuttage
花瓶に花を挿す かびんにはなをさす put flowers in a vase

注す
Ⓚ0287

① **pour (into), fill up**
器に水を注す うつわにみずをさす fill a pitcher with water
② **color**

射す
Ⓚ1327

[also 差す] **shine on**
障子に影が射す しょうじにかげがさす A shadow is cast on the *shoji* (paper sliding-door)

-止す
Ⓚ2545

[verbal suffix] **leave something unfinished, stop in the middle**
言い止す いいさす break off, stop (in the middle of a sentence)

★ The relationship between the above seven verbs is complicated, and lexicographers disagree as to their proper usage. Their recommended, but not necessarily universal, usage is as shown. Study the equivalents and examples under the respective

107

さす

entries. It is interesting to note that さす can be written in a total of 91 different ways!

281 　　　さと

里
®2968

① **hamlet, village**
里芋 さといも taro
村里 むらざと village
古里(=故郷) ふるさと hometown, birthplace
山里 やまざと mountain hamlet [village]
② **countryside**
③ⓐ **one's parents' home**
　ⓑ [sometimes also 郷] **hometown, one's birthplace**
里心 さとごころ homesickness

郷
®0501

[usu. 里] **hometown, one's birthplace**
故郷(=古里) ふるさと hometown, birthplace

282 　　　さとり

悟り
®0379

① **satori, spiritual awakening**
② [formerly 覚り] **comprehension, understanding**

覚り
®2258

[now usu. 悟り] **comprehension, understanding**

283 　　　さとる

悟る
®0379

① **be spiritually awakened, attain (Buddhist) enlightenment [satori]**
悟り さとり satori, spiritual awakening
② [formerly 覚る] **awake to, be aware of, perceive, discern, realize**
悟り さとり satori, spiritual awakening; [formerly 覚り] comprehension, understanding
悟りが早い さとりがはやい be quick to understand

覚る
®2258

[now usu. 悟る] **awake to, be aware of, perceive, discern, realize**
覚り さとり comprehension, understanding
覚りが早い さとりがはやい be quick to understand

284 　　　さびしい

寂しい
®1982

ⓐ **lonesome, lonely, desolate, deserted**
ⓑ **scarce, scanty**
寂しさ さびしさ loneliness
寂しがる さびしがる feel lonely, miss someone
懐が寂しい ふところがさびしい have a scanty supply of money

淋しい
®0476

ⓐ **lonesome, lonely, desolate, deserted**

b **scarce, scanty**

淋しがる さびしがる feel lonely, miss someone

物淋しい ものさびしい lonesome, desolate, dreary

心淋しい うらさびしい lonely, forlorn, melancholy

懐が淋しい ふところがさびしい have a scanty supply of money

285　　さます

覚ます　　Ⓚ2258

① **awake, wake up**

目を覚ます めをさます awake, wake up, awaken

目覚まし めざまし alarm clock

② **disillusion**

③ **make sober**

冷ます　　Ⓚ0061

① **cool, let cool**

熱冷まし ねつさまし antifebrile, antipyretic

② **dampen, spoil**

興を冷ます きょうをさます spoil a person's pleasure, be a wet-blanket

醒ます　　Ⓚ1457

① **awake, wake up**

② **disillusion**

③ **make sober**

286　　さみしい

寂しい　　Ⓚ1982

same as 寂しい さびしい

淋しい　　Ⓚ0476

[usu. 寂しい] **same as** 淋しい さびしい

287　　さめる

覚める　　Ⓚ2258

① **awake, wake up**

眠りから覚める ねむりからさめる awake from one's sleep

② **be disillusioned**

③ **become sober**

酔い覚め よいざめ recovering from intoxication, sobering up

冷める　　Ⓚ0061

a **cool off, get cold**

b **cool down, subside, flag, be dampened**

スープが冷めた すーぷがさめた The soup has cooled

興冷め きょうざめ being wet-blanketed; skeleton at the feast

醒める　　Ⓚ1457

① **awake, wake up**

醒め遣らぬ さめやらぬ lingering (excitement, etc.), not entirely awake

② **be disillusioned, come to one's senses**

興醒め きょうざめ wet blanket, turnoff

③ **become sober**

酔い醒め よいざめ sobering up

晒す
Ⓚ0831

① **bleach, refine**
晒し さらし bleaching; bleached cotton
晒木綿 さらしもめん bleached cotton cloth
洗い晒し あらいざらし faded from washing

② [also 曝す] **expose (to view, to the elements)**
晒し者 さらしもの pilloried criminal exposed to public view; someone subjected to public scorn [humiliation]
恥晒し はじさらし disgrace, shame
野晒し のざらし weather-beaten

③ **soak**
水に晒す みずにさらす soak in water

曝す
Ⓚ1017

[also 晒す] **expose (to view, to the elements)**
恥曝し はじさらし disgrace, shame
雨曝し あまざらし weather-beaten, exposed to the rain
吹き曝し ふきさらし windswept, exposed to the wind

猿
Ⓚ0612

① **monkey, ape**
猿真似 さるまね blind imitation
猿芝居 さるしばい monkey show; shallow-minded trick
猿回し さるまわし monkey showman, monkey show
日本猿 にほんざる Japan monkey
山猿 やまざる wild monkey; country-man, rustic

② **sly person**
猿知恵 さるぢえ shallow cunning

③ⓐ **door bolt**
ⓑ **fastener**

申
Ⓚ2942

ninth sign of the Oriental zodiac: **the Monkey**—(time) 3-5 p.m., (direction) WSW, (season) July (of the lunar calendar)

触り
Ⓚ1376

① **touch, feel**
② **impression (of a person)**
③ **most impressive passage, punch line**

障り
Ⓚ0647

① **hindrance, obstacle**
②ⓐ **harm, bad effect**
ⓑ **sickness**

触る
Ⓚ1376

① **touch, feel**
触り さわり touch, feel; impression (of a person); most impressive passage, punch line
肌触り はだざわり touch, feel

② **become involved in**
触らぬ神に祟り無し さわらぬかみにたたりなし Let sleeping dogs lie

寄ると触ると よるとさわると whenever they come together

障る   Ⓚ0647

① **hinder, interfere with**

障り さわり hindrance, obstacle; harm, bad effect; sickness

差し障り さしさわり obstacle, offense

月の障り つきのさわり menses

② **affect, harm, jar on**

体に障る からだにさわる affect one's health

292   しあわせ

幸せ   Ⓚ1901

[also 仕合わせ, formerly also 倖せ] **happiness, blessing; good fortune**

幸せな しあわせな happy, fortunate

不幸せ ふしあわせ unhappiness, misfortune, ill luck

倖せ   Ⓚ0102

[now usu. 幸せ or 仕合わせ] **happiness, blessing; good fortune**

仕合わせ   Ⓚ0021

[also 幸せ, formerly also 倖せ] **same as** 幸せ

293   しお

潮   Ⓚ0675

① ⓐ **tide, current**
   ⓑ **seawater**

潮干狩り しおひがり shell gathering (at low tide)

引き潮 ひきしお ebb tide, low water

血潮 ちしお blood

潮風 しおかぜ sea breeze, briny air

② **tide** (in the archaic sense of 'favorable occasion'), **opportunity, chance**

潮時 しおどき time of ebb and flow; good chance, favorable opportunity

汐   Ⓚ0197

① ⓐ **tide, current**
   ⓑ **seawater**

汐干狩り しおひがり shell gathering (at low tide)

汐汲み しおくみ drawing water from the sea; person who draws water from the sea

② **tide** (in the archaic sense of 'favorable occasion'), **opportunity, chance**

汐合い しおあい chance, opportunity

294   しかして

而して   Ⓚ1747

[sometimes also 然して] **and, and then**

然して   Ⓚ2423

[usu. 而して] **and, and then**

295   しかも

然も   Ⓚ2423

[formerly also 而も]

ⓐ **moreover, furthermore**

ⓑ **and yet, nevertheless**

而も   Ⓚ1747

ⓐ **moreover, furthermore**

ⓑ **and yet, nevertheless**
道の常は無為にして而も為さざる
は無 みちのつねはむいにしてし
かもなさざるはなし Tao abides
in nonaction, yet nothing is left
undone (Laozi)

296 しげる

茂る   Ⓚ1934

[formerly also 繁る] **grow thick, be luxuri-
ant, be overgrown**
茂み しげみ thicket, bush
生い茂る おいしげる grow luxuriantly
[thickly]

繁る   Ⓚ2484

[now usu. 茂る] **grow thick, be luxuri-
ant, be overgrown**

297 しずく

滴   Ⓚ0640

ⓐ (liquid globule) **drop**
ⓑ **counter for drops**
露の滴 つゆのしずく dewdrop
一滴 ひとしずく a drop

雫   Ⓚ2405

ⓐ (liquid globule) **drop**
ⓑ **counter for drops**
露の雫 つゆのしずく dewdrop
一雫 ひとしずく a drop

298 しずまる

静まる   Ⓚ1539

ⓐ **become quiet, grow still**
ⓑ **calm down, become tranquil, be
lulled**
静まり返る しずまりかえる become
still as death
寝静まる ねしずまる fall fast asleep
嵐が静まった あらしがしずまった The
storm has abated

鎮まる   Ⓚ1570

① **be quelled, be suppressed, subside, be put down**
暴動が鎮まった ぼうどうがしずまった
The riot was put down
② **be alleviated, be relieved, be
soothed**
③ **be enshrined**

299 しずめる

静める   Ⓚ1539

ⓐ (make quiet) **quiet, calm, still**
ⓑ (make calm) **appease, calm, pacify**
気を静める きをしずめる compose
oneself, becalm one's feelings

鎮める   Ⓚ1570

① **quell, suppress, put down, subdue, pacify**
反乱を鎮める はんらんをしずめる
quell a rebellion
② **alleviate (pain), relieve, allay,
soothe**
痛みを鎮める いたみをしずめる
alleviate pain

沈める   Ⓚ0231

ⓐ sink, send to the bottom, sub-
merge

ⓑ sink oneself into (a chair), lower
oneself

ⓒ sink down in the world, go to ruin

敵艦を沈める てきかんをしずめる
sink an enemy ship

椅子に身を沈める いすにみをしずめ
る sink into a chair

苦界に身を沈める くがいにみをしず
める become a prostitute

300   しのぶ

忍ぶ   Ⓚ1899

① bear, endure, suffer, stand, put up
with

忍び難い しのびがたい unbearable,
intolerable

恥を忍ぶ はじをしのぶ abide one's
shame

② ⓐ conceal oneself, hide

　 ⓑ perform by stealth, steal one's
way to (a lover)

忍び しのび stealing (into); art of
mystification; incognito, traveling
incognito

忍び泣く しのびなく shed silent tears

忍び足 しのびあし tiptoeing, stealthy
steps

忍び込む しのびこむ steal in, sneak in

忍びやかな しのびやかな stealthy,
secret

偲ぶ   Ⓚ0118

recall, recollect, remember, remi-
nisce

故人を偲ぶ こじんをしのぶ think of
the dead

昔を偲ばせる品 むかしをしのばせるし
な things reminiscent of bygone
days

301   しば

芝   Ⓚ1867

ⓐ lawn grass, zoysia

ⓑ lawn, turf, sod

芝草 しばくさ lawn

芝地 しばち grass plot

高麗芝 こうらいしば Korean lawn
grass

芝生 しばふ lawn, turf

芝刈り機 しばかりき lawn mower

芝居 しばい play, drama

柴   Ⓚ2309

brushwood, firewood

柴刈り しばかり firewood gathering

柴垣 しばがき brushwood fence

柴犬 しばいぬ (Japanese) midget
Shiba (kind of dog)

302   しぼり

絞り   Ⓚ1236

① iris diaphragm

② ⓐ white spots on a dyed ground,
tie-dyed fabrics

　 ⓑ variegation, spots (in flowers)

搾り   Ⓚ0594

squeezing

絞る ⓚ1236

① ⓐ **wring, wring out**
ⓑ **strain, rack (one's brains)**
絞り しぼり iris diaphragm; white spots on a dyed ground, tie-dyed fabrics; variegation, spots (in flowers)
お絞り おしぼり wet towel, steamed towel
雑巾を絞る ぞうきんをしぼる wring a floorcloth
知恵を絞る ちえをしぼる rack one's brains, think hard

② **tighten, close tight, press**
袋の口を絞る ふくろのくちをしぼる close a bag tight by pulling the drawstring

③ ⓐ **make narrow, focus; lower (the volume)**
ⓑ **narrow down to, focus on**
議論を要点だけに絞る ぎろんをようてんだけにしぼる narrow an argument down

搾る ⓚ0594

① ⓐ **squeeze, press, squash, extract**
ⓑ **squeeze (money from), sweat, screw**
搾り しぼり squeezing
搾り滓 しぼりかす strained lees [draff]
搾り立てのオレンジジュース しぼりたてのおれんじじゅーす fresh orange juice
搾り取る しぼりとる squeeze, extract; squeeze (money from), sweat

② **scold, reprimand**

油を搾る あぶらをしぼる press oil; give a sound scolding

島 ⓚ2820

[also suffix] **island, isle, islet**
島国 しまぐに island country
島巡り しまめぐり tour of the islands, tour of an island
離れ島 はなれじま solitary island
宝島 たからじま treasure island
八丈島 はちじょうじま Hachijo Island

縞 ⓚ1287

stripe, streak
縞模様 しまもよう striped pattern
縞瑪瑙 しまめのう onyx
縞馬 しまうま zebra
縦縞 たてじま vertical stripes
格子縞 こうしじま check pattern
干渉縞 かんしょうじま interference fringe

締まる ⓚ1274

① ⓐ **tighten, become taut; be compact, be firm**
ⓑ **tighten one's belt, be frugal**
締まった体格 しまったたいかく well-knit frame, firm build
締まり屋 しまりや thrifty person, tightfisted person

② **brace oneself up, become steady**
引き締まる ひきしまる tighten, become tight; be braced up

③ (of the market) **become firm**

小締まり こじまり firmer tendency

④ [in compounds] **exercise (tight) control over, regulate**

取り締まる とりしまる manage, control, superintend

閉まる Ⓚ2832

vi **be shut, be closed, shut, close**

閉まり しまり shutting, closing
戸が閉まった とがしまった The door shut [closed]

絞まる Ⓚ1236

be strangled

首が絞まる くびがしまる have one's neck wrung

★ Note that when used independently the words 閉める and 閉まる mean to shut in the sense of moving into a closed position. 締 in that sense, appears in such compounds as 締め切る しめきる 'fasten, shut up' and 戸締まり とじまり 'fastening the doors', and means to fasten or secure with a lock.

306 しみる

染みる Ⓚ2229

① **soak into, permeate**

染み しみ stain, blot, spot
染み込む しみこむ soak into, permeate
染み付く しみつく be dyed in deeply, be stained

② **penetrate (to the bone), come home to one's heart**

身に染みる風 みにしみるかぜ piercing wind

馴染み なじみ familiarity, intimacy; old acquaintance, crony

③ **smart from irritation**

煙が目に染みた けむりがめにしみた My eyes smarted from the smoke

滲みる

ⓐ **permeate, soak into**
ⓑ **penetrate (to the bone), come home to one's heart**
ⓒ **smart from irritation**

滲み込む しみこむ soak into, permeate

凍みる Ⓚ0111

freeze, congeal

307 しめる¹

湿る Ⓚ0555

get damp, get wet

湿り しめり dampness, moisture, humidity; rain
湿った しめった damp, moist, wet
湿っぽい しめっぽい damp, humid; gloomy, depressing

-染める Ⓚ2229

permeate with fluid or smoke

煮染める にしめる boil thoroughly with seasoning
焚き染める たきしめる perfume clothes by burning incense

締める Ⓚ1274

① ⓐ **tighten, tauten**
ⓑ **fasten, tie up, bind**
ベルトを締める べるとをしめる tighten one's belt
締め括る しめくくる bind fast; settle, round off (a passage)
締め金 しめがね buckle, clasp, clamp

② **exercise tight [rigid] control over, exercise close supervision; reprimand**
締め上げる しめあげる screw up; put the screws on
元締め もとじめ manager, controller

③ [also 〆る] **sum, sum [add] up; close the account**
締め しめ summing up; *judo* choking [strangling] techniques
締めて しめて in all, all told
締め切り日 しめきりび closing day, time limit, deadline

④ **economize, save**
家計を締める かけいをしめる economize in the household

⑤ [also 〆る] [in compounds] **fasten, lock (a door or window), shut**
締め出す しめだす shut the door on (a person), shut out
締め切る しめきる close (up); fix a deadline
締め切り(=〆切) しめきり closing day, deadline; Closed, No Entrance

⑥ [also 〆る] **finish off a bout of eating and drinking (with a closing dish)**

⑦ [also 〆る] **pickle, marinate (fish) (with vinegar)**

〆る

① **sum, sum [add] up; close the account**
〆て しめて in all, all told

② [in compounds] **fasten, lock (a door or window), shut**
〆切(=締め切り) しめきり closing day, deadline; Closed, No Entrance

③ **finish off a bout of eating and drinking (with a closing dish)**

④ **pickle, marinate (fish) (with vinegar)**
鯖を酢で〆る さばをすでしめる marinate mackerel with vinegar

閉める Ⓚ2832

vt (**move into closed position**) **shut, close**
蓋を閉める ふたをしめる shut the lid

絞める Ⓚ1236

① **strangle, strangulate, wring**
絞め殺す しめころす strangle to death
首を絞める くびをしめる strangle, wring the neck

② **squeeze**
羽交い絞め はがいじめ pinioning

退ける Ⓚ2665

① (cause to retreat) **drive away, repel, expel, keep away**
要職から退ける ようしょくからしりぞける expel (a person) from an important position

人を退ける ひとをしりぞける keep others away

② **defeat, beat**
敵の攻撃を退ける てきのこうげきを しりぞける beat off an attack by the enemy

③ [sometimes also 斥ける] **reject, refuse, turn down**
提案を退ける ていあんをしりぞける turn down a proposal

斥ける
Ⓚ2565

[usu. 退ける] **reject, refuse, turn down**
提案を斥ける ていあんをしりぞける turn down a proposal

310 ## しるし

印
Ⓚ0733

① **mark, sign; symbol**
目印 めじるし mark, sign, landmark
矢印 やじるし arrow (mark)

② **token (of appreciation)**
感謝の印 かんしゃのしるし token of appreciation

③ **proof**
...の印として …のしるしとして as proof of…

徴
Ⓚ0622

① **effectiveness (of medicine)**
② **symptom, sign, indication**
地震の徴 じしんのしるし signs of an earthquake

311 ## しるす

記す
Ⓚ1321

write down, record, put down in writing
書き記す かきしるす write down, record, register

印す
Ⓚ0733

mark, inscribe

312 ## しろがね

白金
Ⓚ2929

[usu. 銀]
ⓐ **silver**
ⓑ **silver coin**

銀
Ⓚ1534

ⓐ **silver**
ⓑ **silver coin**

313 ## す¹

州
Ⓚ0040

[formerly also 洲] **sandbar, shallows, shoal**
三角州 さんかくす delta
砂州 さす sandbar, sandbank
座州する ざすする strand, run aground

洲
Ⓚ0352

[now usu. 州] **sandbar, shallows, shoal**
砂洲 さす sandbar, sandbank
座洲する ざすする strand, run aground

酢   ⓚ1373

[formerly also 醋] [also suffix] **vinegar**

酢の物 **すのもの** pickled dish
酢蛸 **すだこ** (sliced and) pickled octopus
酢料理 **すりょうり** pickled dish
醸造酢 **じょうぞうす** brewed vinegar

醋

[now replaced by 酢] [also suffix] **vinegar**

醋蛸 **すだこ** (sliced and) pickled octopus

巣   ⓚ1987

ⓐ (structure for birds, insects or animals) **nest, beehive; web; lair, den**
ⓑ (place favoring the growth of something dangerous) **nest, den, hangout (for bandits)**

巣箱 **すばこ** bird box, bird house
巣立つ **すだつ** leave one's nest; become independent
巣食う **すくう** build a nest, nest; haunt, hang out
古巣 **ふるす** old nest, one's former haunt
空き巣 **あきす** sneak thief

栖   ⓚ0844

ⓐ (structure for birds, insects or animals) **nest, beehive; web; lair, den**
ⓑ (place favoring the growth of something dangerous) **nest, den, hangout (for bandits)**

透かす   ⓚ2677

① ⓐ **make transparent**
   ⓑ **look through, peer into**
透かし **すかし** watermark; openwork
闇を透かす **やみをすかす** peer into the darkness
② [formerly also 隙かす] **leave a space [opening], thin (out)**
透かさず **すかさず** without a moment's delay
木を透かす **きをすかす** thin trees
③ *slang* **break wind noiselessly**

空かす   ⓚ1913

① **feel hungry**
腹を空かす **はらをすかす** be hungry
② **make available, make free**
手を空かす **てをすかす** make oneself available

隙かす   ⓚ0614

[now usu. 透かす] **leave a space [opening], thin (out)**
隙かさず **すかさず** without a moment's delay

透き   ⓚ2677

[also 隙] **gap, interval**

隙   ⓚ0614

① [also 透き] **gap, interval**
隙間 **すきま** gap, opening; crack, crevice

手隙 てすき spare time, free time

② **chance, unguarded moment**

隙を見付ける **すきをみつける** seize an opportunity

隙を窺う **すきをうかがう** watch for an unguarded moment

透く   Ⓚ2677

① **be transparent, be seen through**

見え透く **みえすく** be easily seen, be obvious

②ⓐ **become sparse**

ⓑ [formerly also 隙く] **leave a gap**

透いた枝 **すいたえだ** thinned branches

透き(=隙) **すき** gap, interval

透き間(=隙間) **すきま** gap, opening; crack, crevice

空く   Ⓚ1913

become empty, become less crowded

空き **すき** vacancy, interval

空きっ腹 **すきっぱら** hunger

空いた電車 **すいたでんしゃ** uncrowded train

手空きの **てすきの** not busy, unengaged

隙く   Ⓚ0614

[now usu. 透く] **leave a gap**

隙いた枝 **すいたえだ** thinned branches

優れる   Ⓚ0156

① **be superior to, be excellent, be better than, surpass**

優れて **すぐれて** exceedingly, conspicuously, by far

優れた学者 **すぐれたがくしゃ** eminent scholar

② [usu. in negative constructions] **be fine, feel well**

気分が優れない **きぶんがすぐれない** not feel well

勝れる   Ⓚ0918

① **be superior to, be excellent, be better than, surpass**

勝れた業績 **すぐれたぎょうせき** outstanding achievement

② [usu. in negative constructions] **be fine, feel well**

気分が勝れない **きぶんがすぐれない** not feel well

進める   Ⓚ2689

①ⓐ (cause to move forward in position) **advance, move forward**

ⓑ (raise in rank) **advance, raise, promote**

ⓒ **set (a clock) ahead**

軍を進める **ぐんをすすめる** move troops forward

②ⓐ (aid the progress of) **advance, promote, further**

ⓑ **stimulate, hasten**

計画を進める **けいかくをすすめる** carry a plan forward

工事を進める こうじをすすめる hasten [speed up] the works

勧める ®1645

① ⓐ **urge, persuade, advise**
ⓑ [sometimes also 奨める] **encourage, promote, stimulate**
勧め すすめ exhortation, encouragement
切に勧める せつにすすめる urge strongly
行く様に勧める いくようにすすめる encourage someone to go
② **offer, present**
酒を勧める さけをすすめる offer wine; press wine on

奨める ®2474

[usu. 勧める] **encourage, promote, stimulate**
学問の奨め がくもんのすすめ encouragement of learning

薦める ®2097

recommend (a person to a post or a product to a person)
. . . に薦められて …にすすめられて on the recommendation of…

321　すてる

捨てる ®0461

① [sometimes also 棄てる]
ⓐ **discard, throw away, cast aside**
ⓑ **abandon, desert, discard, forsake, give up**
ごみ捨て ごみすて dumping refuse; garbage pit, dumping ground

捨て子 すてご foundling, abandoned child; abandoning one's child
見捨てる みすてる forsake, desert
② **leave unattended**
捨てて置く すておく leave something as it is
③ [in compounds] **act as if getting rid of something**
言い捨てる いいすてる say (something) over one's shoulder

棄てる ®1835

ⓐ **discard, throw away, cast aside**
ⓑ **abandon, desert, discard, forsake, give up**
棄て売り すてうり sacrifice sale
権利を棄てる けんりをすてる abandon one's rights

322　すでに

既に ®1079

① ⓐ [formerly also 已に] **already**
ⓑ **previously**
彼は既に出発していた かれはすでにしゅっぱつしていた He had already started
既に申した様に すでにもうしたように as I have previously stated
② **itself, in itself**
その事が既に そのことがすでに the fact itself, the very fact

已に ®2861

[now usu. 既に] **already**
時已に遅し ときすでにおそし It is too late now

323   すな

砂   Ⓚ1047

[sometimes also 沙] **sand, grit**

砂地 すなじ sandy place
砂浜 すなはま sandy beach, sands
砂場 すなば sandbox

沙   Ⓚ0236

[usu. 砂] **sand, grit**

324   すなわち

即ち   Ⓚ1036

ⓐ **namely, that is, i.e.**
ⓑ **nothing but, precisely**

救世主即ちキリスト きゅうせいしゅす
なわちきりすと the Savior, that is,
Christ

乃ち   Ⓚ2535

ⓐ **thereupon, whereupon, accordingly**
ⓑ **and then**

戦えば乃ち勝つ たたかえばすなわ
ちかつ win every battle (that is
fought)

325   すべて

凡て   Ⓚ2543

① ⓐ **all, everything, the whole**
   ⓑ **entirely, wholly**
凡ての すべての all, entire, whole
② **generally, as a rule**

全て   Ⓚ1743

① ⓐ **all, everything, the whole**
   ⓑ **entirely, wholly**
全ての すべての all, entire, whole
② **generally, as a rule**

総べて   Ⓚ1261

① ⓐ **all, everything, the whole**
   ⓑ **entirely, wholly**
総べての すべての all, entire, whole
② **generally, as a rule**

326   すべる

滑る   Ⓚ0603

① **slide, glide, skate**
滑り すべり sliding, slipping
滑り台 すべりだい (playground) slide;
   launching platform
横滑り よこすべり skid, skidding
② [formerly also 辷る] **slip**
滑り落ちる すべりおちる slip off
口が滑る くちがすべる make a slip of
   the tongue
③ [formerly also 辷る] **flunk an (entrance) examination**
滑り止め すべりどめ tire chains;
   creepers; taking the entrance
   examination to a university as a
   safety measure in case one fails at
   other universities

辷る

① **slip**
辷らす すべらす let slip, slide, glide
地辷り じすべり landslide
口が辷る くちがすべる make a slip of
   the tongue

② **flunk an (entrance) examination**
　辷り止め **すべりどめ** tire chains; creepers; taking the entrance examination to a university as a safety measure in case one fails at other universities

327　　すます

-澄ます　　⑥0674
[also –済ます] [verbal suffix] **perform an action well [perfectly]**
　研ぎ澄ます **とぎすます** sharpen [grind] well
　見澄ます **みすます** observe carefully, watch intently

-済ます　　⑥0478
[also –澄ます] [verbal suffix] **perform an action well [perfectly]**
　成り済ます **なりすます** successfully impersonate

328　　すみ

墨　　⑥2400
ⓐ **India ink, Chinese ink, ink stick**
ⓑ (black substance) **ink, soot, black dye**
　墨色 **すみいろ** India ink color
　墨絵 **すみえ** India ink drawing, painting in India ink
　お墨付き **おすみつき** handwriting; certificate, authorization; paper bearing the signature of the shogun or feudal lord
　墨染め **すみぞめ** dyeing black; (Buddhist priest's) black robe
　眉墨 **まゆずみ** eyebrow pencil

　入れ墨 **いれずみ** tattooing, tattoo, tattoo marks

炭　　⑥1947
charcoal
　炭火 **すみび** charcoal fire
　炭焼き **すみやき** charcoal making
　消し炭 **けしずみ** cinders

329　　すむ

住む　　⑥0047
(of people) **live, reside, dwell**
　住み家(=栖、住み処) **すみか** residence
　住み着く **すみつく** settle, take up residence

栖む　　⑥0844
[usu. 棲む] (of animals) **inhabit, live**

棲む　　⑥0902
[sometimes also 栖む] (of animals) **inhabit, live**
　棲み分け **すみわけ** biol habitat isolation; compartmentalization, segregation
　鳥が棲む森 **とりがすむもり** woods inhabited by birds

330　　する

擦る　　⑥0707
①ⓐ **rub, chafe**
　ⓑ **strike**
　擦り傷 **すりきず** scratch, abrasion

頬擦り **ほおずり** nestling one's cheek to another's

マッチを擦る **まっちをする** strike a match

② **lose, forfeit**

身代を擦る **しんだいをする** lose a person's fortune

磨る
Ⓚ2744

polish, file, rub down

磨りガラス **すりがらす** frosted glass

磨り減らす **すりへらす** wear away [out]; exhaust

摺る
Ⓚ0628

ⓐ **rub against**

ⓑ **print by rubbing**

摺り足 **すりあし** shuffling walk

摺り合わせ **すりあわせ** precision surface finishing; coordinating of ideas [opinions]

摺り鉢 **すりばち** (earthenware) mortar

引き摺る **ひきずる** drag along; trail

手摺り **てすり** handrail, railing

スプーン摺り切り一杯 **すぷーんすりきりいっぱい** level spoonful

摺り本 **すりほん** woodblock-printed book

石摺り **いしずり** print from stone, rubbing, rubbed copy

刷る
Ⓚ1169

print, put in print

刷り **すり** printing

刷り上げる **すりあげる** finish printing, print off

座り
Ⓚ2686

[formerly also 坐り] **stability**

坐り
Ⓚ2970

[now usu. 座り] **stability**

座る
Ⓚ2686

[formerly also 坐る] **sit, take a seat, sit down**

座り **すわり** stability

座り込み **すわりこみ** sit-in, sit-down (strike)

居座る **いすわる** settle down, stay on; remain in the same position unwantedly

坐る
Ⓚ2970

[now usu. 座る] **sit, take a seat, sit down**

坐り **すわり** stability

坐り込む **すわりこむ** sit down (for a prolonged time); do a sit-in

据わる
Ⓚ0455

be set

目が据わって **めがすわって** with set eyes

腹の据わった男 **はらのすわったおとこ** man with plenty of guts

背
Ⓚ2230

① [sometimes also 脊] **back; backside**

背中 せなか back
背骨 せぼね backbone, spine
背負う せおう carry on one's back, shoulder, bear
背を向ける せをむける turn one's back on, pretend not to see
② [sometimes also 脊] **stature, height**
背の順 せのじゅん order of height
③ [sometimes also 脊] **ridge**
山の背 やまのせ ridge (of a mountain)
④ **unclassified compounds**
背広 せびろ business suit

脊 ⓚ2317

① **back; backside**
脊骨 せぼね backbone, spine
② **stature, height**
③ **ridge**

334 せい

背 ⓚ2230

[sometimes also 脊] **stature, height**
背比べ せいくらべ comparison of statures
上背 うわぜい height, stature

脊 ⓚ2317

[usu. 背] **height, stature**

335 せく

堰く ⓚ0510

ⓐ **dam up**
ⓑ **check, prevent**
堰き止める(=塞き止める) せきとめる dam up, stop up; check

堰き止め湖 せきとめこ dammed lake

塞く ⓚ2033

ⓐ **dam up**
ⓑ **check, prevent**
塞き止める せきとめる dam up, stop; check

336 せめ

攻め ⓚ0215

① [also suffix] **attack, offensive, bombardment**
② **batting**

責め ⓚ2176

① **responsibility**
② **blame**
③ [also suffix] **torture, persecution**

337 せめる

攻める ⓚ0215

attack, take the offensive
攻め せめ [also suffix] attack, offensive, bombardment; batting
攻め込む せめこむ attack and invade
攻め滅ぼす せめほろぼす attack and overthrow, utterly destroy
質問攻め しつもんぜめ barrage of questions

責める ⓚ2176

① **blame, condemn, censure, accuse, criticize, reproach**
責め せめ responsibility; blame; [also suffix] torture, persecution

人の怠慢を責める ひとのたいまん
をせめる blame [denounce] a
person for his [her] negligence
② **torture, persecute**
責め道具 せめどうぐ instruments of
torture
責め立てる せめたてる torture se-
verely; urge
水責め みずぜめ water torture
③ **urge, press; tease**
金を払えと責める かねをはらえとせ
める press for payment

---

338 ぜろ

零 ®2433

zero (the number)
零戦 ぜろせん Zero fighter

◯

zero (the numeral)
ゼッケン三◯一四番 ぜっけんさんぜ
ろいちよんばん bib number 3014

---

339 そう

沿う ®0290

ⓐ **lie along (a river), follow along**
ⓑ **be in line with (a policy)**
路線に沿って ろせんにそって along
the route [line]
対外政策に沿って たいがいせいさく
にそって in line with the foreign
policy

添う ®0485

① **accompany, go along with, stay
with**

添い寝 そいね sleeping with (one's
child)
付き添い つきそい attendance; attendant, escort
② **marry**
連れ添う つれそう be man and wife,
be married to
③ **meet (someone's wishes), suit**
人の要求に添う ひとのようきゅうにそ
う meet one's demands
④ **add to, increase**
趣が添う おもむきがそう add color to

---

340 そぐ

削ぐ ®1316

① **chip, cut off**
鼻を削がれる はなをそがれる have
one's nose mutilated [cut off]
②ⓐ **diminish, reduce, dampen**
ⓑ **spoil**
気勢を削ぐ きせいをそぐ diminish
[dampen] the spirit
興を削ぐ きょうをそぐ spoil the fun
of

殺ぐ ®1208

① **chip, cut off**
殺がれた耳 そがれたみみ mutilated
ear
②ⓐ **diminish, reduce, dampen**
ⓑ **spoil**
興を殺ぐ きょうをそぐ spoil the fun
of

341　そなえ

備え ⓚ0126
① provision, preparation
② defense

供え ⓚ0070
offering

342　そなえる

備える ⓚ0126
①ⓐ **provide for, make preparations for, stock**
　ⓑ **provide with, furnish**
　備え そなえ provision, preparation; defense
　万一に備える まんいちにそなえる provide against contingencies
　備え付ける そなえつける provide with, furnish, fit with
② [also 具える] **possess, be endowed with**
　資格を備える しかくをそなえる have a qualification (for)

供える ⓚ0070
offer (to a god), make an offering
　供え そなえ offering
　供え物 そなえもの offering
　墓に花を供える はかにはなをそなえる offer flowers on a tomb

343　そねむ

嫉む ⓚ0584
[also 妬む] **be jealous, be envious**

妬む ⓚ0254
[also 嫉む] **be jealous, be envious**

344　その

園 ⓚ2722
① **garden**
　花園 はなぞの flower garden
② **institution**
　学びの園 まなびのその educational institution

苑 ⓚ1926
① **garden**
② **institution**

345　そば

側 ⓚ0120
[sometimes also 傍] **side, vicinity**
　側に そばに by the side of
　側女 そばめ mistress, concubine

傍 ⓚ0127
[usu. 側] **side, vicinity**
　傍に そばに by the side of

346　そむく

背く ⓚ2230
① [sometimes also 叛く] **go against, disobey, rebel against, violate**
　約束に背く やくそくにそむく break one's promise
② **turn one's back on**

叛く

[usu. 背く] **rebel against, go against, disobey, violate**

親に叛く おやにそむく disobey one's parent(s)

347 そめる

染める Ⓚ2229

①ⓐ **dye**
　ⓑ **color, stain, tinge**

染め そめ dyeing, printing
染物屋 そめものや dyer
染め直す そめなおす redye
頬を染める ほおをそめる blush
血染めの ちぞめの bloodstained

② **have a hand in, dabble in**

手を染める てをそめる have a hand (in)
見染める みそめる fall in love at first glance

-初める Ⓚ1031

[verbal suffix] **begin to (occur); for the first time**

咲き初める さきそめる begin to bloom

348 そらす

反らす Ⓚ2549

vt **bend (backward), curve, warp**

体を反らす からだをそらす bend oneself backward
胸を反らす むねをそらす throw out one's chest, be puffed up with pride

逸らす Ⓚ2688

① **let slip, miss, lose, let go, let pass**

ボールを逸らす ぼーるをそらす miss a ball, let a ball pass
注意を逸らす ちゅういをそらす distract a person's attention

② (cause to deviate) **divert, avert, dodge, evade**

目を逸らす めをそらす avert one's eyes, look away

349 それ

夫れ Ⓚ2909

① [archaic] **emphatic adverb at the beginning of a sentence**

夫れ、秦王虎狼之心有り それ, しんのうころうのこころあり The King of Chin had the heart of tigers and wolves

② [usu. 其れ] *pronoun* **that, it**

夫れ夫れ それぞれ respectively, each

其れ Ⓚ2285

① [sometimes also 夫れ] *pronoun* **that, it**

其れ其れ それぞれ respectively, each
其れから それから and then, after that
其れでも それでも nevertheless, even so
其れなりに それなりに in its own way
其れと無く それとなく indirectly, obliquely

② (interjection used to call attention) **look, there**

350　　ぞめ

–染め
Ⓚ2229

ⓐ **dyeing process**
ⓑ **dyed fabric**

先染め さきぞめ yarn dyeing
友禅染め ゆうぜんぞめ silk printed by the *yuzen* process

–初め
Ⓚ1031

[verbal suffix] **performing an action for the first time (of the year)**

書き初め かきぞめ New Year's writing

351　　たえる

堪える
Ⓚ0514

①ⓐ [sometimes also 耐える] **endure, bear, stand, tolerate**
ⓑ **bear (a burden), hold out, stand**

堪え忍ぶ たえしのぶ endure, bear up, tolerate, put up with
堪え難い たえがたい unbearable
不幸に堪える ふこうにたえる bear up under misfortune
遺憾に堪えない いかんにたえない be really regrettable

② **be fit for, be competent, be equal to**

仕事に堪える しごとにたえる be fit for work

耐える
Ⓚ1178

ⓐ (resist physical forces) **withstand, resist, be proof against**
ⓑ [usu. 堪える] **endure, bear, tolerate**

火に耐える ひにたえる be fireproof

352　　たおす

倒す
Ⓚ0106

① **bring down, fell, knock down, throw to the ground**

押し倒す おしたおす push down

②ⓐ **overthrow, ruin**
ⓑ **defeat**

拝み倒す おがみたおす entreat (a person) into consent, win over by persuasive entreaty

③ [formerly 斃す] **kill**

④ **fail to pay**

踏み倒す ふみたおす trample down; bilk, shirk payment

⑤ [in compounds] **make a show of, sham**

見掛け倒し みかけだおし deceptive appearance, mere show

斃す

[now usu. 倒す] **kill**

敵を斃す てきをたおす kill one's enemy [opponent]

353　　たおれる

倒れる
Ⓚ0106

① **fall over, topple, tumble down, collapse**

後に倒れる うしろにたおれる fall backward

② **succumb, break down, fall senseless**

③ⓐ **go to ruin**
ⓑ **go bankrupt**

共倒れ ともだおれ falling together, joint bankruptcy

内閣が倒れた ないかくがたおれた The cabinet was overthrown

④ [formerly 斃れる] **fall down dead, perish, die**

行き倒れ いきだおれ person dying [dead] on the street

斃れる

[now usu. 倒れる] **fall down dead, perish, die**

凶弾に斃れる きょうだんにたおれる be shot to death by an assassin

354 たく

炊く ⓚ0773

cook, boil

炊き込み御飯 たきこみごはん rice seasoned and cooked with various ingredients

炊き出し たきだし distribution of boiled rice (in emergency)

飯炊き めしたき cooking rice; kitchen maid, cook

煮炊き にたき cooking

焚く ⓚ2418

burn, kindle, build a fire

焚き火 たきび bonfire

焚き付け たきつけ kindling, fire lighter

焚き付ける たきつける kindle, build a fire; instigate, stir up

空焚き からだき heating a pan or bathtub without water in it

追い焚き おいだき reheating (of bath)

355 たくみ

巧み ⓚ0166

skill, dexterity, ingenuity

巧みな たくみな skillful, clever, cunning

巧みな手段 たくみなしゅだん clever trick

匠 ⓚ2581

artisan; woodworker, carpenter

356 たくわえ

蓄え ⓚ2038

[sometimes also 貯え] **store, reserve, stock; savings**

貯え ⓚ1368

[usu. 蓄え] **store, reserve, stock; savings**

357 たくわえる

蓄える ⓚ2038

① [sometimes also 貯える] **store up, lay in stock, save, lay aside**

蓄え たくわえ store, reserve, stock; savings

燃料を蓄える ねんりょうをたくわえる store up fuel

知識を蓄える ちしきをたくわえる store one's mind with knowledge

② **have, wear (a mustache)**

貯える   Ⓚ1368

[usu. 蓄える] **store up, lay in stock, save, lay aside**

貯え たくわえ store, reserve, stock; savings

358   たすける

助ける   Ⓚ1037

① [formerly also 扶ける] **help, aid, assist**

助け たすけ aid, rescue, relief
助け合う たすけあう help each other
手助け てだすけ help, assistance

② **save, rescue, relieve**

助け出す たすけだす rescue (a person) from [out of], deliver [extricate] (a person) from

扶ける   Ⓚ0220

[now usu. 助ける] **help, aid, assist**

扶け起こす たすけおこす help a person to his [her] feet
家計の扶け かけいのたすけ assistance in supporting a family

359   たずねる

尋ねる   Ⓚ2027

①ⓐ [sometimes also 訊ねる] **inquire (about, after), ask, question**
ⓑ **inquire into, investigate into**

理由を尋ねる りゆうをたずねる ask the reason
由来を尋ねる ゆらいをたずねる inquire into the origin

② **search for, look for**

尋ね人 たずねびと missing person
尋ね求める たずねもとめる seek for

お尋ね者 おたずねもの wanted person, person wanted by the police

訊ねる   Ⓚ1320

ⓐ **question, interrogate**
ⓑ **inquire (about, after), ask, question**

訪ねる   Ⓚ1335

visit, call on, pay a visit

友人を訪ねる ゆうじんをたずねる call on a friend

360   たたえる

讃える   Ⓚ1485

praise, laud, admire, commend

称える   Ⓚ1075

praise, extol

誉め称える ほめたたえる admire, applaud, praise

361   たたかい

戦い   Ⓚ1590

① **war, fight, battle**
② **match, game, contest**

闘い   Ⓚ2847

struggle, conflict

362   たたかう

戦う   Ⓚ1590

① **wage war, fight**

戦い たたかい war, fight, battle; match, game, contest

戦い抜く たたかいぬく fight to a finish

敵と戦う てきとたたかう fight one's enemy

議論を戦わす ぎろんをたたかわす have a discussion

② **contest, contend, play a match [game]**

正正堂堂と戦おう せいせいどうどうとたたかおう Let's play the game fairly

闘う
Ⓚ2847

(struggle with) **fight (against), contend with, strive against**

闘い たたかい struggle, conflict

困難と闘う こんなんとたたかう contend with difficulties

363　ただ

唯
Ⓚ0419

[also 只] **only, just, merely, solely**

唯一度 ただいちど only once

唯そこへ行きさえすれば良い ただそこへいきさえすればよい have [need] only to go there

只
Ⓚ1849

① **no charge**

只の ただの free of charge, cost-free, for nothing; ordinary, common, plain

② **ordinariness, plainness**

只の人 ただのひと common [ordinary] person, man in the street

只ならぬ ただならぬ unusual, alarming, serious

③ **doing nothing, being idle**

只では置かないぞ ただではおかないぞ You shall pay dear for that

只–
Ⓚ1849

① **free of charge, cost-free, for nothing**

只働き ただばたらき working for nothing

只乗り ただのり free ride

② **ordinary, common, plain**

只者 ただもの ordinary person, common mortal

只事ではない ただごとではない It is no common case

③ [also 唯] **only, just, merely, solely**

只今 ただいま at present, now; just now; soon; Hello (used by person returning home)

364　ただす

正す
Ⓚ2926

ⓐ **correct, rectify**

ⓑ **set right, reform, redress**

誤りが有れば正せ あやまりがあればただせ Correct mistakes, if any

姿勢を正す しせいをただす straighten oneself

質す
Ⓚ2445

ⓐ **query, question, consult, inquire**

ⓑ **ascertain, verify**

専門家に質す せんもんかにただす consult an expert

子細を質す しさいをただす verify details

糾す　Ⓚ1176

inquire into, investigate into, examine

元を糾す もとをただす inquire into the origin, go to the bottom of an affair

365　たっとい

貴い　Ⓚ2260

① **precious, valuable, priceless**
　貴い命 たっといいのち precious life
② (of noble rank) **noble, high-ranking**
　貴い家柄である たっといいえがらである be of noble birth

尊い　Ⓚ2029

exalted, august, awe-inspiring, sacred

尊い高齢 たっといこうれい sacred old age

366　たっとぶ

貴ぶ　Ⓚ2260

value, set a high value on, have a high regard for

命より名を貴ぶ いのちよりなをたっとぶ value honor above life

尊ぶ　Ⓚ2029

honor, respect, revere
神を尊ぶ かみをたっとぶ revere God

367　たつ¹

断つ　Ⓚ1355

① (detach by severing) **cut off, sever, cut apart**
　断ち切る たちきる cut off, disconnect
② (stop or interrupt the intended course) **cut off, intercept**
　退路を断つ たいろをたつ cut off the retreat
③ **abstain from, give up**
　塩断ち しおだち abstinence from salt as a vow

絶つ　Ⓚ1240

① **break off, discontinue, cut off, sever**
　連絡を絶つ れんらくをたつ sever the connection
② **exterminate, extirpate, eradicate**
　禍根を絶つ かこんをたつ strike at the root of an evil

裁つ　Ⓚ2813

cut out (a garment), cut (paper)
裁ち出す たちだす cut out (a dress) from cloth
裁ち縫い たちぬい cutting and sewing
裁ち板 たちいた (tailor's) cutting board

368　たつ²

立つ　Ⓚ1723

① ⓐ **stand, stand up, rise**
　ⓑ **stand out, be conspicuous**

ⓒ (stand on one's own legs) **establish oneself, begin life**

ⓓ **stand up to (criticism)**

立場 たちば standpoint

立ち上がる たちあがる stand up, rise to one's feet; take action

立ち直る たちなおる regain one's footing, recover; (of the market) improve

目立つ めだつ stand out, be conspicuous

引き立つ ひきたつ be set off, improve in appearance, contrast well

文を以て立つ ぶんをもってたつ live by the pen

面目が立つ めんもく(=めんぼく)がたつ save one's face

② [formerly 起つ] **rise (to action), rouse oneself**

祖国の為に立つ そこくのためにたつ rise to the rescue of one's country

③ begin an action:

ⓐ [sometimes also 発つ] **start (on a journey), leave, depart**

ⓑ (of seasons) **begin, come**

ⓒ (of the market) **open**

先立つ さきだつ precede, go before; die before

旅立ち たびだち departure

秋立つ日 あきたつひ first day [beginning] of autumn

市が立つ日 いちがたつひ market day

④ (of birds) **take wing, rise in the air**

飛び立つ とびたつ rise in the air, take flight

⑤ **evaporate, rise (in vapor), (of smoke) go up**

立ち上る たちのぼる go up, rise, ascend

⑥ (of waves) **run high**

波立つ海 なみだつうみ choppy sea

⑦ (of plans or policies) **be formed, be established; be decided; make sense, hold water**

言い訳が立たない いいわけがたたない admit no excuse

⑧ **be proficient in**

筆が立つ ふでがたつ wield a facile pen

⑨ **stand in good stead, be useful**

役立つ やくだつ be of use, serve a purpose

⑩ (of rumors) **spread**

噂が立っている うわさがたっている A rumor is about

⑪ **get excited**

苛立つ いらだつ be irritated, be nettled, be impatient

浮き立つ うきたつ be enlivened, be exhilarated

腹が立つ はらがたつ get angry, take offense

⑫ *math* **give, make (an integral quotient)**

十六を五で割ると三が立って一が余る じゅうろくをごでわるとさんがたっていちがあまる Sixteen divided by five gives three with a remainder of one

⑬ (of arrows or thorns) **stick into, run into**

喉に骨が立った のどにほねがたった A bone got caught in the throat

建つ

Ⓚ2661

be built, be erected, be established

銅像が建った どうぞうがたった A bronze statue was erected

起つ   Ⓚ2818

[now usu. 立つ] **rise (to action), rouse oneself**

起ち居 たちい one's movement

祖国の為に起つ そこくのためにたつ rise to the rescue of one's country

発つ   Ⓚ2222

[now usu. 立つ] **start (on a journey), leave, depart**

東京を発つ とうきょうをたつ leave Tokyo

経つ   Ⓚ1218

pass, elapse, go by

時間が経つ じかんがたつ Time goes by

---

369   **たつ³**

竜   Ⓚ1805

dragon

辰   Ⓚ2582

fifth sign of the Oriental zodiac: **the Dragon**—(time) 7-9 a.m., (direction) ESE, (season) March (of the lunar calendar)

辰の年 たつのとし the year of the Dragon

辰の刻 たつのこく the fifth hour, 8 a.m.; the Hour of the Dragon

辰巳 たつみ [also 巽] southeast

---

370   **たて¹**

立て-   Ⓚ1723

① ⓐ **standing**

ⓑ [formerly also 竪] **vertical, upright**

立て看板 たてかんばん standing signboard

立て型ピアノ たてがたぴあの upright piano

② **leading**

立て役者 たてやくしゃ leading actor; leader

③ **unclassified compounds**

立て替える たてかえる pay for another; pay in advance

縦   Ⓚ1286

① ⓐ **length, height**

ⓑ [sometimes also 竪-] **vertical, upright**

縦の たての vertical, longitudinal

縦書き たてがき vertical writing

縦縞 たてじま vertical stripes

② **warp**

縦糸 たていと [also 経糸 or 経] warp

竪   Ⓚ2470

ⓐ [now usu. 縦-] **vertical, upright**

ⓑ [now usu. 立て-] **vertical, upright**

竪琴 たてごと harp

竪縞 たてじま vertical stripes

竪穴 たてあな pit

竪樋 たてどい downspout

建て   Ⓚ2661

[in compounds] **business commitment, sales contract**

建て値 たてね official quotations, rates of exchange, market

盾 　Ⓚ2590

[sometimes also 楯] **shield, escutcheon**

盾突く たてつく oppose, defy, rebel

盾座 たてざ the Shield, Scutum

法律を盾に取って ほうりつをたてに
　とって on the authority of law

楯 　Ⓚ0928

[usu. 盾] **shield, escutcheon**

楯突く たてつく oppose, defy; rebel

楯籠る(=立て籠る) たてこもる barri-
　cade [shut] oneself in, hold (a fort)

後ろ楯 うしろだて backing, protec-
　tion; supporter

小楯 こだて small shield, screen

法律を楯に取って ほうりつをたてに
　とって on the authority of law

経 　Ⓚ1218

[also 縦糸 or 経糸] **warp**

縦糸 　Ⓚ1286

[also 経糸 or 経] **warp**

経糸 　Ⓚ1218

[also 経 or 縦糸] **warp**

立てる 　Ⓚ1723

① **stand, make stand, erect, raise, set**

立て掛ける たてかける lean against,
　set against

旗を立てる はたをたてる hoist a flag

候補者を立てる こうほしゃをたてる
　put up a candidate

②ⓐ **establish, set up, form**
　ⓑ **establish (laws), enact, lay
　(plans), develop (a theory)**

計画を立てる けいかくをたてる make
　plans

立て直す たてなおす rally, make over;
　reorganize

献立 こんだて menu, preparations

仮説を立てる かせつをたてる build
　up a hypothesis

③ **establish oneself, support oneself**

身を立てる みをたてる make a suc-
　cess in life

生計を立てる せいけいをたてる make
　a living

④ **look up to, respect**

夫を立てる おっとをたてる treat one's
　husband with due respect

引き立てる ひきたてる favor; set off;
　march (a prisoner) off

⑤ⓐ **do one's duty, be loyal**
　ⓑ **save face**

義理を立てる ぎりをたてる do one's
　duty, be faithful

顔を立てる かおをたてる save (a
　person's) face

⑥ **raise (one's voice)**

音を立てるな おとをたてるな Don't
　make a noise

⑦ **set (a rumor) afloat**

噂を立てられる うわさをたてられる
　be gossiped about

⑧ **make an oath**

誓いを立てている ちかいをたててい
　る be under a vow

⑨ **render (distinguished services)**

手柄を立てる てがらをたてる do a meritorious deed

⑩ sharpen (a saw)
目立をする めたてをする set the teeth of a saw

⑪ [usu. 閉てる] shut (as a paper sliding door)
戸を立てる とをたてる shut a door

⑫ [also 点てる] make tea
抹茶を立てる まっちゃをたてる prepare powdered tea

⑬ make use of
役立てる やくだてる put to use, make use of, turn to account

⑭ become angry
腹を立てる はらをたてる get angry, take offense

建てる　Ⓚ2661

ⓐ build, construct, erect, put up
ⓑ establish (a nation)
建物 たてもの building, structure
建て前 たてまえ erection of house framework; principle, rule, one's position; one's words (as opposed to one's real intentions)
建て直し たてなおし rebuilding, re-erection

点てる　Ⓚ1793

[also 立てる] make tea
野点 のだて open-air tea ceremony

閉てる　Ⓚ2832

[sometimes also 立てる] shut (as a paper sliding door)
開け閉て あけたて opening and shutting

例える　Ⓚ0071

illustrate, give an example
例え(=喩え、譬え) たとえ metaphor, simile, allegory
例えば たとえば for example

譬える

[also 喩える] compare to, liken, speak figuratively
譬え(=喩え、例え) たとえ simile, metaphor, allegory
譬え話 たとえばなし fable, allegory
死を眠りに譬える しをねむりにたとえる compare death to sleep

喩える　Ⓚ0508

[also 譬える] compare to, liken, speak figuratively
喩え たとえ metaphor, simile, allegory
死を眠りに喩える しをねむりにたとえる compare death to sleep

店　Ⓚ2657

① shop, store
店卸し(=棚卸し) たなおろし inventory
大店 おおだな large store

② house for rent
店子 たなこ tenant

棚　Ⓚ0895

ⓐ [also suffix] shelf, rack, ledge, mantelpiece

ⓑ (natural shelflike structure) **shelf, ledge (of rock)**
ⓒ **continental shelf**
棚卸し(=店卸し) たなおろし inventory
棚牡丹 たなぼた windfall, godsend
棚上げする たなあげする shelve (up), pigeonhole
棚引く たなびく trail, hang [lie] over
書棚 しょだな bookshelf
本棚 ほんだな bookshelf
食器棚 しょっきだな cupboard, sideboard
岩棚 いわだな ledge
大陸棚 たいりくだな continental shelf
陸棚 りくだな continental shelf

376 たね

種 ⓚ1128

① **seed, stone, kernel, pip**
菜種 なたね rapeseed, coleseed
②ⓐ **kind, species, variety; quality**
ⓑ **breed, stock**
変わり種 かわりだね novelty, exception, freak
種馬 たねうま stud horse, stallion
一粒種 ひとつぶだね one's only child
③ [formerly also 胤] **paternal blood, offspring**
種違い たねちがい half brother, half sister
④ⓐ **material, matter**
ⓑ **subject, topic, matter, news**
料理の種を仕込む りょうりのたねをしこむ prepare for cooking
特種 とくだね exclusive news, scoop
⑤ **cause, source, origin**
悩みの種 なやみのたね cause of annoyance

⑥ **trick, secret, gimmick**
種明かし たねあかし exposure of a trick

胤 ⓚ0008

[now usu. 種] **paternal blood, offspring**
胤違い たねちがい half brother, half sister

377 たのしい

楽しい ⓚ2460

[sometimes also 愉しい] **pleasurable, pleasant, enjoyable, merry**
楽しさ たのしさ pleasure, joy; pleasantness
楽しい思い出 たのしいおもいで happy [sweet] memory

愉しい ⓚ0534

[usu. 楽しい] **pleasurable, pleasant, enjoyable, merry**
愉しさ たのしさ pleasure, joy; pleasantness
愉しげな たのしげな joyous, merry, pleasant, happy, gay

378 たのしみ

楽しみ ⓚ2460

① [sometimes also 愉しみ]
ⓐ **pleasure, enjoyment**
ⓑ **amusement, diversion, hobby**
② **expectation**

愉しみ ⓚ0534

[usu. 楽しみ]
ⓐ **pleasure, enjoyment**

ⓑ **amusement, diversion, hobby**

379 たのしむ

楽しむ   Ⓚ2460

[sometimes also 愉しむ] **take pleasure in, enjoy (oneself)**

> 楽しみ たのしみ pleasure, enjoyment; amusement, diversion, hobby; expectation
>
> 映画を楽しむ えいがをたのしむ enjoy a movie

愉しむ   Ⓚ0534

[usu. 楽しむ] **take pleasure in, enjoy (oneself)**

> 愉しみ たのしみ pleasure, enjoyment; amusement, diversion, hobby

380 たま¹

魂   Ⓚ0975

[also 霊] **soul, spirit, ghost**

> 魂送り たまおくり sending off the spirits of the dead
>
> 人魂 ひとだま spirit of a dead person

霊   Ⓚ2442

[also 魂] **soul, spirit, ghost**

> 霊送り たまおくり sending off the spirits of the dead
>
> 御霊屋 みたまや mausoleum

381 たま²

玉   Ⓚ2919

① ⓐ [formerly also 珠 or 璧] **gem, jewel, precious stone, pearl; bead**
   ⓑ **something as beautiful or precious as a jewel**

> 玉に疵(=玉に瑕) たまにきず flaw in the crystal, fly in the ointment
>
> 勾玉(=曲玉) まがたま comma-shaped bead
>
> 玉の輿 たまのこし marriage to a man of wealth
>
> 掌中の玉 しょうちゅうのたま apple of one's eye

② various spherical objects, as:
   ⓐ **ball, globe; lump of noodles; egg; lens**
   ⓑ slang **testicles**

> 玉突き たまつき billiards; serial collisions (of cars)
>
> 玉子 たまご [also 卵] egg
>
> 目玉 めだま eyeball; loss leader (of merchandise)
>
> 鉄砲玉(=鉄砲弾) てっぽうだま gunshot, bullet; lost [truant] messenger; bull's-eye
>
> 金玉 きんたま testicles, balls

③ slang
   ⓐ **guy, chap**
   ⓑ **pretty girl, doll**

> 親玉 おやだま big shot, kingpin
>
> 表六玉(=兵六玉) ひょうろくだま nincompoop, simpleton
>
> 大変な玉だ たいへんなたまだ He's a caution!
>
> 上玉 じょうだま pretty girl

弾   Ⓚ0524

bullet, shot, shell

鉄砲弾(=鉄砲玉) てっぽうだま gun-shot, bullet; lost [truant] messenger; bull's-eye

珠

®0854

[now usu. 玉, formerly also 璧] **gem, jewel, precious stone, pearl; bead**

珠暖簾 たまのれん bead curtain

球

®0880

ⓐ **ball (in a sports game)**
ⓑ **light bulb**

球拾い たまひろい picking up balls; poor (ball) player
釣り球 つりだま deceptive pitch
電気の球 でんきのたま electric [light] bulb

璧

®2519

[now usu. 玉, formerly also 珠] **gem, jewel, precious stone, pearl, bead**

382 たまう

給う

®1237

① [sometimes also 賜う] [suffix] *literary* **deign to (perform an action for an inferior)**
② [usu. 賜う] *literary* **deign to give, bestow, grant, award**

賜う

®1433

① [sometimes also 給う] *literary* **deign to give, bestow, grant, award**
② [usu. 給う] [suffix] *literary* **(perform an action for an inferior) deign to**

383 たまご

卵

®0751

①ⓐ [also 玉子] **egg**
  ⓑ **spawn, roe**
  卵焼き たまごやき fried egg, omelette
② (an expert) **in the making**
  文士の卵 ぶんしのたまご hatching writer

玉子

®2919

[also 卵] **egg**

384 ためる

貯める

®1368

[also 溜める] **save (money), lay up (one's income)**
金を貯める かねをためる save money

溜める

®0608

①ⓐ **accumulate, heap up**
  ⓑ **collect (stamps)**
  ⓒ **store (esp. water)**
  溜め ため sink, cesspool; manure sink
  溜め息 ためいき sigh
  切手を溜める きってをためる collect stamps
  溜め池 ためいけ reservoir, irrigation pond, cistern
② **run up (a bill), leave undone**
  家賃を溜める やちんをためる let the rent fall into arrears
③ [also 貯める] **save (money), lay up (one's income)**
  溜め込む ためこむ save [store] up, hoard

385 だて

-立て   Ⓚ1723

① counter for:
  ⓐ number of carriage horses or boat oars
  ⓑ number of films in a multifeature movie
  四頭立ての馬車 よんとうだてのばしゃ carriage and four
  二本立ての映画 にほんだてのえいが double feature movie
② doing on purpose, doing something uncalled for
  隠し立て かくしだて keeping secret, concealment

-建て   Ⓚ2661

① way of building, method of construction
  二階建ての家 にかいだてのいえ two-storied house
② currency of exchange
  ドル建て どるだて quotation in dollars
③ average number of pages (of a newspaper or magazine)
  十六頁建ての新聞 じゅうろくぺーじだてのしんぶん 16-page newspaper

386 ついえる

費える   Ⓚ2261

be wasted
  費え ついえ wasteful expenses
  無為に費えた年月 むいについえたとしつき years spent idly

潰える   Ⓚ0677

ⓐ be routed, be utterly defeated
ⓑ collapse

387 ついたち

朔   Ⓚ1209

[usu. 一日] first day of the (lunar) month

一日   Ⓚ2850

[sometimes also 朔] 1st of the month

388 ついに

遂に   Ⓚ2705

[sometimes also 終に] at last, at length, in the end, finally

終に   Ⓚ1223

[usu. 遂に] at last, at length, in the end, finally

389 つか

柄   Ⓚ0799

hilt, handle
  柄頭 つかがしら pommel

束   Ⓚ2978

① hand breadth
  束の間 つかのま brief space of time, moment
② short support
③ bulk (of a book)

390 つかい

-使い ⓚ0072

[also suffix]
① trainer, tamer
② servant, employee

-遣い ⓚ2717

① spending, spending money
② worrying, being anxious
③ use (of language), spelling
④ manipulating

391 つかう

使う ⓚ0072

① ⓐ use, make use of, employ, handle
ⓑ employ, keep (in one's employ)
使い古す つかいふるす wear out (a thing) by use
使いこなす つかいこなす manage, handle, acquire command of
使い分ける つかいわける use properly, know how to use properly
使い物にならない つかいものにならない be no use
使い手 つかいて user, consumer; (fencing) master
使い捨ての つかいすての throwaway (articles)
魔法使い まほうつかい magician, sorcerer
人を使う ひとをつかう employ, take a person in one's service
② [usu. 遣う] spend, use (time or money)
金を使う かねをつかう spend money

遣う ⓚ2717

① [sometimes also 使う] spend, use (time or money)
金を遣う かねをつかう spend money
② be anxious, worry
気遣う きづかう feel anxious about, worry about, have apprehensions of
③ use (language properly), spell
正しい言葉を遣う ただしいことばをつかう use the correct word
④ manipulate
人形を遣う にんぎょうをつかう manipulate puppets

392 つかまえる

捕まえる ⓚ0387

arrest, nab, capture, catch
犯人を捕まえる はんにんをつかまえる arrest the culprit

捉まえる ⓚ0391

[usu. 摑まえる] grasp, grip, clutch

摑まえる ⓚ0627

[sometimes also 捉まえる] catch, seize, grasp, get hold of
鳥を摑まえる とりをつかまえる catch a bird

393 つかまる

捕まる ⓚ0387

be caught, be arrested
取っ捕まる とっつかまる be caught

捉まる ⓚ0391

[usu. 摑まる] **grasp, grip, clutch**

摑まる ⓚ0627

[sometimes also 捉まる] **hold fast to, cling to**

吊り革に摑まる つりかわにつかまる cling to a strap

394 つぎ

次 ⓚ0039

① **next, following**

次次に つぎつぎに one after another, in succession

② **post town**

東海道五十三次 とうかいどうごじゅうさんつぎ fifty-three stages on the Tokaido highway in former Japan

継ぎ ⓚ1242

a patch

395 つく¹

付く ⓚ0019

① ⓐ **attach itself to, stick (to), adhere (to); be connected with**
ⓑ **come in contact with, touch, reach**

結び付き むすびつき connection, relation, alliance

くっ付く くっつく stick (to), cling, adhere

噛み付く かみつく bite [snap] at

近付く ちかづく approach, near, get near; get acquainted

追い付く おいつく overtake, catch up with

② **be attached to, belong to, join, associate with; take up the cause of**

付き合う つきあう keep company with, get along with

付き合い つきあい friendship, association

敵に付く てきにつく take the side of the enemy

③ **gain (weight, power), become proficient, grow (wise)**

肉が付く にくがつく gain [put on] weight

④ **attend on, go with, accompany**

付き添う つきそう accompany, attend on, escort

⑤ **be installed, be built**

電話が付いた でんわがついた A telephone was installed

⑥ **be written, be registered**

帳面に付いている ちょうめんについている be written [entered] in a book

⑦ **be perceived [detected]**

目に付く めにつく catch one's eye, attract one's attention

気付く きづく notice, become aware of, find out

⑧ **catch fire, be ignited**

火が付く ひがつく catch fire, be ignited

⑨ **take (root)**

根が付く ねがつく take [strike] root

⑩ **cost, amount to**

安く付く やすくつく come cheaper

⑪ **be lucky**

付いている ついている be in luck

⑫ **be settled, be established**

話が付く はなしがつく come to terms, reach agreement

附く Ⓚ0307

[usu. 付く] **same as** 付く **つく**

着く Ⓚ2826

① ⓐ **arrive at, reach, come to hand**
  ⓑ (succeed in touching) **reach, come in contact with, touch**
  駅に着く えきにつく arrive at the station
  行き着く いきつく arrive at, get to
  船着き場 ふなつきば harbor; landing place
  追い着く おいつく catch up with
② (come to rest in a position) **settle, settle [seat] oneself, become situated, settle down (in a place)**
  席に着く せきにつく take a seat
  帰途に着く きとにつく leave for home
  落ち着く おちつく calm down, settle down, be steady; settle in, take up one's residence; harmonize with, match

就く Ⓚ1512

① ⓐ **set about a task, set out, enter upon, take up (a position), assume (office), enter (a business)**
  ⓑ **set out, start, leave**
  就いて ついて about, concerning
  職に就く しょくにつく take up employment
  帰途に就く きとにつく leave for home
② [formerly 即く] **ascend to (the throne)**

位に就く くらいにつく ascend to the throne
③ **study under (a teacher)**
  先生に就く せんせいにつく study under (a teacher)

即く Ⓚ1036

① [now usu. 就く] **ascend to (the throne)**
  位に即く くらいにつく ascend to the throne
② **be in immediate [close] contact, be based on**
  即かず離れずの態度 つかずはなれずのたいど neutral attitude

点く Ⓚ1793

be lighted, be switched on, go on
  ガスが点いている がすがついている The gas is on

396	つく²

突く Ⓚ1918

① (penetrate with a pointed end) **thrust, pierce, stab, prick**
  突き刺す つきさす stab, pierce, thrust
  突き殺す つきころす stab to death
  突き抜く つきぬく pierce through
  突き抜ける つきぬける go [push, thrust] through, penetrate
  突き破る つきやぶる break [smash] through, pierce
  楯突く たてつく oppose, defy; rebel
② ⓐ (strike forcibly with a pointed end) **thrust, push, give a push [thrust]**
  ⓑ [sometimes also 撞く] **poke, strike (a bell)**

突き つき thrust, push; lunge

突き出す つきだす thrust out, push out; push out of a sumo ring

突き当たる つきあたる hit against, run into; come to the end of (a street)

突き当たり つきあたり end [bottom] of a street

突っ込む つっこむ thrust in, ram into, stuff into; dash [run] into

突っ掛ける つっかける slip on, slip into (slippers)

鐘を突く かねをつく strike a bell

③ [sometimes also 衝く] **attack, strike at**
中堅を突く ちゅうけんをつく strike [attack] at the center [heart]

④ [sometimes also 衝く] **brave, face courageously**
嵐を突いて進む あらしをついてすすむ proceed in the face of a storm

⑤ [sometimes also 衝く] **stimulate (the senses), be pungent**
鼻を突く はなをつく assail the nostrils

衝く ⓚ0658

① [usu. 突く] **attack, strike at**
中堅を衝く ちゅうけんをつく strike [attack] at the center [heart]

② [usu. 突く] **brave, face courageously**
嵐を衝いて進む あらしをついてすすむ proceed in the face of a storm

③ [usu. 突く] **stimulate (the senses), be pungent**
鼻を衝く はなをつく assail the nostrils

④ **unclassified compounds**
衝立て ついたて single-leaf screen

撞く ⓚ0668

[usu. 突く] **poke, strike (a bell)**
鐘を撞く かねをつく strike a bell

397 つくり

作り ⓚ0052

① **make, physique, features**
顔の作り かおのつくり features of the face

② **makeup**
濃い作り こいつくり heavy makeup

③ *sashimi*, **sliced raw flesh (esp. of fish)**
お作り おつくり *sashimi*, sliced raw flesh (esp. of fish)

造り ⓚ2679

ⓐ **making, building, constructing (as buildings or ships)**

ⓑ **make, structure, construction**
造り付けの つくりつけの built-in
造りの頑丈な家 つくりのがんじょうないえ house of solid structure

398 つくる

作る ⓚ0052

①ⓐ **make (out of materials), form, prepare**

ⓑ [sometimes also 創る] **create, bring into being**

ⓒ **make (as a document), make out, compose, frame, draw up**

ⓓ **form (an organization), organize, found, establish**

ⓔ **prepare food, cook; slice (raw fish)**

形作る かたちづくる form, shape, make, mold

作り出す つくりだす make, turn out, create

詩を作る しをつくる compose a poem

新内閣を作る しんないかくをつくる form a new Cabinet

刺身を作る さしみをつくる slice (raw fish)

② **raise crops, cultivate, grow, till**
庭で作った野菜 にわでつくったやさい vegetables grown in one's yard

③ **foster, cultivate (a person's character), build up**
良い習慣を作る よいしゅうかんをつくる cultivate a good habit

④ **make [touch] up, apply cosmetics; trim**
酷く作った顔 ひどくつくったかお face with heavy makeup

⑤ **make up (a story), invent, fabricate**
作り話 つくりばなし fable, fiction
作り泣き つくりなき make-believe crying
作り笑い つくりわらい forced laugh

造る Ⓚ2679

① ⓐ **make (as an object that requires time and skill), manufacture, fabricate, fashion**
ⓑ **build (ships or buildings), construct**
船を造る ふねをつくる build a ship

② **make (wine), brew**
酒造り さけづくり sake brewing

③ **coin, mint**
新語を造る しんごをつくる coin a new word

創る Ⓚ1610

[usu. 作る] **create, bring into being**
天地を創る てんちをつくる create the heavens and the earth

接ぐ Ⓚ0460

ⓐ **join, piece together, set (a broken bone), splice (ropes)**
ⓑ **graft (trees)**
骨接ぎ ほねつぎ bonesetting
接ぎ木 つぎき grafting, grafted tree
木に竹を接ぐ きにたけをつぐ graft a bamboo shoot on a tree, sew a fox's skin to the lion's

継ぐ Ⓚ1242

① **succeed (to), accede; inherit**
家を継ぐ いえをつぐ succeed to a house
受け継ぐ うけつぐ inherit, succeed to
跡継ぎ あとつぎ successor, heir
引き継ぐ ひきつぐ take over, hand over; succeed to, inherit

② **couple, link, relay**
継ぎ足す つぎたす add to; extend, piece out
言葉を継ぐ ことばをつぐ continue (to say)

③ **patch (up)**
継ぎ つぎ a patch
継ぎ接ぎ つぎはぎ patching (and darning)

④ **add to, replenish, feed**

次ぐ Ⓚ0039

rank next to, come next [after]

次いで ついで next, secondly; subsequently

相次ぐ あいつぐ succeed one another

取り次ぐ とりつぐ act as agent; transmit; answer the door

注ぐ ⓀＫ0287

pour out, pour in, fill

注ぎ込む つぎこむ pour in [into]; invest in

注ぎ口 つぎぐち spout

400 つける

付ける ⓀＫ0019

① **attach, affix, stick, fasten, add (on), append; set, put (one thing on another)**

付け加える つけくわえる add

付け足す つけたす add on, append

くっ付ける くっつける join, attach; paste, glue

着付け きつけ dressing, fitting

コップに口を付ける こっぷにくちをつける put one's lips to a glass

② **apply, put on**

薬を付ける くすりをつける apply medicine

③ **leave a mark on**

染みを付ける しみをつける stain, blot, smudge

④ **write, make an entry**

付け込む つけこむ take advantage of; make an entry

帳簿に付ける ちょうぼにつける enter in a book

⑤ⓐ **give, impart, direct (one's attention)**

ⓑ **set (a price)**

元気を付ける げんきをつける give courage to, encourage

裏付け うらづけ guarantee, endorsement; support, backing; substantiation, proof

貸し付け かしつけ loaning

値段を高く付ける ねだんをたかくつける put a high price on

⑥ **provide (a person) with an attendant, place a person in attendance (on)**

護衛を付ける ごえいをつける provide (a person) with a bodyguard

⑦ **follow, trail, shadow**

後を付ける あとをつける follow, tag along

⑧ **kindle, set (fire)**

付け木 つけぎ spill (piece of wood for lighting)

⑨ **load, put on, dish up**

干し草を付けた馬 ほしくさをつけたうま horse loaded with hay

⑩ **settle, bring to terms**

話を付ける はなしをつける settle a matter; negotiate, arrange

⑪ [in the form of 付けて つけて] **refer to, relate to, connect with**

それに付けても それにつけても in this connection

⑫ **unclassified compounds**

受付 うけつけ receipt, reception, acceptance; receptionist, information clerk; information office [desk]

附ける ⓀＫ0307

[usu. 付ける] **same as** 付ける つける

着ける Ⓚ2826

① (cause to arrive) **bring (a vehicle or boat) alongside, put ashore, berth**
ボートを岸に着ける ぼーとをきしにつける put a boat ashore
車を門に着ける くるまをもんにつける pull a car up at the gate

② **put on clothes, don, wear, be dressed**
面を着ける めんをつける put a mask on

③ (place a person in a position) **settle, settle [seat] a person, situate, steady**
落ち着ける おちつける calm (down); settle (down)

④ **set about, start, commence**
手を着ける てをつける start; set one's hand to

就ける Ⓚ1512

① **install [place] a person in a position**
役に就ける やくにつける place someone in a position

② [formerly 即ける] **enthrone**
王位に就ける おういにつける place on the throne

③ **make (a person) study under (a teacher)**
良い先生に就ける よいせんせいにつける have one study under a good teacher

即ける Ⓚ1036

[now usu. 就ける] **enthrone**
王位に即ける おういにつける place on the throne

点ける Ⓚ1793

light, turn [switch] on
電灯を点ける でんとうをつける turn [switch] on an electric lamp

漬ける Ⓚ0636

① **pickle (vegetables), salt, preserve**
漬け物 つけもの pickles, pickled vegetable
漬け菜 つけな pickled [salted] greens
菜を漬ける なをつける pickle greens
梅を塩に漬ける うめをしおにつける salt plums; preserve plums in salt

② **immerse, steep, soak, dip**
手を水に漬ける てをみずにつける immerse [dip] one's hand in water
衣服を良く漬けて置け いふくをよくつけておけ Give the clothes a thorough soak

401　つつしむ

慎む Ⓚ0590

ⓐ **be prudent, be discreet, be careful**
ⓑ **restrain oneself, abstain from, be moderate**
慎み つつしみ prudence, modesty, self-control
慎み深い つつしみぶかい discreet, prudent, modest
口を慎む くちをつつしむ be careful in speech
酒を慎む さけをつつしむ abstain from drinking

謹む Ⓚ1462

[usu. in TE-form] **be respectful, be humble**

謹んで つつしんで respectfully, reverently, humbly

402　つとまる

務まる ⓚ1085

be fit [qualified] for

後任が務まる こうにんがつとまる be fit to succeed

勤まる ⓚ1613

be fit for, be equal to (the task)

勤まらない つとまらない be unfit [incompetent] for

403　つとめ

勤め ⓚ1613

① **service, employment, duties**
② **Buddhistic service, sutra chanting**
③ **prostitute service**

務め ⓚ1085

duty, task, responsibility

404　つとめる

勤める ⓚ1613

serve (in an office), hold a job, be in the service of

勤め つとめ service, employment, duties; Buddhistic service, sutra chanting; prostitute service
勤め先 つとめさき (one's place of) employment
勤め上げる つとめあげる serve out one's time, perform one's service

務める ⓚ1085

ⓐ **discharge [perform] one's duties**
ⓑ **play [act, perform] (a part or role)**

務め つとめ duty, task, responsibility
議長を務める ぎちょうをつとめる act as chairman

努める ⓚ2204

[sometimes also 勉める] **endeavor, make efforts, try hard, work diligently**

努めて つとめて with effort, as much as possible
極力努める きょくりょくつとめる do one's best

勉める ⓚ2829

[usu. 努める] **endeavor, make efforts, try hard, work diligently**

勉めて つとめて with effort, as much as possible
極力勉める きょくりょくつとめる do one's best

405　つむ¹

摘む ⓚ0629

① **pick (flowers), pluck, gather**
摘み取る つみとる pick, pluck
摘み草 つみくさ gathering wild greens
茶摘み ちゃつみ tea-picking
②ⓐ **nip**
ⓑ [also 剪む] **cut (one's hair), trim**
芽を摘む めをつむ nip the buds; nip something in the bud
髪を摘む かみをつむ have one's hair cut [trimmed]

剪む

[also 摘む] **cut (one's hair), trim**
髪を剪む かみをつむ have one's hair cut [trimmed]

406　つむ²

積む　Ⓚ1142

① **pile up, heap (up), stack**
積み上げる つみあげる pile [heap] up, accumulate
上積み うわづみ upper load, deck cargo; loading on top, overlaying
② **load, ship, stow aboard**
積み込む つみこむ load (up), put on board, stow aboard
船積み ふなづみ shipment, shipping
③ **accumulate, lay by, save, amass**
積み立て つみたて laying by, reserving, accumulation

詰む　Ⓚ1380

① **be packed, become fine [close]**
目の詰んだ めのつんだ fine(-grained), close
② **be checkmated**
詰み つみ checkmate

407　つり

釣り　Ⓚ1496

① [also suffix] **angling, rod fishing**
釣り糸 つりいと fishing line
釣り師 つりし angler
魚釣り さかなつり angling, fishing
鮪釣り まぐろつり tuna fishing

一本釣り いっぽんづり pole-and-line fishing
② **change (for money)**
お釣り おつり change
釣り銭 つりせん change

釣り–　Ⓚ1496

[also 吊り] **suspended, hanging**
釣り橋 つりばし suspension bridge
釣鐘 つりがね hanging bell, temple bell
釣り合う つりあう balance; match, be in harmony
釣り合い つりあい balance, equilibrium; proportion
釣り下げる つりさげる suspend from

吊り

ⓐ **suspension, hanging; suspender(s)**
ⓑ [also 釣り–] **suspended, hanging**
首吊り くびつり hanging (by the neck)
ズボン吊り ずぼんつり suspenders
吊り棚 つりだな hanging shelf
吊り革 つりかわ (hand) strap
吊り輪 つりわ flying rings

408　つる

釣る　Ⓚ1496

① **angle, fish**
釣り上げる つりあげる fish up, land
② **decoy, allure, take in**
釣り出す つりだす fish out, draw out, decoy

吊る

① [also 釣る] **suspend, hang, swing, sling**
吊り上げる **つりあげる** hang up, suspend; raise, lift
② **lift by the loins (in sumo wrestling)**
吊り出す **つりだす** hold (the opponent) in the arms and carry him out of the ring
③ [formerly 攣る] **cramp, have a cramp**
引き吊り **ひきつり** cramp; scar
④ [formerly 攣る] **turn up, slant upward**
吊り目 **つりめ** slanted [upturned] eyes

攣る

① **cramp, have a cramp**
引き攣り **ひきつり** cramp; scar
足が攣る **あしがつる** have one's leg cramp
② **turn up, slant upward**
攣り目 **つりめ** slanted [upturned] eyes

409　　づくり

–作り　　Ⓚ0052

① (build of the body) **make, physique**
細作りの人 **ほそづくりのひと** slender person
② **suffix indicating material composition**
粘土作りの **ねんどづくりの** made of clay
③ **affectation, pretense**
若作りにする **わかづくりにする** make oneself up to look younger
④ **sliced raw fish, *sashimi***

生け作り(=活け作り) **いけづくり**
freshly-killed fish served whole with its meat cut in slices

–造り　　Ⓚ2679

ⓐ **make, structure; style of building**
ⓑ **building, constructing, developing**
防火造り **ぼうかづくり** fireproof construction
数寄屋造り(=数奇屋造り) **すきやづくり** *sukiya* style of building, style of a tea-ceremony arbor
別荘地造り **べっそうちづくり** developing a villa site

410　　づけ

–付け　　Ⓚ0019

① **attaching, affixing**
糊付け **のりづけ** pasting
② [suffix] **dated**
八日付 **ようかづけ** dated the eighth

–漬け　　Ⓚ0636

ⓐ **pickles**
ⓑ **pickling with, preserving in**
千枚漬け **せんまいづけ** pickled sliced radishes
松前漬け **まつまえづけ** Matsumae pickles
塩漬け **しおづけ** salted [corned] food; pickling with salt
味噌漬け **みそづけ** vegetables preserved in *miso*; preserving in *miso*
ホルマリン漬け **ほるまりんづけ** specimen preserved in formalin

411   てのひら

掌   ⓚ2256

[also 手の平] **palm of the hand**

手の平   ⓚ2907

[also 掌] **palm of the hand**

412   とう

問う   ⓚ2833

① **ask, question, inquire**
問い合わせる といあわせる inquire, make a reference, apply
問い質す といただす inquire, question
問い詰める といつめる press a question, cross-examine

② **accuse, charge**
殺人罪に問われて さつじんざいにとわれて on a charge of murder

③ **care, mind**
経験を問わず けいけんをとわず no experience necessary

訪う   ⓚ1335

call on, visit

413   とうとい

貴い   ⓚ2260

same as 貴い たっとい

尊い   ⓚ2029

same as 尊い たっとい

414   とうとぶ

貴ぶ   ⓚ2260

same as 貴ぶ たっとぶ

尊ぶ   ⓚ2029

same as 尊ぶ たっとぶ

415   とおす

通す   ⓚ2678

① ⓐ **let pass, let go by; run (a thread) through**
ⓑ **let in, admit, usher**
ⓒ **pass through, penetrate, pierce**
通せん坊 とおせんぼう barring (a person's) way
先に通す さきにとおす let (a person) pass first
客を通す きゃくをとおす show a guest in
千枚通し せんまいどおし eyeleteer
水を通さない みずをとおさない be impervious to water

② [also 透す] **be transparent, be pervious to (light)**
光を通す ひかりをとおす be pervious to light

③ **pass [carry] (a bill)**
議案を通す ぎあんをとおす pass [see] a bill (through the House)

④ [also verbal suffix] **carry through, stick to**
押し通す おしとおす push through, carry it through, hold out to the end

⑤ [also verbal suffix] **continue, keep doing, remain**

三日通して みっかとおして for three
days on end

泣き通す なきとおす keep crying

⑥ **do (something) through an intermediary**

仲人を通して なこうどをとおして
through a go-between

透す Ⓚ2677

[also 通す] **be transparent, be pervious to (light)**

光を透す ひかりをとおす be pervious
to light

416 とおり

通り Ⓚ2678

① ⓐ **passage; drainage**

ⓑ **street traffic, coming and going**

通りが良い とおりがよい pass [run]
well

人通り ひとどおり traffic

② **street, avenue, road**

大通り おおどおり main street

③ **reputation; favor**

世間の通り せけんのとおり reputa-
tion

④ **accordance, agreement, conform-
ity**

約束の通り やくそくのとおり true to
one's promise, as promised

透り Ⓚ2677

penetration (as of light)

417 とおる

通る Ⓚ2678

① ⓐ **pass (by), go along [past], get
through**

ⓑ **pass for [as], be known as, pass
current**

通り掛かる とおりかかる happen to
pass by

通り道 とおりみち path

町を通る まちをとおる pass through
town

本物で通る ほんものでとおる pass for
[as] genuine

② [also 透る]

ⓐ **penetrate, pierce, permeate**

ⓑ **be transparent, be pervious to
(light)**

通る声 とおるこえ carrying voice

透き通る すきとおる be transparent

③ ⓐ **pass (an examination)**

ⓑ **pass, be admissible**

議案が通った ぎあんがとおった The
bill passed (the House)

そんな言い訳は通らない そんない
いわけはとおらない Such excuses
will not do

④ **come in, be ushered into**

客間に通る きゃくまにとおる enter
the parlor

⑤ **be understood [comprehensible]**

意味が通らない いみがとおらない
not make sense, be incomprehensible

透る Ⓚ2677

ⓐ **be transparent, be pervious to
(light)**

ⓑ **penetrate, pierce, permeate**

透り とおり penetration (as of light)
光が透るカーテン ひかりがとおる かーてん curtain pervious to light
透る声 とおるこえ carrying voice

418 とかす

解かす ⓚ1375

① [also 溶かす, formerly also 融かす] *vt* **melt (snow or ice), thaw (out)**
氷を解かす こおりをとかす melt ice
② [usu. 梳かす] **comb (one's hair)**
髪を解かす かみをとかす comb one's hair

融かす ⓚ1626

[now usu. 解かす or 溶かす] *vt* **melt (snow or ice), thaw (out)**
氷を融かす こおりをとかす melt ice

溶かす ⓚ0610

① (cause to pass into solution or to turn liquid) **dissolve, melt, liquefy**
砂糖を水に溶かす さとうをみずにとかす dissolve sugar in water
②ⓐ [formerly 熔かす or 鎔かす] **melt (up) (metals), fuse, smelt**
ⓑ [also 解かす, formerly also 融かす] **melt (snow or ice), thaw (out)**
鉄を溶かす てつをとかす melt [fuse] iron
氷を溶かす こおりをとかす melt ice

熔かす

[now usu. 溶かす] *vt* **melt (up) (metals), fuse, smelt**
鉄を熔かす てつをとかす melt [fuse] iron

鎔かす

[now usu. 溶かす] *vt* **melt (up) (metals), fuse, smelt**
鉄を鎔かす てつをとかす melt [fuse] iron

梳かす

[sometimes also 解かす] **comb (one's hair)**
髪を梳かす かみをとかす comb one's hair

419 とき

時 ⓚ0830

①ⓐ **time, hour, moment**
ⓑ **times, age, the day**
ⓒ (former unit of time) **two-hour period**
時が移る ときがうつる Time elapses
一時 ひととき time, while, moment
引け時 ひけどき closing time (of school)
時の ときの then, of the day
戦争の時 せんそうのとき times of war
子の時 ねのとき midnight
②ⓐ **right time, opportunity, occasion, case; season**
ⓑ [also 秋] **critical moment**
時には ときには occasionally
時時 ときどき sometimes, occasionally; each occasion
時を待つ ときをまつ wait for a favorable chance
時と場合によって ときとばあいによって should time and circumstances permit
丁度良い時に ちょうどよいときに just at the right moment

危急存亡の時 ききゅうそんぼうのとき
crisis, critical moment

③ⓐ **when**
ⓑ **in case of, if, in the event of**
家に帰る時 いえにかえるとき when
returning home
五時迄に帰らない時は ごじまでに
かえらないときは if I don't come
back till five o'clock
④ *gram* **tense**
法と時 ほうととき mood and tense

秋 Ⓚ1054

[also 時] **critical moment**
危急存亡の秋 ききゅうそんぼうのと
き crisis, critical moment

420	とく

解く Ⓚ1375

① **undo, unfasten, unloosen, unsew**
解き放す ときはなす set free
髪を解く かみをとく undo one's hair
② **dissolve, cancel, release, lift**
禁を解く きんをとく lift [remove] a
ban
③ **solve, work out**
謎解き なぞとき solution of a riddle
④ [also 梳く] **comb (one's hair)**
髪を解く かみをとく comb one's hair
⑤ *literary* **relieve (a person) of a post**
任を解かれる にんをとかれる be
relieved of one's post

説く Ⓚ1405

① **explain**
説き明かす ときあかす explain, solve;
make clear

② **preach, advocate; persuade**
口説く くどく persuade; seduce

溶く Ⓚ0610

① (cause to pass into solution) **dissolve
(paint)**
絵の具を溶く えのぐをとく dissolve
colors
② **whip an egg**
溶きほぐす ときほぐす whip an egg

梳く

[also 解く] **comb (one's hair)**

421	とぐ

研ぐ Ⓚ1046

[rarely also 砥ぐ] **sharpen, grind, whet,
polish; wash (rice)**
研ぎ とぎ grinding, polish, sharpen-
ing
研ぎ石 とぎいし whetstone, knife
sharpener
研ぎ澄ます とぎすます sharpen
[grind] well

砥ぐ Ⓚ1066

[now always 研ぐ] **sharpen, grind, whet,
polish**

422	とける

解ける Ⓚ1375

① **come loose, come undone**
靴紐が解けた くつひもがとけた The
shoestrings came untied
② **be allayed, relent**

③ **be solved, be resolved, be cleared**
解けない問題 とけないもんだい
insoluble problem
④ [also 溶ける, formerly 融ける] (esp. of snow or ice) **melt, thaw**
雪解け ゆきどけ thawing of snow

融ける
Ⓚ1626
[now usu. 解ける or 溶ける] *vi* (esp. of snow or ice) **melt, thaw**
雪融け ゆきどけ thawing of snow

溶ける
Ⓚ0610
① (pass into solution) **dissolve**
塩は水に溶ける しおはみずにとける
Salt dissolves in water
②ⓐ [formerly 熔ける or 鎔ける] (of metals) **melt (up), fuse, smelt**
ⓑ [also 解ける, formerly 融ける] (esp. of snow or ice) **melt, thaw**
火で溶ける ひでとける melt in the fire
溶け込む とけこむ melt into, fuse into

熔ける
[now usu. 溶ける] *vi* (of metals) **melt (up), fuse, smelt**

鎔ける
[now usu. 溶ける] *vi* (of metals) **melt (up), fuse, smelt**

423　　ところ

所
Ⓚ0752
①ⓐ **place, spot, site; part; room, space; district**
ⓑ **one's place, one's house, one's address**

所々 ところどころ here and there, at places
所を替える ところをかえる change places, change sides
居所 いどころ one's address [residence], one's whereabouts
台所 だいどころ kitchen
所書き ところがき one's address
②ⓐ **time, moment**
ⓑ **occasion, case**
早い所 はやいところ promptly
今の所 いまのところ at present
書いている所だ かいているところだ I am writing now
彼は今来た所だ かれはいまきたところだ He has just arrived
所構わず ところかまわず irrespective of the occasion, indiscriminately
③ **point, feature**
詩人らしい所 しじんらしいところ something of a poet
強い所 つよいところ strong point
④ **extent**
... 所では …ところでは so far as…
倍でも安い所だ ばいでもやすいところだ It would be cheap even at twice the sum
⑤ **passage, part**
面白い所 おもしろいところ interesting passage
⑥ⓐ function word equiv. to relative pronoun: **what, thing that, which, who**
ⓑ [in the form of 所となる ところとなる] **function word indicating the passive voice**
彼の言う所 かれのいうところ what he says
私が愛する所の女性 わたくしがあいするところのじょせい the woman whom I love

人の好む所となる ひとのこのむところ
となる be liked by people

⑦ⓐ when, upon, even if
ⓑ [in the form of 所が ところが] but,
however, on the contrary
ⓒ [in the form of 所で ところで] well,
now, by the way, incidentally

問い合わせた所、嘘だと分かった
といあわせたところ、うそだとわ
かった On inquiry, the report
proved false

損をした所で そんをしたところで
even if one loses

所が失敗した ところがしっぱいした
Nevertheless, I failed

所で猫は好きですか ところでねこ
はすきですか By the way, do you
like cats?

処 　　　　　　　　 Ⓚ2609

[also suffix] **place (for a specific purpose, as eating or resting)**

お食事処 おしょくじどころ (Japanese)
restaurant

年 　　　　　　　　 Ⓚ1752

① [formerly also 歳] **year**

お年玉 おとしだま New Year's (money) gift

今年 ことし this year

毎年 まいとし every year

半年 はんとし(=はんねん) half a year

閏年 うるうどし leap year

② [also 歳, sometimes also 齢] **one's
years, age**

年寄り としより old [aged] person,
the aged; older councilor

年上の としうえの older, senior

年取った としとった old, aged

年頃 としごろ age; marriageable age;
adolescence, puberty

歳 　　　　　　　　 Ⓚ2190

ⓐ [now usu. 年] **year**

ⓑ [also 年, sometimes also 齢] **one's
years, age**

歳を取る としをとる age, grow old

齢 　　　　　　　　 Ⓚ1675

[usu. 年 or 歳] **one's years, age**

閉じる 　　　　　　 Ⓚ2832

① **close, shut**

閉じ込める とじこめる shut in [up],
lock in [up]

閉じ籠もる とじこもる shut oneself
up (in a room)

② (come or bring to an end) **close (a
meeting)**

幕を閉じる まくをとじる close the
curtain; come to an end

綴じる 　　　　　　 Ⓚ1264

ⓐ **bind, file**

ⓑ **sew up, stitch together; mend**

綴じて とじて in bound form

綴じ込み とじこみ file

綴じ本 とじほん bound book

和綴じ わとじ Japanese-style book-
binding

袋綴じ ふくろとじ dual page

綴じ針 とじばり large sewing needle

綴じ蓋 とじぶた mended lid

調う
Ⓚ1417

① **be prepared [ready], be fully equipped**

調度が調う ちょうどがととのう get fully furnished

② **be arranged [settled], be agreed upon**

協議が調った きょうぎがととのった An agreement has been arrived at

整う
Ⓚ2501

be in order, be adjusted [regulated], be made up properly

整った ととのった in good order, well-ordered, well-regulated; well-featured

服装が整っている ふくそうがととのっている be properly dressed

調える
Ⓚ1417

① **prepare, make ready, procure, raise (money)**

夕食を調える ゆうしょくをととのえる get supper ready

旅装を調える りょそうをととのえる prepare for a journey

金を調える かねをととのえる raise money

② **season, flavor**

味を調える あじをととのえる season, flavor

③ (bring to a conclusion) **arrange, settle, conclude**

縁談を調える えんだんをととのえる arrange a marriage

整える
Ⓚ2501

(put in order) **arrange, tidy up, adjust (clothes), regulate**

髪を整える かみをととのえる arrange [tidy up] one's hair

調子を整える ちょうしをととのえる put in tune

止まる
Ⓚ2545

① **come to a stop, stop, halt**

思い止まる おもいとどまる abandon (an idea), refrain from (doing)

② **be limited [confined] to**

単に希望を述べたに止まる たんにきぼうをのべたにとどまる I simply expressed my desire

留まる
Ⓚ2235

stay behind, remain

家に留まる いえにとどまる stay home

止める
Ⓚ2545

① (arrest motion) **stop, arrest**

押し止める おしとどめる stop, check, keep back

② **confine (oneself) to, be restricted to**

. . . と言うだけに止めよう …というだけにとどめよう Suffice it to say that…

留める
Ⓚ2235

① **leave (behind)**

書き留める かきとどめる leave a note behind

② **make stay, detain**

原級に留める げんきゅうにとどめる keep (a student) back (to repeat a grade)

430 とぶ

飛ぶ ⓚ2990

①ⓐ **fly; travel by air**
ⓑ **rush [fly] (to the scene)**
ⓒ **fly about, be scattered**

飛び上がる とびあがる fly up, jump up

飛び込む とびこむ down, jump from, jump [leap] in; dive into

飛び切り とびきり exceptionally, by far

飛び魚 とびうお flying fish

② **skip (pages), skip over**

二頁から四頁へ飛ぶ にページから よんページへとぶ skip from page two to page four

翔ぶ ⓚ1241

soar, fly

翔んでる とんでる groovy, far-out, flipped out

跳ぶ ⓚ1392

ⓐ **jump, leap, spring**
ⓑ **jump [leap] over, vault**

縄跳び なわとび rope skipping, rope jumping

跳び過ぎる とびすぎる overleap, overjump

★ Though when used independently 飛ぶ means to fly and 跳ぶ to leap

or jump, both 飛 and 跳 can mean to jump when used as components of compounds, as for example 飛び掛かる とびかかる 'spring [jump] upon'. 翔ぶ and 飛ぶ both mean to fly, but the former has a more poetic or elegant flavor.

431 とまり

止まり ⓚ2545

ⓐ **stop, stoppage**
ⓑ **end**

泊まり ⓚ0293

①ⓐ **stopover, stay**
ⓑ **night duty**

② **anchorage**

432 とまる

止まる ⓚ2545

①ⓐ **come to a stop, stop, halt**
ⓑ [sometimes also 停まる] (of vehicles) **roll to a stop, stop (at a station)**
ⓒ **be stopped up**

止まり とまり stop, stoppage; end

止まり木 とまりぎ perch, roost; footrail

立ち止まる たちどまる stop, halt, stand still

駅に止まる えきにとまる stop at a station

② (cease acting) **stop, cease; be suspended, be interrupted**

行き止まり いきどまり dead end, blind alley, *cul-de-sac*

血が止まる ちがとまる stop bleeding

留まる

Ⓚ2235

① **be held in position, be fastened**

釘で留まっている くぎでとまっている be fastened with a nail

②ⓐ **remain in one's perception, strike one's senses**

  ⓑ [in compounds] **remain, be left over**

目に留まる めにとまる attract one's attention, strike the eye

歩留まり ぶどまり yield, yield rate

③ **perch on**

木に留まる きにとまる sit in a tree

お高く留まる おたかくとまる assume an air of importance, put on airs

泊まる

Ⓚ0293

① **stay overnight, lodge, stay at**

泊まり とまり stopover, stay; night duty; anchorage

素泊まり すどまり staying overnight without board

② **stay at anchor**

港に泊まる みなとにとまる stay at anchor

③ **be on night duty**

泊まり番 とまりばん night duty

停まる

Ⓚ0121

[now usu. 止まる] (of vehicles) **roll to a stop, stop (at a station)**

停まらずに行く とまらずにいく run without stopping, run past

---

433   **とめる¹**

止める

Ⓚ2545

①ⓐ (arrest motion) **stop, bring to a standstill, arrest**

  ⓑ [sometimes also 停める] (bring a vehicle to a temporary halt) **stop (a bus or train), bring to a halt, brake**

呼び止める よびとめる stop, call to stop

受け止める うけとめる stop, catch; receive

塞き止める せきとめる dam up, stop; check

車を止める くるまをとめる bring a car to a halt

② (cause an action to cease) **stop (an engine), turn off; arrest, stop, hold**

止め処無く とめどなく endlessly, ceaselessly

ガスを止める がすをとめる turn off the gas

通行止め つうこうどめ suspension of traffic

消し止める けしとめる put out, extinguish

客止め きゃくどめ full house

打ち止め うちどめ close, end

③ⓐ **stop an action from occurring, check, arrest**

  ⓑ **stop a person from doing, dissuade**

食い止める くいとめる check, hold back

差し止める さしとめる prohibit, forbid; suspend (a paper)

口止めする くちどめする forbid to mention, hush up

留める
®2235
① ⓐ **keep in place, retain, fix, fasten**
  ⓑ **keep (a parcel) until called for**
  ⓒ **keep in custody, detain**
  ⓓ (keep a vehicle from moving) **park**
  留め金 とめがね clasp, latch, fasten-ing
  取り留めの無い とりとめのない wandering, rambling, incoherent
  局留め きょくどめ poste restante
  引き留める ひきとめる detain
  足留めする あしどめする keep in-doors, induce to stay
  車を留める くるまをとめる park a car
② **keep in mind**
  気に留める きにとめる mind, give heed to, pay attention to
③ **keep (a quarrel) from intensifying, stop**
  留め男 とめおとこ man who stops a quarrel

泊める
®0293
① **lodge, give shelter, accommodate**
  友達を泊める ともだちをとめる put a friend up for the night
② **anchor a ship**

停める
®0121
[now usu. 止める] (bring a vehicle to a temporary halt) **stop (a bus or train), bring to a halt, brake**
  車を停める くるまをとめる bring a car to a halt

---

434   とめる²

-止める
®2545
[also –留める] **kill**
  射止める いとめる shoot to death; win, acquire
  突き止める つきとめる ascertain, run to the ground; [archaic] stab [thrust] to death

-留める
®2235
① **kill**
  仕留める しとめる kill, shoot dead
② **write down, register**
  書留 かきとめ registered mail
★ Both forms are used in compounds in the sense of kill, but –留める is preferred in the word 仕留める しとめる 'kill, shoot dead'. とめる is not used independently in this sense.

435   とも

友
®2553
[sometimes also 朋] **friend, companion, pal**
  友達 ともだち friend, companion
  竹馬の友 ちくばのとも childhood friend, old playmate

朋
®0784
[usu. 友] **friend, companion, pal**

供
®0070
attendant, retinue
  供回り ともまわり train of attendants, retinue

お供する おともする go with, accompany, follow

共 ⓚ2122

① [in compounds]
ⓐ **joint, together, simultaneous**
ⓑ **of the same quality [kind]**
ⓒ **both, neither; including**
共稼ぎ ともかせぎ working together (for a living), working in double harness
共倒れ ともだおれ falling together, joint bankruptcy
共共 ともども together, in common
共布 ともぬの same cloth
両方共 りょうほうとも both, the two
送料共 そうりょうとも including postage
② **same cloth**
共のハンカチ とものハンカチ handkerchief of the same cloth

436 ともしび

灯 ⓚ0730

[also 灯火, sometimes also 燭] **light, lamp, flame**
風前の灯 ふうぜんのともしび candle flickering before the wind; extremely precarious position

燭 ⓚ1008

[usu. 灯 or 灯火] **light, lamp, flame**

437 ともす

点す ⓚ1793

[sometimes also 灯す] **light (a lamp), set alight, turn on (a light)**
松明を点す たいまつをともす kindle a torch

灯す ⓚ0730

[usu. 点す] **light (a lamp), set alight, turn on (a light)**
灯火 ともしび [also 灯, sometimes also 燭] light, lamp, flame
松明を灯す たいまつをともす kindle a torch

438 ともに

共に ⓚ2122

① [formerly also 倶に] **together**
共に天を戴かず ともにてんをいただかず cannot live together under the canopy of heaven
② **both, alike**
母子共に ぼしともに both mother and child

倶に ⓚ0093

[now usu. 共に] **together**
倶に天を戴かず ともにてんをいただかず cannot live together under the canopy of heaven

439 とら

虎 ⓚ2766

① **tiger**

虎の巻 とらのまき key, crib, pony; secret (of a trade)

② **drunkard**

寅 ⓚ1981

third sign of the Oriental zodiac: **the Tiger**—(time) 3-5 a.m., (direction) ENE, (season) January (of the lunar calendar)

寅の刻 とらのこく around four o'clock in the morning

丑寅 うしとら [also 艮] one of the four supplementary signs of the Oriental zodiac: **northeast**

440 とらえる

捕らえる ⓚ0387

①ⓐ **catch, seize, grasp**

ⓑ (capture by force) **catch, capture, arrest**

袖を捕らえる そでをとらえる catch a person by the sleeve

泥棒を捕らえる どろぼうをとらえる arrest a thief

引っ捕らえる ひっとらえる capture, arrest, seize

② [also 捉える] (take hold as if with the hand) **grasp (an idea), seize (an opportunity)**

捕らえ所の無い とらえどころのない elusive, subtle, slippery

捉える ⓚ0391

[also 捕らえる] (take hold as if with the hand) **grasp (an idea), seize (an opportunity)**

捉え所の無い とらえどころのない elusive, subtle

心を捉える こころをとらえる impress, charm

意味を捉える いみをとらえる grasp the meaning

言葉尻を捉える ことばじりをとらえる cavil at a person's words

441 とらわれる

捕らわれる ⓚ0387

①ⓐ **be caught, be arrested**

ⓑ [also 囚われる] **be imprisoned, be taken captive**

捕らわれ とらわれ captivity, imprisonment

敵に捕らわれる てきにとらわれる be caught by the enemy

② [also 囚われる] **adhere to (tradition), be swayed by**

捕らわれた考え とらわれたかんがえ conventional ideas, prejudiced opinion

囚われる ⓚ2618

① **be imprisoned, be taken captive**

囚われ とらわれ captive, imprisonment

② **adhere to (tradition), be swayed by**

囚われた考え とらわれたかんがえ conventional ideas, prejudiced opinion

442 とり

鳥 ⓚ2822

ⓐ [sometimes also 禽] **bird, fowl**

ⓑ [also 鶏] **chicken; fowl, poultry**

鳥居 とりい torii, Shinto shrine arch-way (开)

海鳥 うみどり seabird
小鳥 ことり small [little] bird
渡り鳥 わたりどり migratory bird
水鳥 みずとり waterfowl
大鳥 おおとり [also 鳳, 鴻 or 鵬] large wild bird such as crane or white stork; huge bird such as a mythical Chinese phoenix
鳥肉 とりにく chicken
鳥屋 とりや bird dealer; poulterer
雌鳥 めんどり hen

鶏 Ⓚ1577

[also 鳥] chicken; fowl, poultry
若鶏 わかどり spring chicken

禽 Ⓚ1837

[usu. 鳥] bird, fowl

酉 Ⓚ2969

tenth sign of the Oriental zodiac: **the Bird**—(time) 5-7 p.m., (direction) west, (season) August (of the lunar calendar)
酉年 とりどし Year of the Rooster
酉の方角 とりのほうがく west

443 とりで

塁 Ⓚ2250

[now usu. 砦, formerly also 塞] **fort, fortress, stronghold**

砦 Ⓚ2328

[formerly also 塁 or 塞] **fort, fortress, stronghold**
砦を築く とりでをきずく construct a fort

塞 Ⓚ2033

[now usu. 砦] **fort, fortress, stronghold**

444 とる

取る Ⓚ1162

① ⓐ **take, take hold of, seize**
ⓑ **take off, take away, remove, delete, leave out**
ⓒ (take (a life) away, kill
ⓓ (ingest food) **take, have, eat**
ⓔ (secure by payment) **take (in) (a newspaper), subscribe to; buy, order**
ⓕ (take in crops) **harvest, reap, gather**
ⓖ (take money for) **charge, ask**
取れる とれる can be held; come off, fall off; be removed; be produced; be understood; be interpreted
取り柄 とりえ merit, worth, recommendable feature
取り上げる とりあげる take [pick] up; take away, confiscate; deliver a baby; accept, listen to; adopt (a proposal)
取り分け とりわけ especially, above all
塵取り ちりとり dustpan
遣り取り やりとり giving and taking, exchanges
手に取る てにとる take in one's hand
色取る いろどる [also 彩る] color, paint, dye; make up
取り外す とりはずす remove, dismantle
汲み取る くみとる draw [dip] up, drain; take into consideration
帽子を取る ぼうしをとる take off one's hat

蚊取り線香 かとりせんこう mosquito-repellent incense

朝食を取る ちょうしょくをとる take breakfast

朝日新聞を取る あさひしんぶんをとる take in [subscribe to] the *Asahi* (newspaper)

取り入れる とりいれる take in; harvest; accept, adopt, introduce

食費を取る しょくひをとる charge for one's meal

② get or cause to come into one's possession:
   ⓐ **take, receive, get, obtain, accept, acquire**
   ⓑ **take possession of (a castle), seize, capture, conquer**
   ⓒ **take away from, deprive, steal**
   ⓓ (reserve) **take, book, engage**

取り戻す とりもどす take back, regain, restore

取り込む とりこむ take in, introduce, incorporate; be in confusion

関取 せきとり ranking sumo wrestler

受け取る うけとる receive, accept; understand

満点を取る まんてんをとる get full marks

連絡を取る れんらくをとる get in touch with

城を取る しろをとる take a castle

寝取る ねとる steal another's wife [husband, lover]

席を取って置く せきをとっておく book [take] a seat

③ cause an abstract thing or action to shift towards oneself or elsewhere:
   ⓐ **take down (notes), write, record**
   ⓑ **take on (responsibility), assume**
   ⓒ **take (the meaning of a passage), make out, interpret**
   ⓓ **take count, measure**

ⓔ **undergo, suffer**

書き取る かきとる write down, note down

ノートを取る のーとをとる note down, take notes

責任を取る せきにんをとる take responsibility for

気取る きどる make an affected pose, assume airs

意味を取る いみをとる understand the meaning of, follow the sense

脈を取る みゃくをとる take a pulse

不覚を取る ふかくをとる suffer a defeat

④ **take (time), take up (space), require**

手間を取る てまをとる take time, be detained

場所を取る ばしょをとる take up [occupy] space

採る   Ⓚ0459

① ⓐ **gather, collect, extract (oil), produce (wine out of grapes)**
   ⓑ **admit (light)**

山菜を採る さんさいをとる gather edible wild plants

葡萄からワインを採る ぶどうからわいんをとる make wine from grapes

明かり採り あかりとり skylight, dormer; transom

② ⓐ **pick (out), choose, prefer**
   ⓑ **adopt, take, engage**

採り上げる とりあげる adopt, accept, listen to

可否を採る かひをとる take the ayes and noes

新卒者を採る しんそつしゃをとる engage a new graduate

執る

®1501

① **perform (duties), conduct, trans-act, take (trouble)**

執り行う とりおこなう carry out, perform

事務を執る じむをとる do [attend to] business

② **perform an action while holding an object (such as a pen)**

筆を執る ふでをとる write, pen, draw

③ **persist in, insist on**

固く自説を執る かたくじせつをとる persist in one's views

捕る

®0387

catch, take, seize

捕り物 とりもの capture, arrest

魚を捕る さかなをとる catch fish

分捕る ぶんどる loot, grab

撮る

®0671

photograph, shoot, film, videotape

写真を撮る しゃしんをとる take a picture

隠し撮り かくしどり sneaking a shot

445　　どめ

-止め

®2545

① **device for stopping, stopper**

車止め くるまどめ bumping post, bumper

歯止め はどめ drag, pallet; brake

滑り止め すべりどめ tire chains; creepers; taking the entrance examination to a university as a safety measure in case one fails at other universities

② **something that prevents, preven-tive**

咳止め せきどめ cough medicine

錆止め さびどめ anticorrosive, rust preventive

-留め

®2235

clip, fastener, retainer

帯留め おびどめ sash clip [fastener]

土留め どどめ sheathing, retaining (wall)

446　　ども

-共

®2122

belittling or humble plural suffix

私共 わたくしども we

大人共 おとなども adults

餓鬼共 がきども those damn kids

-供

®0070

plural suffix— now used only in 子供 こども without implying plurality

子供 こども child, kid; son, daughter

★ Note that こども is correctly written 子供, *not* 子共.

447　　どり

-取り

®1162

① **arrangement, placement**

間取り まどり room arrangement

日取り ひどり schedule

② **manner, style**

足取り あしどり one's manner of walking; trace (of a culprit's move-ment); (price) movement

-撮り ⓚ0671

counter for number of shots [pictures] available in a film

十二枚撮りのフィルム じゅうにまいどりのふぃるむ film for 12 shots

448 な

-名 ⓚ1857

[sometimes also -字] **character, letter**

仮名 かな kana, Japanese syllabary

-字 ⓚ1860

[usu. -名] **character, letter**

仮字 かな kana, Japanese syllabary

449 ない

無い ⓚ1832

① ⓐ **there is no, do not exist, have not**
  ⓑ **be missing, lack**

無しで なしで without

金が無い かねがない have no money

資本無しで しほんなしで without capital

子が無い こがない have no children

無くす なくす lose, be deprived of; get rid of, remove, do away with

無くなる なくなる disappear, be gone; run short; get lost, be missing

財布が無い さいふがない My purse is missing

② **not, do not**

行きたく無い いきたくない do not want to go

寒くも無いし暑くも無い さむくもないしあつくもない It is neither hot nor cold

亡い ⓚ2874

not in this world, dead

亡くす なくす lose (a parent), be bereft of

亡くなる なくなる die, pass away, breathe one's last

450 なお

尚 ⓚ1919

① ⓐ (in increasing degree) **still (more), all the more**
  ⓑ **further, in addition, by the way**

尚の事 なおのこと all the more, still more

尚一層悪い事は なおいっそうわるいことは what is worse still

この方が尚良い このほうがなおよい This is still better

尚更 なおさら still more, all the more

尚又 なおまた further, besides

尚且つ なおかつ and yet

② ⓐ **still, yet**
  ⓑ **even, still**

春尚浅し はるなおあさし Spring is not yet far advanced

昼尚暗い ひるなおくらい be dark even in the daytime

③ literary **as, just like, no more...than**

鯨の魚にあらざるは尚馬の魚にあらざるが如し くじらのさかなにあらざるはなおうまのさかなにあらざるがごとし A whale is no more a fish than a horse is

猶   Ⓚ0566

① ⓐ (in increasing degree) **still (more), all the more**
   ⓑ **further, in addition, by the way**

猶の事 なおのこと all the more, still more

猶良い なおよい still better

猶一層悪い事は なおいっそうわるいことは what is worse still

② ⓐ **still, yet**
   ⓑ **even, still**

春猶浅し はるなおあさし Spring is not yet far advanced

昼猶暗い ひるなおくらい be dark even in the daytime

③ *literary* **as, just like, no more…than**

鯨の魚にあらざるは猶馬の魚にあらざるが如し くじらのさかなにあらざるはなおうまのさかなにあらざるがごとし A whale is no more a fish than a horse is

451   なおす

直す   Ⓚ2539

① ⓐ **fix, repair, mend, set right**
   ⓑ **fix up, adjust, put in order**

直し物 なおしもの mending, thing to be mended

パンクを直す ぱんくをなおす fix a flat tire

化粧直し けしょうなおし adjusting one's makeup

② **correct, rectify, remedy, reform, cure (a bad habit)**

誤りを直す あやまりをなおす correct an error

行儀を直す ぎょうぎをなおす mend one's manners

③ ⓐ **alter, change**

   ⓑ **convert**
   ⓒ **render, translate**

時間割りを直す じかんわりをなおす alter the schedule

キロをポンドに直す きろをぽんどになおす convert kilograms to pounds

日本語に直す にほんごになおす render into Japanese

治す   Ⓚ0297

cure, heal

風邪を治す かぜをなおす cure a cold

452   なおる

直る   Ⓚ2539

① **be fixed, be mended, be repaired**

直らない なおらない irreparable, beyond repair

② **be corrected, be reformed, be cured (of a bad habit)**

悪癖が直る あくへきがなおる get over a bad habit

③ ⓐ **be restored, return to normal**
   ⓑ **improve in status, change for the better**

仲直り なかなおり reconciliation

立ち直る たちなおる regain one's footing, recover; (of the market) improve

開き直る ひらきなおる switch to a defiant attitude

治る   Ⓚ0297

be cured, get well, recover

治り なおり recovery

傷が治った きずがなおった The wound has healed up

中
Ⓚ2902

① **inside, interior**
　中へ入る なかへはいる step into, go [come] inside, enter
　中味 なかみ interior, content, substance
　中庭 なかにわ courtyard

②ⓐ **middle, the second**
　ⓑ **middle course, mean**
　中の兄 なかのあに middle brother
　中指 なかゆび middle finger
　中継ぎ(=中次ぎ) なかつぎ intermediation; agent; relay
　真ん中 まんなか center, middle
　背中 せなか back
　中を取る なかをとる take the middle course [mean]

③ⓐ **within the confines of a given range**
　ⓑ **amidst an undesirable event**
　中に なかに in; in the middle of; between, among
　中には なかには some (of them), among (them)
　町中で まちなかで in the streets
　夜中 よなか midnight, dead of night
　世の中 よのなか the world, society, life
　多くの中から選ぶ おおくのなかからえらぶ choose among many things
　雨の中で あめのなかで in the rain

仲
Ⓚ0028

① **personal relations, relationship, (familiar) terms, fellowship, friendship**

仲が良い なかがよい be on good terms
仲良くする なかよくする become friendly with, make friends with
仲間 なかま company, fellow, comrade, associate
仲直り なかなおり reconciliation
恋仲 こいなか love relationship

② **intermediary, go-between**
　仲に入る なかにはいる act as an intermediary
　仲買 なかがい brokerage; middleman
　仲買人 なかがいにん broker
　仲立ち なかだち intermediation
　仲居 なかい parlormaid, waitress

③ [in compounds] **inner, middle**
　仲見世通り なかみせどおり shopping street in the precincts of a shrine [temple]

勿れ
Ⓚ2547

[sometimes also 莫れ] **do not, not, never**
　勿れ主義の道徳 なかれしゅぎのどうとく negative virtues
　事勿れ主義 ことなかれしゅぎ peace-at-any-price principle
　恐るる勿れ おそるるなかれ Be not afraid!

莫れ
Ⓚ1971

[usu. 勿れ] **do not, not, never**

長い
Ⓚ2212

ⓐ (of considerable extent) **long, lengthy, prolonged**

b (of considerable duration) **long**

長さ ながさ length

長袖 ながそで clothes with long sleeves

長らく ながらく for a long time

長引く ながびく be prolonged, drag on

長持ちする ながもちする last [keep] long, endure

長続きする ながつづきする last for a long time

長話をする ながばなしをする have a long talk

永い ⓚ1695

(lasting forever) **eternal, everlasting, long**

永年(=長年) ながねん many years, long time

末永く すえながく forever

日永 ひなが a long day

456 なぎさ

渚 ⓚ0481

[sometimes also 汀] **strand, beach, waterside, shore**

渚伝い なぎさづたい along the shore

汀 ⓚ0174

[usu. 渚] **strand, beach, waterside, shore**

汀伝い なぎさづたい along the shore

457 なく

泣く ⓚ0300

cry, weep, sob

泣き なき weeping, lamenting

泣き顔 なきがお tear-stained face

泣き声 なきごえ tearful voice, crying

泣き叫ぶ なきさけぶ cry, scream, wail

咽び泣く むせびなく sob, be choked with tears

鳴く ⓚ0616

(of animals, birds or insects) **cry, chirp, ululate, howl, yelp, meow**

鳴き声 なきごえ cry, song, chirping

鳴き交わす なきかわす cry [howl] to each other, exchange wooing cries

長鳴き ながなき long crowing [warbling]

458 なくす

無くす ⓚ1832

a **lose, be deprived of**
b **get rid of, remove, do away with**

亡くす ⓚ2874

lose (a parent), be bereft of

459 なくなる

無くなる ⓚ1832

a **disappear, be gone; run short**
b **get lost, be missing**

亡くなる ⓚ2874

die, be dead

嘆き
Ⓚ0577

[formerly also 歎き] **grief, lamentation**

歎き
Ⓚ1652

[now usu. 嘆き] **grief, lamentation**

嘆く
Ⓚ0577

[formerly also 歎く] **sigh (in grief or despair), grieve, lament; deplore**

嘆き なげき grief, lamentation
嘆き悲しむ なげきかなしむ grieve and moan
政治の腐敗を嘆く せいじのふはいを なげく deplore the corruption of politics

歎く
Ⓚ1652

① **sigh (in grief or despair), grieve, lament; deplore**

歎き なげき grief, lamentation

② **sigh in admiration, exclaim, admire, praise**

成す
Ⓚ2964

① **form, make, constitute**

円を成す えんをなす form a circle
山成す やまなす mountainlike, a mountain of

② **achieve, accomplish, succeed**

成し遂げる なしとげる complete, carry out, accomplish

名を成す なをなす make a name, become famous

為す
Ⓚ2994

do, perform, carry out

不善を為す ふぜんをなす do evil, commit vice

生す
Ⓚ2933

give birth, bear

生さぬ仲の なさぬなかの with no blood relation

嘗めずる
Ⓚ2268

[also 舐めずる] **lick around (one's lips)**

舌嘗めずりする したなめずりする lick one's lips; await eagerly

舐めずる

[also 嘗めずる] **lick around (one's lips)**

舌舐めずりする したなめずりする lick one's lips; await eagerly

嘗める
Ⓚ2268

① ⓐ **taste, have a taste**
ⓑ **taste, undergo, experience (hardship, etc.)**

塩を嘗める しおをなめる taste the salt
辛酸を嘗める しんさんをなめる experience hardships

② **lick, lap, suck**

嘗め尽くす なめつくす lick thoroughly; burn to the ground

べろべろ嘗める べろべろなめる lick up with one's tongue

③ **burn down, consume, devour**

総嘗め そうなめ annihilation; a sweeping victory

④ **make light of, treat with contempt**

舐める

① ⓐ **taste, have a taste**

ⓑ **taste, undergo, experience (hardship, etc.)**

塩を舐める しおをなめる taste the salt

辛酸を舐める しんさんをなめる experience hardships

② **lick, lap, suck**

舐め尽くす なめつくす lick thoroughly; burn to the ground

べろべろ舐める べろべろなめる lick up with one's tongue

③ **burn down, consume, devour**

総舐め そうなめ annihilation; a sweeping victory

④ **make light of, treat with contempt**

465   ならう

習う

Ⓚ2324

learn, be taught, study; practice

習い事 ならいごと practice

見習い みならい apprenticeship, apprentice

倣う

Ⓚ0095

copy after, copy from, imitate, follow an example

前例に倣う ぜんれいにならう follow [copy after] a precedent

以下これに倣う いかこれにならう The undermentioned to follow this example

466   ならす

慣らす

Ⓚ0624

[sometimes also 馴らす] **inure, habituate, accustom, make used to**

足慣らし(=足馴らし) あしならし walking exercise, warming up

使い慣らす つかいならす accustom oneself to using (a thing), train

体を寒さに慣らす からだをさむさにならす inure oneself to cold

馴らす

Ⓚ1616

① **tame, domesticate**

馴らし手 ならして tamer

飼い馴らす かいならす tame (an animal), domesticate

② [usu. 慣らす] **inure, habituate, accustom, make used to**

足馴らし あしならし walking practice, warming up

均す

Ⓚ0207

① **level, make even, roll**

土を均す つちをならす level the ground

② **average**

均し ならし average

成る ⓚ2964

① **be accomplished, succeed, be attained, materialize**

成るべく なるべく as…as possible, if possible

成程 なるほど I see, really, indeed

工事が成った こうじがなった The work was finished

丸で成ってない まるでなってない not good at all

② **form, constitute, consist of, be composed of**

成り立つ なりたつ consist of; be realized, be concluded, materialize

成り行き なりゆき course [turn] of events, issue

委員会は五人から成る いいんかいはごにんからなる The committee consists of five members

③ **honorific auxiliary verb**

山田さんがお見えに成りました やまださんがおみえになりました Mr. Yamada is here to see you

④ **bear, put up with**

そんな事をされて成る物か そんなことをされてなるものか I can't put up with such a thing

⑤ (of chessmen) **be promoted**

成り駒 なりこま promoted chessman

成り上がる なりあがる suddenly rise to a higher position

為る ⓚ2994

①ⓐ **become, turn into, grow, get**
ⓑ **begin to (do), come to (do)**

病気に為る びょうきになる fall [be taken] ill

泳げる様に為る およげるようになる learn how to swim

②ⓐ **result in, turn out**
ⓑ **amount [come] to**

幾らに為りますか いくらになりますか How much will that be?

③ⓐ (of seasons) **come, set in**
ⓑ **elapse, pass**

④ **serve [act] as**

生る ⓚ2933

bear fruit, fruit

生り年 なりどし year of large crop

生業 なりわい (=せいぎょう) livelihood; calling, occupation

末生り うらなり fruit grown near the top end of the vine; pale-faced man

鈴生りに生る すずなりになる grow in clusters

慣れる ⓚ0624

[sometimes also 馴れる] [also suffix] **grow accustomed to, get used to, become inured to, become experienced in**

慣れ なれ habituation, practice, experience

慣れた なれた practiced, experienced, familiar

慣れ親しむ なれしたしむ get used to, become familiar with

見慣れる みなれる get used to seeing

場慣れ ばなれ experience, poise in a critical situation

馴れる

① **become tame [domesticated]**

馴れた **なれた** tame, domesticated

馴染む **なじむ** become familiar; grow accustomed; get (clothing) to fit

人馴れ **ひとなれ** being used to people, being tame

② [usu. 慣れる] [also suffix] **grow accustomed to, get used to, become inured to, become experienced in**

不馴れ **ふなれ** inexperienced, unfamiliar (with)

場馴れ **ばなれ** experience, poise in a critical situation

見馴れる **みなれる** become used to seeing

③ [in compounds] **become familiar [friendly] with; become overfamiliar with**

馴れ合う **なれあう** collude, conspire; establish clandestine liaisons

馴れ馴れしい **なれなれしい** overfamiliar, unceremonial

馴れ初め **なれそめ** start of a romance, beginning of love

469 なんじ

汝

Ⓚ0193

[sometimes also 爾] **thou, you**

汝の隣人を愛せよ **なんじのりんじんをあいせよ** Love thy neighbor

汝自身を知れ **なんじじしんをしれ** Know thyself

爾

Ⓚ3001

[usu. 汝] **thou, you**

470 におい

臭い

Ⓚ2289

ⓐ **stench, stink**

ⓑ **smack, inkling (of something disagreeable)**

臭い消し **においけし** deodorant

不正の臭い **ふせいのにおい** smack of evil

匂い

Ⓚ2548

ⓐ **smell, scent, fragrance, aroma**

ⓑ **flavor, touch (of something agreeable)**

匂い袋 **においぶくろ** sachet

文学的な匂い **ぶんがくてきなにおい** literary flavor

471 におう

臭う

Ⓚ2289

stink, reek

ガスが臭う **がすがにおう** There is a smell of gas

匂う

Ⓚ2548

① **smell (sweet), give out a smell [fragrance]**

匂い立つ **においたつ** be enveloped in a smell; be radiant, be attractive

香水が髪から匂った **こうすいがかみからにおった** Her hair emitted a fragrance

② (of blossoms) **glow, be shiningly beautiful**

桜が咲き匂う **さくらがさきにおう** Cherry trees are in beautiful bloom

472　ねたましい

妬ましい　　　Ⓚ0254

ⓐ **enviable**
ⓑ **jealous, envious**

嫉ましい　　　Ⓚ0584

ⓐ **enviable**
ⓑ **jealous, envious**

473　ねたむ

妬む　　　Ⓚ0254

[also 嫉む] **be jealous, be envious**
　妬み ねたみ jealousy, envy

嫉む　　　Ⓚ0584

[also 妬む] **be jealous, be envious**

474　ねる

練る　　　Ⓚ1256

①ⓐ **train, drill, exercise**
　ⓑ **polish (one's style), refine**
　練り上げる ねりあげる train up,
　　discipline
　文を練る ぶんをねる polish one's
　　style
② **gloss, boil off, soften**
　練り絹 ねりぎぬ glossed silk
③ **walk in procession**
　練り歩く ねりあるく parade, march
④ [formerly 煉る] **knead**
　練り ねり kneading; gloss; tempering
⑤ [formerly 錬る] **temper (metals),
　forge, refine, smelt**

錬る　　　Ⓚ1553

[now usu. 練る] **temper (metals), forge,
refine, smelt**

煉る　　　Ⓚ0939

[now also 練る] **knead**

475　の

之　　　Ⓚ2886

possessive particle
　鳥之巣 とりのす bird's nest
　実業之日本社 じつぎょうのにほん
　　しゃ Jitsugyo no Nihon Sha (name
　　of a publisher)

乃　　　Ⓚ2535

possessive particle
　日乃丸 ひのまる Rising Sun flag
　波乃花 なみのはな crest of a wave;
　　salt

476　のがれる

逃れる　　　Ⓚ2666

**escape, get away; get clear of;
escape, evade, shirk**
　責任を逃れる せきにんをのがれる
　　shirk one's responsibility
　言い逃れ いいのがれ evasion, subter-
　　fuge, excuse

遁れる　　　Ⓚ2782

flee, escape; evade, shirk away

乗せる Ⓚ2992

① **take (a person) on board, carry (passengers), pick up (passengers)**
乗客を乗せる じょうきゃくをのせる take passengers on board

② **let (a person) take part in (a scheme)**
その仕事に私も一口乗せてくれないか そのしごとにわたしもひとくちのせてくれないか Let me in on that job, won't you?

③ **take in, impose upon**
そんな話に乗せられる物か そんなはなしにのせられるものか You can't come round me with such yarns

④ **bring into harmony**

載せる Ⓚ2814

① **load (a vehicle or ship with cargo), lade, carry**
船に貨物を載せる ふねにかもつをのせる load a ship with cargo

② **place on, put on**
棚に本を載せる たなにほんをのせる place a book on a shelf

③ **put in print, publish, carry, put on record**
記録に載せる きろくにのせる put on record

望む Ⓚ2390

① ⓐ **desire, wish, crave for**
　 ⓑ **hope (for), expect, look forward to**

望み のぞみ desire, wish; hope, expectation, prospect; preference
望ましい のぞましい desirable, welcome
平和を望む へいわをのぞむ crave for peace
成功を望む せいこうをのぞむ hope to succeed
待ち望む まちのぞむ expect, look forward to

② **expect (a person) to do, ask for**
自重を望む じちょうをのぞむ ask for prudence

③ **look afar, gaze into the distance, command a view of**
富士を望む家 ふじをのぞむいえ house commanding a view of Mt. Fuji

臨む Ⓚ1470

① **be present at, be on the spot, attend, come to, visit**
会合に臨む かいごうにのぞむ be present at a meeting

② **come face to face, meet, be confronted with**
別れに臨んで わかれにのぞんで at parting (with)

③ **overlook, face, border on**
海に臨んだホテル うみにのぞんだほてる hotel on the sea

宣わく Ⓚ1940

[formerly 曰わく] *literary* [honorific] **say that…**
子宣わく しのたまわく Confucius says…

曰わく

[now also 宣わく] [honorific] *literary* **say that…**

子曰わく しのたまわく Confucius says…

480 のっと

節 ®2349

[also 浬] **knot, nautical mile**

時速二十節 じそくにじゅうのっと speed of 20 knots per hour

浬 ®0397

[also 節] **nautical mile per hour, knot**

481 のど

喉 ®0506

①ⓐ **throat**
　ⓑ **singing voice**

喉元 のどもと throat
喉越し のどごし feeling of a drink going down one's throat
喉仏 のどぼとけ Adam's apple
喉笛 のどぶえ windpipe
喉ちんこ のどちんこ *colloq* uvula
喉自慢 のどじまん proud of one's voice

② **gutter (margin) (in printing)**

ページの喉側 ページののどがわ gutter side of a page

咽 ®0309

①ⓐ **throat**
　ⓑ **singing voice**

咽から手が出る のどからてがでる want something desperately

② **gutter (margin) (in printing)**

482 のばす

伸ばす ®0054

①ⓐ **stretch, elongate, extend, spread**
　ⓑ **expand, let grow, develop**

引き伸ばす ひきのばす stretch out, elongate; enlarge (photographs)
才能を伸ばす さいのうをのばす develop one's ability

② **straighten**

体を伸ばす からだをのばす stretch (unbend) oneself

③ **dilute**

スープを伸ばす すーぷをのばす thin soup with water

④ **knock out**

伸ばしてしまえ のばしてしまえ Knock him out!

延ばす ®2646

① **extend (in space or time), prolong, spread**

引き延ばす ひきのばす extend, draw out; enlarge; prolong, filibuster
寿命を延ばす じゅみょうをのばす prolong one's life
期限を延ばす きげんをのばす extend the term

② **postpone, delay, defer**

返事を延ばす へんじをのばす delay one's answer

伸び ®0054

① ⓐ stretching, elongation
  ⓑ development, growth
② spread (as of paint)

延び ®2646

① extension
② postponement

伸びる ®0054

① ⓐ stretch, lengthen, extend, spread
  ⓑ expand, increase, grow, develop, advance

伸び のび stretching, elongation; development, growth; spread (as of paint)

背伸び せのび stretching one's back

伸び悩む のびなやむ be held in check, fail to grow

伸び率 のびりつ growth rate; coefficient of extension

伸び伸び のびのび at ease

② spread (as of paint)

良く伸びるクリーム よくのびるくりーむ easily-spreadable cream

③ be exhausted, be knocked out

殴られて伸びる なぐられてのびる be knocked out cold

延びる ®2646

① extend (in space or time), be extended, be prolonged

延び のび extension; postponement

延び率 のびりつ growth rate

この鉄道は国境迄延びている このてつどうはこっきょうまでのびている This railway extends as far as the frontier

② be postponed, be delayed

延び延び のびのび repeated delays, dragging on and on

出発が延びた しゅっぱつがのびた The departure was postponed

伸べる ®0054

ⓐ extend, stretch out (one's arm)
ⓑ spread out (bedding)

手を差し伸べる てをさしのべる extend one's arm, hold out one's hand

差し伸べる さしのべる stretch out (one's hand), extend (one's arm)

床を伸べる とこをのべる spread [make] a bed

延べる ®2646

① [also 伸べる]
  ⓐ extend, stretch out (one's arm)
  ⓑ spread out (bedding)

手を延べる てをのべる stretch one's arm

② postpone, delay

日延べ ひのべ postponement, adjournment

上せる ®2876

ⓐ bring up (a proposal for discussion)

ⓑ **enter, put on record**

梓に上せる しにのぼせる publish, bring (a book) into the world

逆上せる　　　Ⓚ2662

① **have a rush of blood to the head, feel dizzy**

② **get excited; run mad after; become conceited**

487　　のぼり

上り　　　Ⓚ2876

ⓐ **going up, going upstream**

ⓑ **ascent, uphill road**

ⓒ **upward-bound train, Tokyo-bound train**

上り下り のぼりくだり going up and down

上り坂 のぼりざか ascent, upward slope

上り勾配 のぼりこうばい upgrade, uphill grade

上り列車 のぼりれっしゃ up train [line]

登り　　　Ⓚ2251

climbing, ascent

488　　のぼる

上る　　　Ⓚ2876

①ⓐ **go up (stairs), walk up (a hill); go [swim] upstream**

ⓑ **go up to the capital**

階段を上る かいだんをのぼる go up the stairs

煙が立ち上る けむりがたちのぼる Smoke ascends to the sky

逆上る さかのぼる [usu. 遡る] go upstream; go back (to the past); retroact

鮭が川を上る さけがかわをのぼる Salmon run up the rivers

京に上る きょうにのぼる go up to Kyoto

② **reach, amount to, add up to**

かなりの数に上る かなりのかずにのぼる amount to a considerable number

③ **come up, be brought up (for discussion)**

噂に上る うわさにのぼる be gossiped about

登る　　　Ⓚ2251

(move up, esp. by using the hands and feet)

climb, mount, ascend, scale

登り のぼり climbing, ascent

登り口 のぼりぐち starting point (for the ascent of a mountain)

山登り やまのぼり mountain climbing

演壇に登る えんだんにのぼる mount the platform

昇る　　　Ⓚ2139

ⓐ (rise up to the sky) **ascend, rise**

ⓑ **ascend to a higher rank, rise in rank, be promoted**

太陽は東から昇る たいようはひがしからのぼる The sun rises in the east

煙が昇って行く けむりがのぼっていく Smoke is going up

位が昇る くらいがのぼる rise in rank

★ In the sense of moving upwards, the above three verbs are easily confused. Whereas 上る refers only to the process of going up (as a hill or steps), 登る implies that an effort is made to reach the top, as when climbing a mountain. 昇る refers to something rising toward the sky, such as smoke or the rising sun, or a soul rising to heaven.

489 のむ

飲む ⓚ1510

① ⓐ **drink**
  ⓑ [also 呑む] **drink alcoholic beverages**
  飲み込む のみこむ swallow, gulp down; grasp, take in
  飲み物 のみもの beverage
  飲み水 のみみず drinking [potable] water
  飲み屋 のみや bar, tavern
② **smoke**
  一服飲む いっぷくのむ have a smoke

呑む ⓚ2131

① ⓐ **swallow, gulp**
  ⓑ **swallow (one's feelings), hold back**
  呑み込み のみこみ understanding, comprehension
  鵜呑み うのみ accepting (a story) unthinkingly; swallowing whole
  丸呑み まるのみ swallowing whole
  蛇が卵を呑んだ へびがたまごをのんだ The snake swallowed an egg
  息を呑む いきをのむ hold one's breath, gasp
  涙を呑む なみだをのむ choke back one's tears, pocket an insult

② [also 飲む] **drink (esp. alcoholic beverages)**
  呑み助 のみすけ guzzler, boozer
  湯呑み ゆのみ teacup
  酒呑み さけのみ drinking; (heavy) drinker
  乳呑み児 ちのみご unweaned baby
③ **accept**
  清濁併せ呑む せいだくあわせのむ be broad-minded enough to accept both good and bad
  条件を呑む じょうけんをのむ accept the conditions
④ **look down on, make light of**
  呑んで掛かる のんでかかる hold lightly, make light of
⑤ **conceal**
  どすを呑む どすをのむ wear a dagger in one's bosom

490 のり

法 ⓚ0295

[sometimes also 則] **law, rule, regulation; model, pattern; religious doctrine; sacred teachings of Buddha**
法を越える のりをこえる violate the laws of nature

則 ⓚ1311

[usu. 法] **law, rule, regulation; model, pattern; religious doctrine; sacred teachings of Buddha**
則を越える のりをこえる violate the laws of nature

のり

491　のる

乗る

ⓚ2992

① ⓐ **ride, ride in, travel**
　ⓑ (be carried) **ride (the winds), be borne**

乗組員 のりくみいん crew

乗り入れ のりいれ extension (of a railway line) into

乗り換え のりかえ change, transfer

乗り越し のりこし riding past one's stop

乗っ取る のっとる take possession of; capture, hijack

乗り物 のりもの vehicle, conveyance

電車に乗る でんしゃにのる take a train

風に乗る かぜにのる ride upon the winds

② (take a place on a vehicle or animal) **get on, board, mount**

乗り込む のりこむ board, go on board; march into

馬に乗る うまにのる get on (mount) a horse

③ (move or be placed on something) **get on, step on, mount**

乗り出す のりだす lean forward; start, set out; embark on, launch into

踏み台に乗る ふみだいにのる step on a footstool

④ **join, participate in, get a share in**

相談に乗る そうだんにのる take part in a consultation

⑤ **be deceived, be taken in**

計略に乗る けいりゃくにのる play into another's hands, fall into a trap

⑥ **feel like doing**

乗り気になる のりきになる get enthusiastic about, be keen to do

乗り気 のりき keenness [enthusiasm] to do

気乗りする きのりする be interested in, feel like (doing)

⑦ **be in harmony with**

歌が曲に乗る うたがきょくにのる The song is in harmony with the melody

⑧ **be spread on**

乗り のり spread

乗りが良い のりがいい spread well

載る

ⓚ2814

① **appear in print, be published, be recorded**

新聞に載る しんぶんにのる appear in the newspaper

② **be placed upon**

棚の上に載っている たなのうえにのっている be [lie] on a shelf

③ **be loaded (on a vehicle)**

492　は

端

ⓚ1131

[in compounds] **odd thing, fragment, piece**—historically sometimes interchangeable with 葉, as in the word はがき, which is now always written 葉書

端数 はすう fraction, odd sum

端役 はやく minor role [part]

半端 はんぱ fragment, odd item; incompleteness

下っ端 したっぱ underling, subordinate

葉

[in compounds] **fragment, piece**—historically sometimes interchangeable with 端, as in the word **はがき**, which is now always written 葉書

葉書 はがき postcard

言葉 ことば word, term; wording; language

493 はえる

映える

Ⓚ0793

① **shine, excel in brilliance**
照り映える てりはえる glow (in the sun), be lighted up
面映ゆい おもはゆい abashed, made self-conscious

② [also 栄える] **look better [to advantage], go well with**
映えない色 はえないいろ dull color
映え はえ glory, splendor

栄える

Ⓚ2231

[also 映える] **look better [to advantage], go well with**
栄えない色 はえないいろ dull color
その木のお蔭で庭が栄える そのきのおかげでにわがはえる The tree sets off the garden

494 はかる

計る

Ⓚ1309

① **compute, calculate, estimate**
所要時間を計る しょようじかんをはかる calculate the time required

② **guess, surmise, fathom**

計り知れない はかりしれない unfathomable, inestimable

③ **plan, design, scheme**
国の将来を計る くにのしょうらいをはかる plan [provide] for the future of the country

④ **deceive, play upon, take in**
計られる はかられる be taken in

測る

Ⓚ0558

(measure the physical dimensions of)
measure, gauge (length, depth, distance or area)
標高を測る ひょうこうをはかる measure the height of (a mountain)

量る

Ⓚ2180

① (determine the weight or volume of)
measure, weigh
量り はかり measurements; weighing
量り売り はかりうり sale by measure; sale by weight
肉の目方を量る にくのめかたをはかる weigh the meat

② [in compounds] **guess, surmise, fathom**
推し量る おしはかる conjecture, surmise, guess

図る

Ⓚ2645

① **strive for, work for, promote, look to, provide for, seek**
相互理解を図る そうごりかいをはかる strive for mutual understanding
公益を図る こうえきをはかる labor for the public good
安全を図る あんぜんをはかる provide for safety

② **bring about, attempt**
便宜を図る べんぎをはかる accommodate, suit the convenience of
自殺を図る じさつをはかる attempt suicide
③ [in negative constructions] **expect, look forward to**
図らずも はからずも unexpectedly

謀る   Ⓚ1439

scheme, plot, conspire, contrive
暗殺を謀る あんさつをはかる plot an assassination

諮る   Ⓚ1443

consult, confer, ask (a person's) opinion
委員会に諮る いいんかいにはかる submit (a plan) to a committee for deliberation

---

495   **はく¹**

掃く   Ⓚ0464

① **sweep, brush, clean up**
掃き出す はきだす sweep out
掃き集める はきあつめる sweep up together
② [also 刷く] **brush, apply with a brush**
紅を掃く べにをはく give [have] a brush of rouge (to one's cheeks)
③ **gather silkworms**
掃き立て はきたて being newly swept; gathering silkworms from the egg paper

刷く   Ⓚ1169

[also 掃く] **brush, apply with a brush**

刷毛 はけ brush
紅を刷く べにをはく give [have] a brush of rouge (to one's cheeks)

---

496   **はく²**

履く   Ⓚ2736

put on footwear, wear (shoes)
履物 はきもの footwear, footgear; clogs, sandals
履き違える はきちがえる put on another's shoes; be mistaken

穿く   Ⓚ1941

put on (trousers or socks), wear (a skirt)
下穿き したばき undershorts, underpants
スカートを穿く すかーとをはく put on a skirt

---

497   **はげしい**

激しい   Ⓚ0696

① (acting with extreme force) **violent, fierce, vehement**
激しさ はげしさ intensity, severity
激しい風 はげしいかぜ strong wind
② (of great intensity) **intense, violent, severe**
激しい競争 はげしいきょうそう hot competition

烈しい   Ⓚ2308

① (acting with extreme force) **violent, fierce, vehement**
烈しさ はげしさ intensity, severity
烈しい風 はげしいかぜ strong wind

② (of great intensity) **intense, violent, severe**

烈しい競争 はげしいきょうそう hot competition

498　はこ

箱　　　　　　　　　Ⓚ2366

①ⓐ [sometimes also 函] [also suffix] **box, case, chest, bin**
　ⓑ **counter for boxes**

箱入りの はこいりの cased, boxed
箱入り娘 はこいりむすめ innocent [naive] girl of a good family
小箱 こばこ small box; casket
郵便箱 ゆうびんばこ mailbox
巣箱 すばこ bird box, bird house
本箱 ほんばこ bookcase
救急箱 きゅうきゅうばこ first-aid kit
二箱 ふたはこ two boxes

② *slang* **railway car**

箱師 はこし train pickpocket

③ *slang* **shamisen**

函　　　　　　　　　Ⓚ2587

[now usu. 箱] **box, case, mailbox**

私書函 ししょばこ post office box (P.O.B.)
暗函 あんばこ camera obscura
通い函 かよいばこ reusable shipping carton

499　はさむ

挟む　　　　　　　　Ⓚ0335

①ⓐ **hold between, hold**
　ⓑ **pinch, nip**

テーブルを挟んで話し合う てーぶるをはさんではなしあう hold a conversation across the table
箸で漬け物を挟む はしでつけものをはさむ hold a pickle with chopsticks
紙挟み かみばさみ paper clip, paper holder
ペンを唇に挟む ぺんをくちびるにはさむ nip a pen between one's lips

② [formerly also 挿む] **put (something) between, insert, interpose**

挟み込む はさみこむ insert
雑誌に挟む ざっしにはさむ place in a magazine
口を挟む くちをはさむ interject, cut into (a conversation)

挿む　　　　　　　　Ⓚ0390

[now usu. 挟む] **put (something) between, insert, interpose**

本に栞を挿む ほんにしおりをはさむ put a bookmark between the pages of a book

鋏む　　　　　　　　

snip, clip

枝を鋏む えだをはさむ trim [prune] a tree

500　はし

橋　　　　　　　　　Ⓚ0991

[also suffix] **bridge**

橋渡し はしわたし mediation, good offices
釣り橋 つりばし suspension bridge
丸木橋 まるきばし log bridge

吉野川橋 よしのがわばし Yoshinoga-
wa Bridge

梯 ⓀＯ875

[in compounds] **ladder**
梯子 はしご [sometimes also 梯] ladder
梯子車 はしごしゃ hook-and-ladder
truck
梯子酒 はしござけ barhopping
縄梯子 なわばしご rope ladder

端 Ⓚ1131

① **end, extremity, tip**
紐の端 ひものはし end of a string
両端 りょうはし both ends
② **edge, margin, brink, border; side**
端端に はしばしに here and there, in
some parts
道の端 みちのはし edge of a street
右端 みぎはし right side, right margin
③ **beginning**
端書き はしがき preface, introduction
④ **unwanted piece, scrap, fragment**
端くれ はしくれ fag end
木の端 きのはし fragment of wood

箸 Ⓚ2363

chopsticks
箸置き はしおき chopstick rest
箸使い はしづかい chopstick usage
箸休め はしやすめ palate-cleansing
side dish
箸にも棒にも掛からない はしにも
ぼうにもかからない incorrigible,
hopeless
割り箸 わりばし half-split (disposable)
chopsticks

火箸 ひばし tongs
握り箸 にぎりばし gripping both
chopsticks in one's fist

501	はじ

恥 Ⓚ1200

[sometimes also 羞] **shame, disgrace,
humiliation**
恥知らず はじしらず shameless
person
恥曝し はじさらし disgrace, shame

羞 Ⓚ2823

[usu. 恥] **shame, disgrace, humiliation**

502	はじめ

初め Ⓚ1031

① (initial period) **beginning (of the
month), outset, first stage, early
period**
初めは はじめは at first; originally
年度初め ねんどはじめ beginning of
the (fiscal) year
② **including, as well as, not to speak
of**
田中氏初め六人 たなかしはじめろく
にん Mr. Tanaka and five others

始め Ⓚ0252

① (act or point of commencement) **beginning, start**
② (source) **beginning, origin**

初めて Ⓚ1031

for the first time; not…until
初めての はじめての first, first-time
初めまして はじめまして I am glad to meet you
健康は失って初めてその価値が分かる けんこうはうしなってはじめてそのかちがわかる We don't know the value of health till we lose it

始めて Ⓚ0252

begin and… (TE-form of 始める はじめる)

甫めて Ⓚ2972

literary **barely, just**
我齢は甫めて九つなるに わがよわいははじめてここのつなるに I was barely nine years old

恥じらう Ⓚ1200

[sometimes also 羞じらう] **be shy [coy], look abashed**
恥じらい はじらい shyness

羞じらう Ⓚ2823

[usu. 恥じらう] **be shy, be coy, look abashed**
羞じらい はじらい shyness

恥じる Ⓚ1200

[sometimes also 羞じる] **feel ashamed**
恥じ入る はじいる feel quite ashamed

羞じる Ⓚ2823

[usu. 恥じる] **feel ashamed**

恥ずかしい Ⓚ1200

[sometimes also 羞ずかしい] **shy; ashamed; shameful, disgraceful**
恥ずかしがる はずかしがる be shy [coy], be abashed
気恥ずかしい きはずかしい feel ashamed, feel awkward

羞ずかしい Ⓚ2823

[usu. 恥ずかしい] **shy; ashamed; shameful, disgraceful**

畑 Ⓚ0812

[formerly also 畠] **(plowed or cultivated) field, farm, vegetable garden, plantation**
畑地 はたち farmland
畑作 はたさく dry field farming, dry field crop
田畑 たはた (=でんぱた) fields and rice paddies

畠 Ⓚ2234

[now usu. 畑] **(plowed or cultivated) field, farm, vegetable garden, plantation**
　田畠 たはた (=でんぱた) fields (of rice and other crops)

508　はた²

旗 Ⓚ0958

[sometimes also 幡] **flag, banner, standard, ensign**
　旗揚げ はたあげ raising an army; launching business
　手旗 てばた semaphore [hand] flag

幡 Ⓚ0656

① [usu. 旗] **flag, banner, standard, ensign**
　幡幢 はたほこ (=はたぼこ) long-handled spear bearing a small flag used in Buddhist services and court ceremonies
② *patākā*: **pendant streamer hung before a temple in honor of Buddha**

509　はた³

端 Ⓚ1131

[also suffix] **edge, side**
　池の端で いけのはたで near [by] the pond
　道端 みちばた roadside, wayside
　海岸端 かいがんばた seaside

傍 Ⓚ0127

bystander, outsider

傍の者達 はたのものたち bystanders, onlookers

510　はたけ

畑 Ⓚ0812

① **(plowed or cultivated) field, farm, vegetable garden, plantation**
　畑を作る はたけをつくる cultivate a field, farm
② **one's field, one's specialty**
　畑違いだ はたけちがいだ be out of one's field

畠 Ⓚ2234

① **(plowed or cultivated) field, farm, vegetable garden, plantation**
　畠を耕す はたけをたがやす plow a field
② **one's field, one's specialty**
　畠違いだ はたけちがいだ be out of one's field

511　はだ

肌 Ⓚ0731

① ⓐ **skin, body**
　　ⓑ **surface; grain (of wood)**
　肌身 はだみ body
　肌着 はだぎ underwear
　肌を許す はだをゆるす surrender one's chastity to a man
　肌色 はだいろ flesh-color
　赤肌 あかはだ abraded skin
　山肌 やまはだ surface of a mountain
　美しい肌の材 うつくしいはだのざい wood of fine grain
② ⓐ **disposition, temperament**

ⓑ [suffix] **turn of mind**
肌が合わない はだがあわない cannot
go together (with)
学者肌 がくしゃはだ scholarly bent
of mind

膚 　　　　　　　　Ⓚ2788
①ⓐ **skin, body**
ⓑ **surface; grain (of wood)**
膚身 はだみ body
赤膚 あかはだ abraded skin
山膚 やまはだ surface of a mountain
膚の美しい材 はだのうつくしいざい
wood of fine grain
②ⓐ **disposition, temperament**
ⓑ [suffix] **turn of mind**
学者膚 がくしゃはだ scholarly bent
of mind

512　　はな¹

花 　　　　　　　　Ⓚ1894
①ⓐ [also prefix] **flower, blossom; cher-ry blossom**
ⓑ **flower arrangement**
花見 はなみ flower [cherry blossom]
viewing
花嫁 はなよめ bride
花火 はなび fireworks, firecrackers
花形 はながた floral pattern; star, lion;
leading, popular, favorite
花時計 はなどけい flower clock
草花 くさばな flowering plant
お花 おはな flower arrangement
②ⓐ [also 華] (figuratively) **flower (of life),
essence, cream**
ⓑ **honor, success, glory**
若い内が花だ わかいうちがはなだ
Youth is a treasure

花を持たせる はなをもたせる let (a
person) have the credit for (the
success)
③ **Japanese playing cards with floral
patterns**
花を引く はなをひく play *hana* cards
④ [in compounds] **geisha, prostitute**
花代 はなだい tip to a geisha girl
花街 はなまち red-light district

華 　　　　　　　　Ⓚ1973
①ⓐ [also 花] (figuratively) **flower (of
life), essence, cream**
ⓑ **flower of youth, prime of life**
武士道の華 ぶしどうのはな flower of
chivalry [Bushido]
若い内が華 わかいうちがはな Youth
is a treasure
② [in compounds] **flowery, beautiful,
gallant**
華やかな はなやかな flowery, gay,
bright, brilliant, gorgeous
華華しい はなばなしい brilliant, mag-
nificent, spectacular

513　　はな²

鼻 　　　　　　　　Ⓚ2362
①ⓐ **nose, snout, trunk**
ⓑ [also 端] **end, protruded point**
鼻血 はなぢ nosebleed
鼻水 はなみず nasal discharge
鼻柱 はなばしら bridge of the nose;
self-assertion
鼻息 はないき snorting; temper; vigor
鼻紙 はながみ tissue paper (for wip-
ing the nose)
鼻摘まみ はなつまみ disgusting
fellow

鼻が高い はながたかい be proud (have one's nose up)

鼻持ちならない はなもちならない be intolerable; stink

目鼻が付く めはながつく take a concrete shape, materialize

② [also 端] **beginning**

出鼻 でばな outset, start; point of going out

端　　　　　ⓚ1131

① **outset, beginning**

寝入り端に ねいりばなに just when one has fallen asleep

② **end, protruded point**

離す　　　　　ⓚ1663

①ⓐ **separate, part, divide**
　ⓑ **detach, keep apart, isolate**

切り離す きりはなす cut [chop] off, sever, detach

引き離す ひきはなす draw apart, separate; get a lead on

② **estrange**

放す　　　　　ⓚ0754

ⓐ (set free) **let go, release, free, turn loose**
ⓑ (release one's hold) **let go (one's hold of), leave go**

放し飼い はなしがい grazing; letting (a dog) run free

見放す みはなす desert, abandon, give up

手放す てばなす release [let go] one's hold

離れる　　　　ⓚ1663

①ⓐ **separate, be separated, become disjointed**
　ⓑ **be (a long time or distance) away**

離れ離れになる はなればなれになる get separated, be dispersed

遠く離れて とおくはなれて at a long distance

現実離れする げんじつばなれする become disconnected from reality

② **be estranged from, cut oneself off**

③ **leave, quit, go away**

都会を離れる とかいをはなれる leave town

放れる　　　　ⓚ0754

free oneself of, get free

狼が鎖を放れた おおかみがくさりをはなれた The wolf freed itself of its chain

跳ねる　　　　ⓚ1392

①ⓐ **leap, spring, jump, hop**
　ⓑ **bound, rebound, recoil**
　ⓒ (of the market) **jump (to)**

跳ね起きる はねおきる jump up, spring up

跳び跳ねる とびはねる jump up and down, hop

跳ね返る はねかえる rebound, bounce; (of the market) recover

② (of the theater) **be over, close**

撥ねる

①@ **flip, splash**
　ⓑ **strike, knock down**
　車に撥ねられる **くるまにはねられる**
　　be struck by a car
② **reject, turn down**
　突っ撥ねる **つっぱねる** reject [refuse]
　　flatly
　試験で撥ねられる **しけんではねられ**
　　る get flunked in an examination
③ **take a percentage for one's own**
　上前を撥ねる **うわまえをはねる** take
　　a cut, take a kickback
④ **sweep up (in brush stroke of kanji)**
⑤ **pronounce** ん **as a syllabic conso-**
　nant

517　　　　　はば

幅　　　　　　　　　ⓚ0523

[also suffix] **width, breadth, range;**
influence, power; difference (in
price)
　幅広い **はばひろい** wide, broad
　幅跳び **はばとび** broad jump
　幅利き **はばきき** man of influence
　大幅に **おおはばに** sharply, by a large
　　margin
　小幅 **こはば** single breadth, narrow
　　range
　横幅 **よこはば** breadth
　値幅 **ねはば** difference (in price)

巾　　　　　　　　　ⓚ2879

[usu. 幅] **width, breadth, range**
　半巾 **はんはば** half-width (approx.
　　18 cm)

阻む　　　　　　　　ⓚ0308

[formerly also 沮む] **obstruct, impede,**
hinder, check, prevent
　道を阻む **みちをはばむ** obstruct
　　one's way
　成長を阻む **せいちょうをはばむ** hin-
　　der [check] the growth of (plants)

沮む

[now replaced by 阻む] **obstruct, im-**
pede, hinder, check, prevent

519　　　　　はまる

嵌まる

① **fit, be fit for, suit**
　当て嵌まる **あてはまる** be applicable,
　　come under (a category), fulfill
　　(criteria)
②@ **be trapped, be ensnared**
　ⓑ **be addicted, be deep (into)**
　嵌まり込む **はまりこむ** get stuck in,
　　be mired in; be addicted to
　穴に嵌まる **あなにはまる** fall in a pit

填まる　　　　　　　ⓚ0581

① **fit, be fit for, suit**
②@ **be trapped, be ensnared**
　ⓑ **be addicted, be deep (into)**
　穴に填まる **あなにはまる** fall in a pit
　填まり込む **はまりこむ** get stuck
　　[mired] in; be addicted to

嵌める

① ⓐ **put in, set in, insert, fit**
　ⓑ **put on, slip on**
　嵌め込み はめこみ insertion, inlaying
② **entrap, ensnare; trick, deceive**
　旨く嵌められた うまくはめられた I
　　was cleverly taken in

塡める Ⓚ0581

① ⓐ **put in, set in, insert, fit**
　ⓑ **put on, slip on**
　塡め込み はめこみ insertion, inlaying
② **entrap, ensnare; trick, deceive**
　旨く塡められた うまくはめられた I
　　was cleverly taken in

早– Ⓚ2120

① **early**
　早起き はやおき early rising
　早立ち(=早発ち) はやだち early
　　morning departure
　早引き はやびき early leaving
　早寝する はやねする go to bed early
② ⓐ [also prefix] [sometimes also 速–]
　　quick, fast, rapid
　ⓑ [prefix] **hasty, rash**
　早見表 はやみひょう list, chart
　早業 はやわざ quick work, (clever)
　　feat
　早口 はやくち fast [rapid] talking
　早合点 はやがてん hasty conclusion
　早呑み込み はやのみこみ hasty
　　conclusion

速– Ⓚ2674

[usu. 早–] **quick, fast, rapid**
　速口 はやくち fast [rapid] talking
　速業 はやわざ quick work, (clever)
　　feat
　速分かり はやわかり quick under-
　　standing; guide, handbook
★ Though 早い and 速い as independ-
　ent *kun* words can be discriminated
　as shown above, they are often in-
　terchangeable in the formation of
　compounds related to speed.

早い Ⓚ2120

① **early, premature**
　早く はやく early, soon; early age
　　[time]
　早早と はやばやと early, promptly
　お早う おはよう Good morning!
　日暮れが早い ひぐれがはやい Dusk
　　falls early
　親に早く死なれる おやにはやくしなれ
　　る be orphaned while still young
② [sometimes also 速い] (requiring little
　time) **quick, prompt**
　早い話が はやいはなしが in short
　早い事 はやいこと quickly
　耳が早い みみがはやい be quick-
　　eared
　手っ取り早く てっとりばやく expedi-
　　tiously, with dispatch

速い Ⓚ2674

ⓐ (acting or moving quickly) **quick,
　speedy, fast, rapid, swift**
ⓑ [usu. 早い] (requiring little time) **quick,
　prompt**

速さ はやさ speed
足速い あしばやい swift-footed, light-footed
素速い すばやい quick, nimble, agile
耳が速い みみがはやい be quick-eared

523 はやまる

早まる ⓀK2120

① take place ahead of time
梅雨明けは早まるだろう つゆあけは はやまるだろう The rainy season will end early

② be rash, be too hasty, act rashly
早まって はやまって in one's hurry

速まる ⓀK2674

vi quicken, accelerate, speed up
速まる鼓動 はやまるこどう quickening heartbeat

524 はやめる

早める ⓀK2120

perform an action early, do ahead of time
期日を早める きじつをはやめる advance the date (of)

速める ⓀK2674

vt quicken, accelerate, speed up, hasten
足を速める あしをはやめる quicken one's pace [steps]

525 はり

針 ⓀK1488

① ⓐ [also suffix] **needle**
  ⓑ **needle-shaped object as the hand of a clock or pointer of an instrument**
針仕事 はりしごと needlework, sewing
針山 はりやま pincushion
針箱 はりばこ needlecase, sewing box
針状の はりじょうの needle-shaped, pointed
針で刺す はりでさす prick with a needle
縫い針 ぬいばり needle
木綿針 もめんばり needle for cotton thread
鉤針 かぎばり hook, crochet needle
針金 はりがね wire
釣り針 つりばり (fish)hook

② **sting, sarcasm**
針を含んだ言葉 はりをふくんだことば stinging [scathing] words

鍼

ⓐ **acupuncture**
ⓑ **acupuncture needle**
鍼医 はりい acupuncturist
鍼治療 はりちりょう acupuncture

526 はる

張る ⓀK0431

① (open to the full extent) **spread (out), extend over, stretch**

縄張り なわばり roping off; one's sphere of influence, one's territory

翼を張る つばさをはる spread the wings

② ⓐ **strain, stretch, tighten**
ⓑ **be stretched [tightened], become taut**
ⓒ **be under strain, be tense, be anxious; be enthusiastic**

張り はり tension; will power, pluck

引っ張る ひっぱる pull, draw; drag

糸を張る いとをはる stretch a string

張り裂ける はりさける burst (open), break, split

乳が張る ちちがはる The breasts swell

頬張る ほおばる cram one's mouth (with food)

突っ張る つっぱる become taut; thrust (one's opponent); stick to (one's opinion), insist on; *slang* be delinquent

気が張る きがはる feel nervous

欲を張る よくをはる lust for

張り詰めた はりつめた high-strung, tense

張り切る はりきる be in high spirits, be enthusiastic; stretch to the full

強張る(=硬ばる) こわばる become stiff, stiffen

③ [also 貼る]
ⓐ **stick, paste; apply to**
ⓑ **cover, line**
張り付ける はりつける stick on, paste
タイルを張る たいるをはる tile a floor

④ **stick out, project**
張り出す はりだす project, jut out
角張った顔 かくばったかお squarish face

⑤ **keep watch, guard**

張り込む はりこむ look out for, ambush

見張る みはる watch, guard

⑥ ⓐ **insist, persist**
ⓑ **display, demonstrate**
頑張る がんばる persist, be tenacious, hold out
意地を張る いじをはる be obstinate
威張る いばる put on airs, be haughty; boast, brag
見栄を張る みえをはる show off

⑦ **hold, give (a banquet), run, manage**
世帯を張る しょたいをはる keep [set up] house

⑧ *slang* **slap, smack**
張り倒す はりたおす knock down

⑨ **rival, compete**
張り合う はりあう compete, challenge
向こうを張る むこうをはる vie with one's opponent

貼る Ⓚ1369

ⓐ **stick, paste; apply to**
ⓑ **cover, line**
貼り付ける はりつける stick on, paste
貼り合わせる はりあわせる paste together
貼り紙 はりがみ sticker, label, poster
切り貼り きりばり cutting and pasting, patching (up)
下貼り したばり undercoat, first coat
床にタイルを貼る ゆかにたいるをはる tile a floor

527 はれる

腫れる Ⓚ0951

[sometimes also 脹れる] **swell, become swollen; tumefy**

腫れ はれ swelling, boil
腫れ上がる はれあがる swell up
腫れ物に触るように はれものにさわるように with great caution, gingerly
惚れた腫れた ほれたはれた head over heels in love

脹れる Ⓚ0916

[usu. 腫れる] **swell, become swollen; tumefy**

脹れ はれ swelling, boil
脹れぼったい はれぼったい somewhat swollen, puffy
みみず脹れ みみずばれ wale, welt

528 ばえ

-映え Ⓚ0793

① **glow**
夕映え ゆうばえ evening [sunset] glow
② [also –栄え] **looking better**
代わり映えがしない かわりばえがしない It's none the better for the change
③ [usu. –栄え] **result, effect**
出来映え できばえ result, effect, workmanship

-栄え Ⓚ2231

① [also –映え] **looking better**

見栄え みばえ improvement in appearance, good show
② [sometimes also –映え] **result, effect**
出来栄え できばえ result, effect, workmanship

529 ばたけ

-畑 Ⓚ0812

① [also suffix] **field, farm, vegetable garden, plantation**
花畑 はなばたけ flower garden
段段畑 だんだんばたけ terraced fields, terraced farm
コーヒー畑 こーひーばたけ coffee plantation
② [suffix] **one's field, one's specialty**
技術畑の人 ぎじゅつばたけのひと man in the technical line, career technician

-畠 Ⓚ2234

① [also suffix] **field, farm, vegetable garden, plantation**
段段畠 だんだんばたけ terraced fields, terraced farm
② [suffix] **one's field, one's specialty**
工学畠 こうがくばたけ engineering field

530 ばり

-張り Ⓚ0431

① [suffix] **fashion, manner**
川端張りの小説 かわばたばりのしょうせつ novel written in imitation of Kawabata's
② [sometimes also –貼り] [also suffix] **covered with, lined with**

絹張り きぬばり lined with silk
③ **unit for expressing the power of a bow in terms of number of persons**

-貼り
Ⓚ1369

[usu. -張り] [also suffix] **covered with, lined with**
絹貼り きぬばり lined with silk
紙貼り かみばり lined with paper

| 531 | ひ¹ |

日
Ⓚ2606

① [sometimes also 陽] **sun, sunlight**
日の丸 ひのまる Rising Sun Flag
日時計 ひどけい sundial
日の出 ひので sunrise
日の入り ひのいり sunset
日陰 ひかげ the shade
日影 ひかげ sunshine; shadow
日向 ひなた sunshine, sunny place
日差し ひざし rays of the sun, sunlight
朝日 あさひ [sometimes also 旭] rising sun, morning sun; rays of the morning sun

② **day, date, time**
日日 ひび daily; days
日日 ひにち date; number of days
日付 ひづけ date, dating
日頃 ひごろ usually; always
日替わり ひがわり changing on a daily basis
日に日に ひにひに day by day, every day
曜日 ようび day of the week
生年月日 せいねんがっぴ date of birth

陽
Ⓚ0572

[usu. 日] **sun, sunlight**
夕陽 ゆうひ setting sun

| 532 | ひ² |

火
Ⓚ2911

① ⓐ [also prefix and suffix] **fire, flame**
　ⓑ **firelight**
火元 ひもと origin [source] of a fire
火花 ひばな spark
火加減 ひかげん condition of the fire
灯火 ともしび [also 灯, sometimes also 燭] light, lamp, flame
花火 はなび fireworks, firecrackers
口火 くちび fuse; pilot burner; cause (of a war)
不審火 ふしんび suspected case of arson

② **heat**
火を通す ひをとおす heat, cook

灯
Ⓚ0730

(source of illumination) **light, lantern, lamp**
灯を付ける ひをつける turn on the light

| 533 | ひかえ |

控え
Ⓚ0453

① **note, memo; counterfoil, stub**
控え書き ひかえがき notes, memo
捕り物控え とりものひかえ detective's memoirs
領収書の控え りょうしゅうしょのひかえ counterfoil of a receipt

② **duplicate, copy**

控え を取る ひかえをとる take a copy of

控え見本 ひかえみほん duplicate sample

③ **waiting; reserve, substitute, alternate**

控えの間 ひかえのま antechamber, anteroom

控え室 ひかえしつ anteroom, waiting room

控えの力士 ひかえのりきし sumo wrestler waiting at the ringside

控え選手 ひかえせんしゅ reserve, substitute player

④ **prop, stay**

主控え しゅびかえ mainstay

扣え

① **note, memo; counterfoil, stub**
② **duplicate, copy**
③ **waiting; reserve, substitute, alternate**
④ **prop, stay**

534　ひかえる

控える　　Ⓚ0453

① (keep in check) **hold back, keep**

馬を控える うまをひかえる hold back a horse

②ⓐ (refrain from) **hold back (from), restrain oneself, refrain**
　ⓑ **be moderate, be sparing**

差し控える さしひかえる be moderate in; withhold, desist from, refrain from

手控える てびかえる hang [hold] back, hold off, refrain

食べ物を控える たべものをひかえる be temperate in eating

控え目な ひかえめな modest, temperate, reserved

③ **be in waiting, wait**

別の間に控える べつのまにひかえる wait in another room

④ **note down, write down, take notes**

電話番号を控える でんわばんごうをひかえる jot down a phone number

⑤ **have (something at hand)**

選挙を控えて せんきょをひかえて with the election around the corner

扣える

① (keep in check) **hold back, keep**
②ⓐ (refrain from) **hold back (from), restrain oneself, refrain**
　ⓑ **be moderate, be sparing**
③ **be in waiting, wait**
④ **note down, write down, take notes**

535　ひき¹

引き　　Ⓚ0160

① [sometimes also 抽-] **drawing**

引き出し ひきだし drawer; withdrawal (of money)

② **patronage, backing, pull**

良い引きが有る よいひきがある have a strong pull

抽-　　Ⓚ0267

[usu. 引き] **drawing**

抽出し ひきだし (desk) drawer

匹   Ⓚ2558

① [formerly also 疋] **counter for animals**

犬五匹 いぬごひき five dogs

数匹 すうひき several animals

② [also 疋] *hiki*: **unit of measure for cloth equiv. to 2** *tan* (反)

絹一匹 きぬいっぴき one *hiki* of silk

疋   Ⓚ2922

① *hiki*:
  - ⓐ [also 匹] **unit of measure for cloth equiv . to 2** *tan* (反)
  - ⓑ **former monetary unit equiv. to 10 (later 25)** *mon* (文)

② [now usu. 匹] **counter for animals**

引く   Ⓚ0160

① ⓐ [formerly also 曳く or 牽く] **draw, pull, haul, tug;** [formerly also 曳く] **drag, trail**
  - ⓑ (cause to retreat) **draw in, pull in**

引 ひく PULL (marking on doors)

引っ張る ひっぱる pull, draw; drag

引き上げる ひきあげる draw [pull] up; promote; increase

引き出す ひきだす draw out; lure out

引き分け ひきわけ draw; drawn game [match]

引き摺る ひきずる drag along; trail

引き止める ひきとめる detain, keep

引き攣る ひきつる have a cramp

引き戻す ひきもどす bring back; pull back; restore

引き締める ひきしめる tighten; brace oneself; cut down

引き締め ひきしめ tightening

弓を引く ゆみをひく draw a bow

船を引く ふねをひく tow a boat

手を引く てをひく wash one's hands of; lead by the hand

② [formerly also 惹く]
  - ⓐ **draw (attention or sympathy), attract, catch**
  - ⓑ **catch (a cold)**

引き付ける ひきつける attract, charm, keep at hand; have a convulsive fit

客引き きゃくひき touting; tout, barker, pander

注意を引く ちゅういをひく draw attention

風邪を引いている かぜをひいている have a cold

③ ⓐ **draw (off) (water), tap, conduct, lead (a stream through a field)**
  - ⓑ **lay on (gas or water), install (a telephone)**

川から水を引く かわからみずをひく draw water off a river

電話を引く でんわをひく install a telephone

④ **draw (a line or diagram)**

図面を引く ずめんをひく draw a plan

⑤ **draw lots**

福引き ふくびき lottery

籤引 くじびき drawing of lots

⑥ [also 退く]
  - ⓐ **retreat, withdraw**
  - ⓑ **retire, resign**

引っ込む ひっこむ draw back, retire; sink, fall in

駆け引き かけひき bargaining; tactics

後へ引く あとへひく retreat, recede

役所を引く やくしょをひく leave office, resign one's post in an office

⑦ [also 退く] **subside, abate, go down**

熱が引いた ねつがひいた The fever has abated

⑧ **subtract, deduct, deduce; allow discount**
引き算 ひきざん subtraction
三引く二は一 さんひくにはいち Three minus two equals one
割引 わりびき discount, reduction

⑨ **quote, cite, refer to**
例を引く れいをひく cite an example

⑩ **look up, consult (a dictionary)**
生き字引 いきじびき walking dictionary

⑪ **lay on, apply, oil**
油を引く あぶらをひく oil

⑫ **succeed to, take over**
引き継ぐ ひきつぐ take over, hand over; succeed to, inherit
引き継ぎ ひきつぎ taking over (someone's duties)
引き受ける ひきうける undertake; answer for, guarantee
引き取る ひきとる take over, receive; retire
皇室の血を引いている こうしつのちをひいている be descended from the Imperial House

⑬ **lift, steal**
万引き まんびき shoplifting; shoplifter

⑭ **unclassified compounds**
取り引き とりひき transaction, dealings

挽く Ⓚ0384

① **grind (meat or coffee)**
挽き肉 ひきにく ground [minced] meat

挽き立てのコーヒー ひきたてのこーひー freshly ground coffee
粗挽き あらびき coarsely ground (coffee, grain), coarsely minced (meat)
合い挽き あいびき beef and pork ground together

② **saw, cut with a saw**
木挽き歌 こびきうた sawyer's song
縦挽き鋸 たてびきのこ ripsaw

弾く Ⓚ0524

play on (stringed instruments)
弾き手 ひきて player, performer
弾き語り ひきがたり reciting to one's own accompaniment
爪弾く つまびく pluck the strings (of a guitar)

轢く

run over (with a vehicle), knock down
轢き逃げ ひきにげ hit-and-run
轢き殺す ひきころす kill by running over

牽く Ⓚ1816

[now usu. 引く, sometimes also 曳く] **draw, pull, haul, tug**
一頭牽き いっとうびき one-horse (carriage)

惹く Ⓚ2015

ⓐ **draw (attention or sympathy), attract, catch**
ⓑ **catch (a cold)**
惹き付ける ひきつける attract, charm
心惹かれる こころひかれる feel attracted [fascinated] by

注意を惹く ちゅういをひく draw attention

風邪を惹いている かぜをひいている have a cold

退く ⓚ2665

① ⓐ **retreat, withdraw**
　 ⓑ **retire, resign**
　 後へ退く あとへひく retreat, recede
　 役所を退く やくしょをひく leave office, resign one's post in an office

② **subside, abate, go down**
　 熱が退く ねつがひく The fever abates

曳く ⓚ2961

ⓐ [sometimes also 牽く] **draw, pull, haul, tug**
ⓑ **drag, trail**
　 曳山 ひきやま festival float
　 曳き船 ひきふね tugboat, towing
　 綱曳き つなひき tug of war; forward puller (of a rickshaw)
　 曳き網 ひきあみ dragnet, seine

538　ひつじ

羊 ⓚ1870

sheep, ram, ewe
　 羊飼い ひつじかい shepherd
　 羊雲 ひつじぐも floccus
　 子羊 こひつじ lamb

未 ⓚ2941

eighth sign of the Oriental zodiac: **the Ram**—(time) 1-3 p.m., (direction) SSW, (season) June (of the lunar calendar)

539　ひとみ

瞳 ⓚ1144

ⓐ **pupil**
ⓑ **one's eyes**
　 瞳の ひとみの pupilary
　 瞳を凝らす ひとみをこらす strain one's eyes

眸 ⓚ1082

ⓐ **pupil, the apple of one's eye**
ⓑ **one's eyes**
　 黒い眸 くろいひとみ (beautiful) dark eyes

★ Both these characters have the same meaning, but the latter has a more literary flavor.

540　ひとり

独り ⓚ0354

ⓐ **alone, solitary, by oneself**
ⓑ **single, unmarried**
　 独りぼっちの ひとりぼっちの solitary
　 独り旅 ひとりたび traveling alone, solitary journey
　 独り者 ひとりもの single [unmarried] man [woman]

一人 ⓚ2850

ⓐ **one person**
ⓑ **only (child, son or daughter)**

541　ひどい

酷い ⓚ1414

① **cruel, harsh, rough**

酷さ ひどさ harshness, severity
酷い仕打ち ひどいしうち cruel treatment
② **severe, intense, heavy**
酷く暑い ひどくあつい It's awfully hot

非道い
Ⓚ0790

[also 酷い] **same as 酷い**

542 ひま

暇
Ⓚ0923

① **free time, spare time, leisure; dullness, slackness; dismissal, discharge**
暇潰し ひまつぶし time killer; waste of time
暇が無い ひまがない have no (free) time, be busy
暇な商売 ひまなしょうばい dull business
暇が出る ひまがでる be discharged
② [sometimes also 隙] **time spent on doing something**
手間暇 てまひま time and effort, trouble

隙
Ⓚ0614

① [usu. 暇] **time spent on doing something**
手間隙 てまひま time and effort, trouble
② [archaic]
ⓐ **gap, space**
ⓑ **discord**
ⓒ **inattention, oversight**

543 ひめ

姫
Ⓚ0368

①ⓐ **daughter [young lady] of noble [gentle] birth, princess**
ⓑ [sometimes also 媛] **courtesy title after names of young ladies of noble birth**
姫君 ひめぎみ princess, highborn young lady
姫様 ひめさま daughter of a nobleman
姫宮 ひめみや princess
千姫 せんひめ Princess Sen
シンデレラ姫 しんでれらひめ Cinderella
② [sometimes also 媛] *elegant* **girl, charming girl**
歌姫 うたひめ songstress, chanteuse
舞姫 まいひめ dancing girl, dancer

媛
Ⓚ0519

① *elegant* **damsel, beautiful young lady**
② **courtesy title after names of young ladies of noble birth**
橘媛 たちばなひめ name of a woman in a Japanese myth

544 ひらく

開く
Ⓚ2835

①ⓐ **open, open up; unfold, flower**
ⓑ **open up, commence operations**
ⓒ **open (a conference), hold (a meeting)**
開き直る ひらきなおる switch to a defiant attitude

店を開く みせをひらく open a business

パーティーを開く ぱーてぃーをひらく give a party

② [sometimes also 拓く] **open up (land), clear, reclaim, develop**

道を切り開く みちをきりひらく open a path

③ **differ, widen the margin between**

距離を開く きょりをひらく open the distance

④ [sometimes also 啓く] **enlighten, edify**

蒙を開く もうをひらく enlighten (a person's mind)

拓く
Ⓚ0282

[usu. 開く] **open up (land), clear, reclaim, develop**

荒れ地を拓く あれちをひらく open up unbroken land

自分の道を拓く じぶんのみちをひらく hew one's way out

啓く
Ⓚ2408

[usu. 開く] **enlighten, edify**

蒙を啓く もうをひらく enlighten (a person's mind)

545　　　ひる

干る
Ⓚ2863

① [formerly also 乾る] **get dry, parch**

干魚 ひうお(=ほしざかな) dried fish

干涸びる ひからびる dry up completely

干上がる ひあがる dry up, parch; ebb away

② (of tides) **ebb, recede**

潮干狩り しおひがり shell gathering (at low tide)

乾る
Ⓚ1500

[now usu. 干る] vi **get dry, parch**

乾物 ひもの dried fish

546　　　ひろがる

広がる
Ⓚ2613

ⓐ **spread out, stretch, unfold**
ⓑ **expand, extend**
ⓒ **spread, reach, go about**

広がった枝 ひろがったえだ spreading branches

広がり ひろがり extent, expanse, stretch, spread

火が燃え広がった ひがもえひろがった The fire spread

拡がる
Ⓚ0273

ⓐ **spread out, stretch, unfold**
ⓑ **expand, extend**
ⓒ **spread, reach, go about**

拡がり ひろがり extent, expanse, stretch, spread

火が燃え拡がった ひがもえひろがった The fire spread

547　　　ひろげる

広げる
Ⓚ2613

①ⓐ **spread (out), outstretch**
ⓑ **unfold, unroll, open**

地図を広げる ちずをひろげる spread a map

広げた腕 ひろげたうで outstretched arms

本を広げる ほんをひろげる open a book

繰り広げる くりひろげる roll out, unfold, spread out; develop

② **widen, enlarge, expand, extend**
運動場を広げる うんどうじょうをひろげる enlarge the playground

拡げる
Ⓚ0273

① ⓐ **spread (out), outstretch**
ⓑ **unfold, unroll, open**
地図を拡げる ちずをひろげる spread a map
拡げた腕 ひろげたうで outstretched arms
繰り拡げる くりひろげる roll out, unfold, spread out; develop

② **widen, enlarge, expand, extend**

548　ひろまる

広まる
Ⓚ2613

[sometimes also 弘まる] **spread, be diffused, be in general circulation, become popular**
広まり ひろまり spread
噂が広まった うわさがひろまった A rumor went about [spread]

弘まる
Ⓚ0169

[usu. 広まる] **spread, be diffused, be in general circulation, become popular**

549　ひろめる

広める
Ⓚ2613

[sometimes also 弘める] **spread, disseminate; extend, broaden, widen**
お広め(=お披露目) おひろめ début
仏教を広める ぶっきょうをひろめる propagate Buddhism
知識を広める ちしきをひろめる extend one's knowledge

弘める
Ⓚ0169

[usu. 広める] **spread, disseminate; extend, broaden, widen**

550　ふえる

増える
Ⓚ0619

vi **(grow in number or in quantity) increase, accrue, multiply**
体重が増える たいじゅうがふえる gain weight
量が増える りょうがふえる gain in quantity

殖える
Ⓚ0907

vi **(increase of its own accord) multiply, increase, propagate**—said esp. of wealth or living things
蝿が殖える はえがふえる Flies multiply
財産が殖える ざいさんがふえる become rich

551　ふく

吹く
Ⓚ0204

① ⓐ **blow, breathe out**

ⓑ **blow (as a trumpet), play on a wind instrument**
吹き込む ふきこむ blow into, breathe into
吹き出す ふきだす blow out; begin to blow
笛吹き ふえふき flute player

② **(of wind) blow**
吹き荒れる ふきあれる blow violently
吹き溜まり ふきだまり snowdrift, drift of dust [sand]

③ **(of germs or buds) sprout**
芽吹く めぶく bud

④ **brag**
吹聴する ふいちょうする make public, announce
ほら吹き ほらふき boaster, braggart

噴く Ⓚ0649

spout, emit, spurt, gush out
噴き出す ふきだす spout, spurt, gush out; break into laughter

膨らむ Ⓚ0999

[sometimes also 脹らむ] **expand, swell (out), get big, become inflated**
膨らみ ふくらみ swelling, bulge, puff
膨らます ふくらます cause to bulge, expand, dilate; raise
膨らし粉 ふくらしこ baking powder

脹らむ Ⓚ0916

[usu. 膨らむ] **expand, swell (out), get big, become inflated**
脹らみ ふくらみ swelling, bulge, puff
脹ら脛 ふくらはぎ calf

膨れる Ⓚ0999

① **expand, swell (out), get big, become inflated**
青膨れ あおぶくれ dropsical swelling
着膨れる きぶくれる be thickly clad

② **get sulky, sulk, fret, get peevish**
膨れっ面 ふくれっつら sulky look [face], sullen look

脹れる Ⓚ0916

① **expand, swell (out), get big, become inflated**
脹れ上がる ふくれあがる swell up
下脹れの しもぶくれの full-cheeked, round-faced

② **get sulky, sulk, fret, get peevish**
脹れっ面 ふくれっつら sulky look [face], sullen look

伏す Ⓚ0030

prostrate, fall prostrate, lie down, bend down
伏し目 ふしめ downcast look
ひれ伏す ひれふす prostrate oneself before a person

臥す Ⓚ1307

same as 臥せる ふせる
臥し所 ふしど bed

防ぐ
Ⓚ0242

① **prevent, keep off, ward off**
伝染を防ぐ でんせんをふせぐ prevent infection

② **defend, protect, resist**
侵略を防ぐ しんりゃくをふせぐ defend against an invasion

禦ぐ

[now replaced by 防ぐ] **ward off, prevent, keep off; defend, protect, resist**
侵略を禦ぐ しんりゃくをふせぐ defend against an invasion

伏せる
Ⓚ0030

① ⓐ **turn downward, lay upside down, turn over**
ⓑ **put something over (another)**
ⓒ **lay under the ground**
身を伏せる みをふせる lie face down
説き伏せる ときふせる argue down, persuade, convince
鶏に籠を伏せる にわとりにかごをふせる coop hens
待ち伏せる まちぶせる lie in wait, ambush, conceal oneself in ambush

② **keep secret**
伏せ字 ふせじ omission, blank, asterisk

臥せる
Ⓚ1307

① **lie down**

② **be confined to one's bed, be sick in bed**
風邪で臥っている かぜでふせっている be laid up with a cold

二
Ⓚ1688

[in compounds] **two**
二言 ふたこと two words; repetition
二人 ふたり two persons
二心 ふたごころ(=にしん) duplicity, double dealing; divided loyalty

双
Ⓚ0013

[in compounds] **set of two, pair**
双子 ふたご twins
双葉 ふたば bud, cotyledon

太る
Ⓚ1846

[sometimes also 肥る] **grow fat, fatten, gain weight**
太った ふとった fat, stout, plump

肥る
Ⓚ0783

[usu. 太る] **grow fat, fatten, gain weight**
肥った ふとった fat, stout, plump

船-
Ⓚ1229

[also 舟-] [also prefix] **ship**
船乗り ふなのり sailor, seaman
船旅 ふなたび voyage

船便 ふなびん surface [sea] mail; shipping service
船火事 ふなかじ fire on a ship

舟- Ⓚ2965

[also 船-] [also prefix] **small boat**
舟着き場 ふなつきば wharf
舟人 ふなびと sailor
舟大工 ふなだいく boatbuilder

560 ふね

船 Ⓚ1229

① **ship, boat, vessel, seacraft**
船に乗る ふねにのる board a ship
② [also 槽] **tub, tank, vessel**
湯船 ゆぶね bathtub

舟 Ⓚ2965

small boat [craft], (row)boat
小舟 こぶね small craft

槽 Ⓚ0981

[also 船] **tub, tank, vessel**
湯槽 ゆぶね bathtub

561 ふやす

増やす Ⓚ0619

vt **(cause to grow in number or quantity) increase, add**
人手を増やす ひとでをふやす add to the staff

殖やす Ⓚ0907

vt **(cause to multiply of its own accord) multiply, increase, propagate, augment**—said esp. of wealth or living things
貯金を殖やす ちょきんをふやす increase one's savings
家畜を殖やす かちくをふやす breed cattle

562 ふるう

振るう Ⓚ0388

①ⓐ [formerly also 揮う] **wield, brandish, manipulate, master**
ⓑ **wield (authority), exercise, exhibit (one's powers)**
ⓒ **shake**
槍を振るう やりをふるう wield a spear
腕を振るう うでをふるう display one's ability, exercise one's talent
振るい落とす ふるいおとす shake off
②ⓐ **be in high spirits, be invigorated**
ⓑ **flourish, thrive, be prosperous**
軍の士気が振るう ぐんのしきがふるう The morale of the army is high
振るわない ふるわない be dull, be in a bad way
振るった ふるった original, striking, extraordinary

揮う Ⓚ0538

[now usu. 振るう] **wield, brandish, manipulate, master**
筆を揮う ふでをふるう drive a quill [pen], wield the writing brush

震う K2443
tremble, quiver, shudder
> 震い ふるい trembling, shaking, shivering
> 身震い みぶるい shivering

奮う K2090
rouse up, rouse oneself, arouse
> 奮って ふるって with energy, strenuously; heartily, willingly
> 勇気を奮い起こす ゆうきをふるいおこす muster up one's courage

-船 K1229
[also -舟] [also suffix] **ship, vessel**
> 助け船 たすけぶね lifeboat; help
> 乗り合い船 のりあいぶね ferryboat

-舟 K2965
[also -船] [also suffix] **small boat**
> 釣り舟 つりぶね fishing boat
> 渡し舟 わたしぶね ferryboat

遜る K2786
[also 謙る] **be humble, be modest**

謙る K1461
[also 遜る] **be humble, be modest**

火- K2911
[also 灯-] **fire**
> 火影(=灯影) ほかげ shadows from firelight
> 火照る ほてる feel hot, flush

灯- K0730
[also 火-] **fire**
> 灯影 ほかげ(=とうえい) firelight in the dark; shadows by the firelight

惚ける K0440
① ⓐ **grow senile**
  ⓑ **be mentally slow, be befuddled**
② [verbal suffix] **be engrossed in (doing something)**
> 遊び惚ける あそびほうける be absorbed in play; spend one's time in idle amusement

呆ける
① ⓐ **grow senile**
  ⓑ **be mentally slow, be befuddled**
② [verbal suffix] **be engrossed in (doing something)**
> 遊び呆ける あそびほうける be absorbed in play; spend one's time in idle amusement

放る K0754
[sometimes also 抛る] **throw, toss, fling, cast; throw up, neglect**

放り出す ほうりだす throw out; dismiss, expel

放って置く ほうっておく neglect, leave alone

放ったらかす ほったらかす neglect, let aside

抛る

ⓐ **toss, throw, fling, cast**
ⓑ **throw up, neglect**

外
Ⓚ0163

① [also 他] **something other than, the rest**

外の ほかの other, another, different, else

外ならぬ ほかならぬ nothing but, no other than

山田外 やまだほか Yamada and others [et al.]

② **some other place, outside**

外で ほかで elsewhere, somewhere else

外を探す ほかをさがす search somewhere else

③ **outside, beyond, besides; except, but**

恋は思案の外 こいはしあんのほか Love and reason do not go together

その外 そのほか besides, in addition; the rest, others

そうする外は無い そうするほかはない There is nothing for it but to do so

他
Ⓚ0023

[also 外] **something other than, the rest**

他の ほかの other, another, different, else

他ならぬ ほかならぬ nothing but, no other than

山田他 やまだほか Yamada and others [et al.]

矛
Ⓚ1732

ⓐ [sometimes also 鋒 or 戟] **ancient halberd or spear consisting of a long shaft and a double-edged blade**
ⓑ [formerly 戈] **arms**

矛先 ほこさき [sometimes also 鋒] spearhead; the aim (of an attack); the brunt (of an argument)

戟
Ⓚ1514

[usu. 矛, sometimes also 鋒] **halberd**

鉾

decorative halberd

山鉾 やまぼこ festival float mounted with a decorative halberd

蒲鉾 かまぼこ steamed fish paste

鋒
Ⓚ1545

[usu. 矛, sometimes also 戟] **halberd**

戈

[now usu. 矛] **arms**

戈を収める ほこをおさめる lay down arms, sheathe one's sword

570　ほしいまま

恣　　　Ⓚ2304

[sometimes also 擅] **self-indulgent, selfish; arbitrary**

擅

[usu. 恣] **self-indulgent, selfish; arbitrary**

571　ほす

干す　　　Ⓚ2863

① **dry (up), desiccate, air (clothes)**
干し物 ほしもの clothes for drying
物干し ものほし clotheshorse, clothes-drier
日干しの ひぼしの sun-dried
② [formerly also 乾す]
  ⓐ **draw off (liquids), drain off**
  ⓑ **drink up, drain dry**
  役を干される やくをほされる be deprived of one's role
  飲み干す のみほす drink up

乾す　　　Ⓚ1500

ⓐ **draw off (liquids), drain off**
ⓑ **drink up, drain dry**
池を乾す いけをほす drain off a pond
干乾し ひぼし starving
飲み乾す のみほす drink up

572　ほのお

炎　　　Ⓚ2145

ⓐ **flame, blaze**
ⓑ (figuratively) **flames (as of passion)**
炎を上げて燃える ほのおをあげてもえる flame up
嫉妬の炎 しっとのほのお flames of jealousy

焔　　　Ⓚ0908

ⓐ [now replaced by 炎] **flame, blaze**
ⓑ [now usu. 炎] (figuratively) **flames (as of passion)**
嫉妬の焔 しっとのほのお The Flames of Jealousy (movie title)

573　ほめる

褒める　　　Ⓚ1841

[sometimes also 誉める or 賞める] **praise, commend, admire, compliment, eulogize**
褒め称える ほめたたえる admire, applaud, praise

誉める　　　Ⓚ2193

[usu. 褒める, sometimes also 賞める] **praise, commend, admire, compliment, eulogize**
誉め称える ほめたたえる admire, applaud, praise

賞める　　　Ⓚ2274

[usu. 褒める, sometimes also 誉める] **praise, commend, admire, compliment, eulogize**
人の勤勉さを賞める ひとのきんべんさをほめる praise a person for his [her] diligence

堀 Ⓚ0423

① **ditch, canal**
堀川 ほりかわ canal
堀割り ほりわり canal, ditch
用水堀 ようすいぼり irrigation ditch
釣り堀 つりぼり fishing pond, fish-
pond
② [sometimes also 濠 or 壕] **moat**
堀端 ほりばた edge of the moat
外堀 そとぼり outer moat

濠

[usu. 堀, sometimes also 壕] **moat**
内濠 うちぼり inner moat

壕 Ⓚ0703

① [usu. 堀] **ditch, canal**
② [usu. 堀, sometimes also 濠] **moat**
外壕 そとぼり outer moat, castle
moat

掘る Ⓚ0454

ⓐ **dig, bore, excavate**
ⓑ **dig up, dig out, unearth**
掘り返す ほりかえす turn up (the soil),
tear up (a road)
掘り下げる ほりさげる dig down;
investigate, probe, delve into

彫る Ⓚ1503

ⓐ (cut so as to form designs or figures)
engrave, carve, chisel
ⓑ **tattoo**

彫り物 ほりもの carving; tattoo
木彫り きぼり woodcarving
浮き彫り うきぼり relief, embossed
carving

滅びる Ⓚ0606

[sometimes also 亡びる] **go to ruin, meet
with destruction, cease to exist; be
overthrown**
滅びて行く民族 ほろびていくみんぞ
く dying race

亡びる Ⓚ2874

[usu. 滅びる] **go to ruin, meet with
destruction, cease to exist; be
overthrown**
亡びて行く民族 ほろびていくみんぞ
く dying race

滅ぶ Ⓚ0606

[sometimes also 亡ぶ] **literary form of** 滅
びる ほろびる

亡ぶ Ⓚ2874

[usu. 滅ぶ] **literary form of** 亡びる ほ
ろびる

滅ぼす Ⓚ0606

[sometimes also 亡ぼす] **destroy, ruin,
annihilate; overthrow**
敵を滅ぼす てきをほろぼす destroy
the enemy

亡ぼす
Ⓚ2874

[usu. 滅ぼす] **destroy, ruin, annihilate; overthrow**

敵を亡ぼす てきをほろぼす destroy the enemy

579 ぼける

惚ける
Ⓚ0440

① ⓐ **grow senile**
   ⓑ **be mentally slow, be befuddled**

惚け防止 ぼけぼうし dementia prevention

惚け ぼけ being out of it, dementia, senility; idiot, fool; funny man (of a comedy duo)

寝惚ける ねぼける be half asleep, be half awake

時差惚け じさぼけ jet lag

② **be out of focus, become unclear [indistinct]**

古惚ける ふるぼける become old-looking, become worn out

呆ける

① ⓐ **grow senile**
   ⓑ **be mentally slow, be befuddled**

呆け ぼけ being out of it, dementia, senility; idiot, fool; funnyman (of a comedy duo)

② **be out of focus, become unclear [indistinct]**

古呆ける ふるぼける become old-looking, become worn out

580 まいない

賄
Ⓚ1390

ⓐ **bribe; bribery**
ⓑ [archaic] **offering, gift of gratitude**

賂
Ⓚ1389

ⓐ **bribe; bribery**
ⓑ [archaic] **offering, gift of gratitude**

581 まく¹

蒔く
Ⓚ2042

① [also 播く] **sow**
種を蒔く たねをまく sow seed

② **scatter (powder)**
蒔絵 まきえ (gold [silver]) lacquer(ing)
ばら蒔く ばらまく scatter; spend recklessly

撒く
Ⓚ0670

① **scatter, sprinkle**
撒き散らす まきちらす scatter, spread
撒き餌 まきえ scattered animal feed, ground bait
ばら撒き ばらまき scattering; spending recklessly
水撒き みずまき watering, sprinkling

② **give (someone) the slip**

播く
Ⓚ0669

[also 蒔く] **sow**
種を播く たねをまく sow seeds
粗播き あらまき sparse sowing [seeding]

582　まく²

巻く　　Ⓚ2298

[sometimes also 捲く] **roll up, roll; wind, reel; wrap**

巻き上げる まきあげる roll up; hoist, heave up; take away; blow up (dust)

巻き込む まきこむ roll (up), wrap; involve, drag in

巻き起こす まきおこす create (a sensation); give rise to

巻き付ける まきつける wind or tie around, coil

巻き返し作戦 まきかえしさくせん rollback operation

巻き添え まきぞえ involvement, entanglement

渦巻き うずまき eddy, whirlpool; coil

捲く　　Ⓚ0451

[usu. 巻く] **roll up, roll; wind, reel; wrap**

捲き上げる まきあげる roll up, hoist, heave up; take away; blow up (dust)

捲き線 まきせん coil, winding

高捲き たかまき detour (in gorge-climbing)

583　まこと

誠　　Ⓚ1382

① **sincerity, true heart, honesty, fidelity**

誠を尽くす まことをつくす do with sincerity

② [sometimes also 実 or 真] **truth, reality**

誠の まことの true, genuine

誠に まことに truly, really; very, extremely

誠しやかに まことしやかに plausibly, with seeming truth

嘘か誠か うそかまことか true or false

実　　Ⓚ1911

[usu. 誠, sometimes also 真] **truth, reality**

実の心 まことのこころ one's real intention

実しやかに まことしやかに plausibly, as if it were true

真　　Ⓚ1813

[usu. 誠, sometimes also 実] **truth, reality**

真に まことに truly, really; very, extremely

嘘か真か うそかまことか true or false

584　まさに

正に　　Ⓚ2926

just, exactly; surely, certainly; really

正に春だ まさにはるだ Spring is really here

当に　　Ⓚ1865

[always followed by 可し べし] **properly, naturally; it is proper to, ought to**

当に人類を救う可き時だ まさにじんるいをすくうべきときだ Now is the time to save the human race

将に　　Ⓚ0415

be about to, on the verge of

将に滅びんとしている まさにほろびんとしている be on the brink of ruin

585　まさる

勝る　Ⓚ0918

[sometimes also 優る] **excel, be better than, surpass**
男勝りの おとこまさりの (of a woman) strong-minded, spirited
全てに於て勝る すべてにおいてまさる excel in every respect

優る　Ⓚ0156

[usu. 勝る] **excel, be better than, surpass**
優るとも劣らない まさるともおとらない not at all inferior to

586　まざる

混ざる　Ⓚ0475

same as 混じる **まじる**
混ざり物 まざりもの impurity

交ざる　Ⓚ1738

same as 交じる **まじる**
英語が交ざった文 えいごがまざったぶん writing interspersed with English

587　まじる

混じる　Ⓚ0475

vi **be blended, get mixed (with the constituents blending into each other)**
混じり合う まじりあう be blended, be mixed together
混じり気 まじりけ a dash of (something), impurity

交じる　Ⓚ1738

vi **be mingled, be mixed, intermingle (with the constituents remaining distinct)**
白髪交じりの髪 しらがまじりのかみ grizzly hair
子供に交じって遊ぶ こどもにまじってあそぶ join children at play
★ 混じる and 交じる are often used interchangeably.

588　ます¹

増す　Ⓚ0619

[sometimes also 益す] *vi* & *vt* **increase, augment, multiply**
増し刷り ましずり additional printing, reprinting
信用が増す しんようがます gain more confidence

益す　Ⓚ1978

[usu. 増す] *vi* & *vt* **increase, augment, multiply**
益益 ますます increasingly

589　ます²

升　Ⓚ2906

①ⓐ **measure, measuring box**
ⓑ **box (seat)**
升目 ますめ measure; square (of graph paper)

五升升 ごしょうます 5-*sho* measure

② **square (as of graph paper)**

升形 ますがた square (shape)

枡

①ⓐ **measure, measuring box**
　ⓑ **box (seat)**

枡目 ますめ measure; square (of
　graph paper)

五升枡 ごしょうます 5-*sho* measure

② **square (as of graph paper)**

枡形 ますがた square (shape)

590　　　まぜる

混ぜる
Ⓚ0475

ⓐ (combine together into a single mass)
　blend, mix, adulterate

ⓑ **mix by stirring, scramble, toss,
　churn**

混ぜ合わす まぜあわす mix together;
　blend, compound

混ぜ返す まぜかえす banter, make
　fun of (what a person says)

搔き混ぜる (=搔き交ぜる) かきまぜる
　mix by stirring, mix up, scramble,
　toss, churn

交ぜる
Ⓚ1738

vt **(combine together, with the constituents remaining distinct) mix,
shuffle**

交ぜ織り まぜおり mixed weave

ない交ぜ ないまぜ intertwinement,
　blend

591　　　また¹

股
Ⓚ0785

ⓐ **crotch (of the human body), inner
thigh**

ⓑ [sometimes also 叉 or 俣] (place of
furcation) **crotch (of a tree), fork (of
a road)**

股下 またした length of the legs,
　inseam

股旅 またたび wandering life of a
　gambler

股に掛ける またにかける travel all
　over, be active in places widely
　apart

内股 うちまた inside of a thigh;
　pigeon-toe; throwing down the
　opponent with one's leg between
　his [her] legs (in judo)

大股 おおまた straddle; long stride;
　thigh-scooping body drop (in
　sumo)

二股 ふたまた bifurcation; *slang* two-
　timing

三股 さんまた forked stick

俣
Ⓚ0081

[usu. 股, sometimes also 叉] [in compounds]
**bifurcation, fork (as of a body of
water)**

二俣 ふたまた bifurcation; *slang* two-
　timing

水俣病 みなまたびょう Minamata
　disease

叉
Ⓚ2870

[usu. 股, sometimes also 俣] (place of
furcation) **crotch (of a tree), fork (of
a road)**

木の又 きのまた crotch of a tree
二又 ふたまた bifurcation; *slang* two-timing
三つ又 みつまた three-pronged fork, trident, trifurcation

592 また²

又 ⓚ2853

① [formerly also 復] **again, once more [again], repeatedly**
又会う日迄 またあうひまで till we meet again
又しても またしても once again

② [formerly also 亦] [often preceded by も] **also, too, as well**
私も又 わたくしもまた I also, me too
それも又結構だ それもまたけっこうだ That's also good

③ⓐ **and, besides, further**
ⓑ **on the other hand**
ⓒ [often followed by particle は] **or, in other words**
勝利又勝利 しょうりまたしょうり victory after victory
夫は病弱だが妻は又元気が良い おっとはびょうじゃくだがつまはまたげんきがよい The husband is invalid, while the wife is robust
又は または or, in other words
言っても良いし、又言わなくても良い いってもよいし、またいわなくてもよい You can either say it or not say it

④ **adverb expressing surprise or doubt**
これは又何の騒ぎだ これはまたなんのさわぎだ Well, what's this row?
そりゃ又酷い話だ そりゃまたひどいはなしだ What a shame!

亦 ⓚ1734

[now usu. 又] [often preceded by も] **also, too, as well**
彼も亦良い人だ かれもまたいいひとだ He is a nice man, too
私も亦 わたしもまた I also, me too

復 ⓚ0527

[now replaced by 又] **again, once more [again], repeatedly**
復いらっしゃい またいらっしゃい Call again!

593 まち

町 ⓚ1028

① [also suffix]
ⓐ **town**
ⓑ (unit of local administration) **town**
ⓒ **suffix after names of towns**
町へ行く まちへいく go to town
町工場 まちこうば town factory
町外れ まちはずれ outskirts of a town
港町 みなとまち port town
温泉町 おんせんまち spa town, hot spring resort
町役場 まちやくば town office
水上町 みなかみまち town of Minakami

②ⓐ (subdivision in the Japanese addressing system) *machi*, **town section**
ⓑ **suffix after names of town sections** (*machi*)
信濃町 しなのまち Shinanomachi

③ [usu. 街] **(busy) city quarter(s), city streets**
町筋 まちすじ street
町並み まちなみ rows of stores and houses on a street

まち

下町 したまち (downtown) business
quarters, old part of Tokyo

街 Ⓚ0528

(busy) city quarter(s), city streets
街の女 まちのおんな streetwalker
街角(=町角) まちかど street corner
街着 まちぎ street clothes
商人街 しょうにんまち business street
北野街 きたのまち Kitano shopping
center

594　　まつる

祭る Ⓚ2329

ⓐ **worship as god, deify**
ⓑ **enshrine**
先祖を祭る せんぞをまつる worship
one's ancestors

祀る

ⓐ **worship as god, deify**
ⓑ **enshrine**
先祖を祀る せんぞをまつる worship
one's ancestors

595　　まもる

守る Ⓚ1861

① [formerly also 護る] **protect, defend,
guard, watch over**
身を守る みをまもる defend oneself
見守る みまもる watch, keep watch
over
②ⓐ **observe, obey, keep to, abide by**
ⓑ **adhere to**
ⓒ **keep (a promise), fulfill**

規則を守る きそくをまもる keep to
the regulations

護る Ⓚ1481

[now usu. 守る] **protect, defend, guard,
watch over**
身を護る みをまもる defend oneself

596　　まり

鞠 Ⓚ1602

[also 毬] **ball**
鞠靴 まりぐつ ancient football shoes
鞠突き まりつき ball-bouncing game
蹴鞠 けまり ancient football game

毬 Ⓚ2773

[also 鞠] **ball**
毬歌 まりうた (children's) handball
song

597　　まる

丸 Ⓚ2883

①ⓐ **round or spherical shape**
　ⓑ [sometimes also 円] **circle**
日の丸 ひのまる Rising Sun Flag
② **wholeness, completeness**
丸の儘 まるのまま whole, in its
entirety
丸で まるで just like; completely,
perfectly
③ [also ○] **check mark for correct
answers (similar to ✓)**
丸を付ける まるをつける mark a
correct answer with a circle
④ **small circle corresponding to a
period in a sentence**

⑤ **within the castle walls**

二の丸 にのまる outworks of a castle

本丸 ほんまる **keep of a castle, donjon**

円 Ⓚ2555

① [usu. 丸] **circle**

② *slang* **money, dough**—used in telegrams

○

① **zero (the numeral)**

② [also 丸] **check mark for correct answers (similar to ✓)**

③ **indicates omitted or unprintable letters [characters]**

丸い Ⓚ2883

① ⓐ (shaped like a ball) **round, spherical**

ⓑ [also 円い] (shaped like a circle) **round, circular**

丸み まるみ **roundness**

背が丸い せがまるい **round-backed**

丸くなって まるくなって **in a circle [ring]**

② **rounded, amicable, harmonious**

丸く治まる まるくおさまる **become reconciled, settle peacefully**

円い Ⓚ2555

[also 丸い] (shaped like a circle) **circular, round**

円さ まるさ **roundness**

円く輪になって踊る まるくわになっておどる **dance in a circle**

希な Ⓚ1763

[usu. 稀な] **rare, uncommon, scarce, unique**

稀な Ⓚ1099

[sometimes also 希な] **rare, uncommon, scarce, unique**

回す Ⓚ2630

① **turn (round), rotate**

独楽を回す こまをまわす **spin a top**

② ⓐ **send [pass] around, circulate; forward, transfer**

ⓑ **send round, forward, transfer**

回し まわし **sumo wrestler's loincloth; gang rape**

塩を回して下さい しおをまわしてください **Pass me the salt, please**

③ **lend money at interest**

金を上手く回す かねをうまくまわす **invest one's money profitably**

④ **arrange, prepare**

手回し てまわし **preparations**

⑤ **perform gang rape**

廻す Ⓚ2660

① **turn (round), rotate**

② ⓐ **send [pass] around, circulate; forward, transfer**

③ **lend money at interest**

④ **arrange, prepare**

⑤ **perform gang rape**

回り Ⓚ2630

① ⓐ **indicates direction of turning**
　ⓑ **counter for rounds**
　時計回りの とけいまわりの clockwise
　西回り にしまわり west circuit
　三回り みまわり three rounds

② **a size (larger or smaller)**
　一回り小さな ひとまわりちいさな a
　　size smaller

③ **via, by way of**
　欧州回りで合衆国へ行く おうしゅう
　　まわりでがっしゅうこくへいく go to
　　the U.S. via Europe

④ **cycle of 12 years**
　彼は私より一回り若い かれはわたく
　　しよりひとまわりわかい He is my
　　junior by 12 years

⑤ **girth, circumference**
　胴回り どうまわり girth

廻り Ⓚ2660

[now usu. 回り] **same as** 回り

周り Ⓚ2585

ⓐ **periphery, surroundings, circumference**
ⓑ **border, fringe**
　周りの人 まわりのひと surrounding
　　people
　地球の周り ちきゅうのまわり cir-
　　cumference of the earth; space
　　around the earth
　池の周りを一回りする いけのまわり
　　をひとまわりする go round a pond

回る Ⓚ2630

① ⓐ **turn round, revolve, rotate**
　ⓑ **go round, circulate, make a
　round**
　ⓒ **detour, go round (to)**
　回り まわり rotation; detour; close
　　surroundings; spreading (of
　　flames); efficacy
　回り舞台 まわりぶたい rotative stage
　見回る みまわる make one's rounds
　回りくどい まわりくどい roundabout,
　　circuitous, indirect
　回り道 まわりみち roundabout [long]
　　way, detour

② **swing over to, come round to, be
transferred**
　反対に回る はんたいにまわる go into
　　opposition

③ **be past (a certain hour)**
　もう十一時を回った もうじゅういちじ
　　をまわった It is already past 11

④ **pass (from hand to hand), circulate, spread; take effect**
　火が回る ひがまわる Fire spreads
　酔いが回る よいがまわる get drunk,
　　become tipsy

⑤ **yield interest**
　利回り りまわり (investment) yield,
　　interest, profits

廻る Ⓚ2660

① ⓐ **turn round, revolve, rotate**
　ⓑ **go round, circulate, make a
　round**
　ⓒ **detour, go round (to)**

廻り まわり rotation; detour; close surroundings; spreading (of flames); efficacy
② **swing over to, come round to, be transferred**
③ **be past (a certain hour)**
④ **pass (from hand to hand), circulate, spread; take effect**
⑤ **yield interest**

603　みえ

見え　　Ⓚ2201

① **appearance**
② [usu. 見栄] **show, ostentation, vanity**
③ [usu. 見得] **pose, posture**

見栄　　Ⓚ2201

[sometimes also 見え] **show, ostentation, vanity**

見得　　Ⓚ2201

[sometimes also 見え] **pose, posture**

604　みず

水　　Ⓚ0003

① ⓐ **water, cold water**
　　ⓑ [in compounds] **liquid, watery**
　水洗い みずあらい washing with water
　水着 みずぎ bathing [swimming] suit
　水色 みずいろ sky blue, turquoise
　雨水 あまみず rainwater
　水飴 みずあめ starch syrup
② *sumo* **break**
　水入りの相撲 みずいりのすもう sumo match with a break

③ **damper, wet blanket, barrier**
　水を注す みずをさす pour water (into); estrange (people); throw cold water
　水入らずで みずいらずで by ourselves [themselves]

瑞-　　Ⓚ0943

young and fresh, vigorous
　瑞瑞しい みずみずしい young and fresh, fresh-looking, juicy
　瑞穂の国 みずほのくに Land of Vigorous Rice Plants, Japan

605　みたす

満たす　　Ⓚ0553

① **fill (up), pack**
　水を満たす みずをみたす fill (a glass) with water
② **fill, fulfill, satisfy, meet (the demand)**
　腹を満たす はらをみたす satisfy one's appetite
　条件を満たす じょうけんをみたす answer the requirement

充たす　　Ⓚ1737

① **fill (up), pack**
　コップを充たす こっぷをみたす fill a glass
② **fill, fulfill, satisfy, meet (the demand)**
　条件を充たす じょうけんをみたす answer the requirement

606 みち

道 ⓚ2701

① ⓐ [formerly also 路] [also prefix and suffix] **way, road, path, street; highway, track**
 ⓑ (distance in general) **way, distance, journey**
 ⓒ **halfway**
 道端 みちばた roadside, wayside
 道順 みちじゅん route, itinerary
 道案内 みちあんない guiding, guide; guidepost
 道草を食う みちくさをくう loiter, dawdle; waste one's time on the way
 坂道 さかみち slope
 筋道 すじみち reason, thread (of an argument), coherence; systematic method, due formality
 散歩道 さんぽみち walk, promenade, esplanade
 五キロの道 ごきろのみち distance of five kilometers
 帰り道で かえりみちで on one's way home

② **way of doing, means, course of action**
 自活の道 じかつのみち independent living
 地道な じみちな steady, straight, fair
 使い道 つかいみち use, application

③ **the way of moral conduct, path of righteousness, moral principles, morality, right way of life**
 道ならぬ みちならぬ improper, illicit
 人たる道に背く ひとたるみちにそむく stray from the path of righteousness

④ **art, line (of work), career**

剣の道 けんのみち swordsmanship
歌の道 うたのみち art of tanka poetry
その道 そのみち the line (of business), the profession, the art, the field

路 ⓚ1394

[now usu. 道] **road, avenue, boulevard**
 町を貫く路 まちをつらぬくみち road passing through the town

607 みどり

緑 ⓚ1259

① **green; verdure**
 緑色 みどりいろ green
 緑に覆われた山 みどりにおおわれたやま mountain robed in verdure
 緑の黒髪 みどりのくろかみ glossy black hair (of a young woman)
 浅緑 あさみどり(=せんりょく) light green
② *elegant* **young leaves**

翠 ⓚ2361

① **green; verdure**
② *elegant* **young leaves**

608 みなと

港 ⓚ0552

[sometimes also 湊] **port, harbor**
 港町 みなとまち port town
 港祭り みなとまつり port festival

湊 ⓚ0557

[usu. 港] **port, harbor**

609 みね

峰   Ⓚ0372

① ⓐ (summit or vicinity of a summit) **peak, summit, ridge**
   ⓑ **high mountain**
   峰峰 みねみね peaks
   峰伝いに みねづたいに along the ridges
   峰続き みねつづき succession of peaks
② **back of a sword**
   峰打ち みねうち striking with the back of a sword

嶺   Ⓚ2102

① ⓐ (summit or vicinity of a summit) **peak, summit, ridge**
   ⓑ **high mountain**
② **back of a sword**

610 みのり

実り   Ⓚ1911

[sometimes also 稔り] **crop, ripening**

稔り   Ⓚ1115

[usu. 実り] **crop, ripening**

611 みのる

実る   Ⓚ1911

[sometimes also 稔る] **bear fruit, ripen**
   実り みのり crop, ripening
   実っている みのっている be in bearing
   実らなかった努力 みのらなかったどりょく fruitless [resultless] efforts

稔る   Ⓚ1115

[usu. 実る] **bear fruit, ripen**
   稔り みのり crop, ripening

612 みる

見る   Ⓚ2201

① ⓐ **see, look (at), have a look**
   ⓑ [sometimes also 観る] **view (flowers), watch (a movie), see, observe, appreciate**
   ⓒ **read (casually), skim through**
   見付ける みつける find (out), locate, spot, turn up
   見付かる みつかる be found (out), be discovered, come to light; be caught
   見出だす みいだす find out, discover
   見本 みほん sample, specimen
   見通し みとおし perspective, vista; prospect, outlook
   見合い みあい meeting with a view to marriage; looking at each other
   見当たる みあたる be found
   見事(=美事)な みごとな splendid, admirable, beautiful
   見送り みおくり seeing someone off
   見上げる みあげる look up (at); look up to, respect
   見下ろす みおろす look down; overlook
   見直す みなおす reconsider, review; change one's opinion for the better; have another look
   見比べる みくらべる compare (with one's eye), judge
   見習う みならう learn (by observation), follow someone's example
   見分け みわけ distinction; identification, recognition

見掛け みかけ looks, appearance

見渡す みわたす look out over

見落とす みおとす overlook, pass by; fail to notice

見詰める みつめる stare

見出し みだし headline, heading, caption; title; index

見舞い みまい inquiry (after a person's health); expression of sympathy; visit

見た目 みため outward appearance

見ず知らずの みずしらずの strange, unknown

見蕩れる みとれる be fascinated by, look admiringly at

見窄らしい みすぼらしい shabby, poor-looking, miserable

見す見す みすみす before one's very eyes

見る見る みるみる in a moment [instant]

見方 みかた (point of) view, way of looking, viewpoint

見所 みどころ good point, merit; highlight

見晴らす みはらす command a view, look out onto

余所見する よそみする look away, take one's eyes off

脇見 わきみ looking aside

花見 はなみ flower [cherry blossom] viewing

② [sometimes also 視る] **look over, examine; look up, refer to**

見積もり みつもり estimate, assessment

見極める みきわめる see through, discern; ascertain, grasp

見届ける みとどける make sure, see with one's own eyes

下見 したみ preliminary inspection; preview

書類を見る しょるいをみる examine papers

③ **take (for), regard (as), judge, estimate**

見なす みなす regard as, presume

見込み みこみ hope, promise; prospect, possibility

見限る みかぎる give up, abandon; desert

見縊る みくびる look down on, hold someone cheap

④ⓐ **attend (to), manage**
ⓑ [sometimes also 看る] **take care of, look after**

事務を見る じむをみる attend to business

面倒見が良い めんどうみがよい take good care of, be very helpful

⑤ **experience, undergo**

憂き目を見る うきめをみる have a bitter experience, have a hard time of it

血を見る争い ちをみるあらそい struggle with bloodshed

⑥ [following the TE-form of verbs]
ⓐ **try (doing something), do and see**
ⓑ [usu. in the form of 見ると] **upon doing, when (the action is achieved), once**

やって見る やってみる try (to do)

聞いて見ましょう きいてみましょう Let's ask (him)

知って見ると詰まらない しってみると つまらない When you know it, its charm is gone

視る   ⓚ0884

[usu. 見る] **look over, examine; look up, refer to**

診る   ⓚ1364

examine (a patient)
脈を診る みゃくをみる examine one's pulse

観る   ⓚ1659

[usu. 見る] **view (flowers), watch (a movie), see, observe, appreciate**
花を観る はなをみる view (cherry) blossoms

看る   ⓚ2771

[usu. 見る] **take care of, look after**
看取る みとる nurse, tend [care for] (the sick)

613   むくい

報い   ⓚ1515

ⓐ [formerly also 酬い] **recompense, return**
ⓑ **punishment, retribution**

酬い   ⓚ1399

[now usu. 報い] **recompense, return**

614   むくいる

報いる   ⓚ1515

① [formerly also 酬いる]
  ⓐ **requite, repay**
  ⓑ **recompense, reward**

報い むくい recompense, return; punishment, retribution
労に報いる ろうにむくいる recompense a person for his [her] labor
② **revenge oneself on, retaliate**

酬いる   ⓚ1399

ⓐ **requite, repay**
ⓑ **recompense, reward**
酬い むくい recompense, return
労に酬いる ろうにむくいる recompense a person for his [her] labor

615   むす

生す   ⓚ2933

[also 産す] **grow**
苔生した こけむした moss-grown, mossy

産す   ⓚ2812

[also 生す] **grow**
苔産した こけむした moss-grown, mossy

蒸す   ⓚ2043

① vt **steam, heat with steam; foment**
蒸し むし steaming
蒸し菓子 むしがし steamed cake
② vi **be sultry, be stuffy**
蒸し暑い むしあつい sultry, sweltering

616   むなしい

空しい   ⓚ1913

①ⓐ **empty, void**

ⓑ **vain, futile**

空しさ むなしさ emptiness, futility

空しい名声 むなしいめいせい empty name

努力も空しく どりょくもむなしく after efforts in vain

② **dead, lifeless**

空しくなる むなしくなる die, expire

虚しい　Ⓚ2778

①ⓐ **empty, void**
　ⓑ **vain, futile**

虚しさ むなしさ emptiness, futility

虚しい名声 むなしいめいせい empty name

努力も虚しく どりょくもむなしく after efforts in vain

② **dead, lifeless**

虚しくなる むなしくなる die, expire

617　むね

旨　Ⓚ1744

① **effect, purport**

その旨を書き送る そのむねをかきおくる write to (a person) to that effect

② **order**

③ [formerly also 宗] **principle, aim**

正確を旨とする せいかくをむねとする aim at accuracy

宗　Ⓚ1915

[now usu. 旨] **principle, aim**

618　むら

群　Ⓚ1400

ⓐ [in compounds] **group, crowd, flock**
ⓑ **counter for groups or flocks**

群雀 むらすずめ flock of sparrows

一群 ひとむら a flock, a bunch

叢　Ⓚ2277

ⓐ [in compounds] **group, crowd, flock**
ⓑ **counter for groups or flocks**

叢雲 むらくも cloud masses

竹叢(=篁) たかむら bamboo grove

稲叢 いなむら rick, stack (of rice straw)

草叢 くさむら [also 叢] grass, grassy place

一叢 ひとむら a copse; a crowd, a herd

619　むらがる

群がる　Ⓚ1400

[sometimes also 叢がる] **crowd together, throng, flock together, swarm**

蜂が群がる はちがむらがる be swarmed with bees

叢がる　Ⓚ2277

[usu. 群がる] **crowd together, throng, flock together, swarm**

蜂が叢がる はちがむらがる be swarmed with bees

雌‒

Ⓚ0971

ⓐ (of plants) **female**
ⓑ [sometimes also 牝‒] (of animals) **female**
ⓒ [also 女] **the weaker or smaller of two**
  雌花 めばな female flower
  雌蕊 めしべ pistil
  雌捻子(=雌螺子) めねじ female screw
  雌牛 めうし cow
  雌滝 めだき the smaller waterfall (of the two)

牝‒

[usu. 雌] (of animals) **female**
  牝牛 めうし cow
  牝鹿 めじか doe

女

Ⓚ2884

① *elegant* **the fair sex, woman, female**
  女神 めがみ goddess
  賤の女 しずのめ woman of lowly birth
② [in compounds] **the weaker or smaller of two**
  女々しい めめしい effeminate, unmanly
  女波 めなみ the smaller waves
  女滝(=雌滝) めだき the smaller waterfall (of the two)

目

Ⓚ2619

①ⓐ [sometimes also 眼] **eye; eyesight**
  ⓑ **looking, seeing, watching**
  ⓒ **look, stare, expression**
  ⓓ **point of view**
  目玉 めだま eyeball; loss leader (of merchandise)
  目先 めさき before one's eyes; near future; foresight; appearance
  目薬 めぐすり eye lotion, eyewash, eyedrops
  目覚める めざめる wake (up); come to one's senses; be awakened
  目覚ましい めざましい striking, remarkable, phenomenal; marvelous
  目覚まし時計 めざましどけい alarm clock
  目眩 めまい dizziness, giddiness
  目印 めじるし mark, sign, landmark
  目処 めど aim, goal; prospects, outlook
  お目に掛かる おめにかかる [humble] see, meet; have the honor of seeing
  目指す(=目差す) めざす aim for, have an eye on
  一目 ひとめ a look, a glimpse
  非難の目を向ける ひなんのめをむける turn a look of reproach
  外人の目から見ると がいじんのめからみると from a foreigner's point of view
②ⓐ **watchful eye, attention, notice**
  ⓑ **discerning eye, judgment, an eye for**
  目に触れる めにふれる catch the eye, attract attention
  目をくらます めをくらます blind the eyes of; deceive
  目立つ めだつ stand out, be conspicuous
  目が効く めがきく have an eye for
  大目に見る おおめにみる overlook
  素人目 しろうとめ untrained eye

③ **experience, treatment**

憂き目を見る うきめをみる have a bitter experience, have a hard time of it

酷い目に遇う ひどいめにあう have a bad time

④ (linear pattern) **texture, weave; grain (of wood); mesh (of a net)**

目の粗い めのあらい coarse (texture or grain)

編み目 あみめ stitch

網目 あみめ meshes (of a net)

⑤ **cross of a go board; territory (in a go game)**

相手の目 あいてのめ the opponent's territory

駄目 だめ *go* cross that does not constitute a territory; no good, useless; No!

⑥ **pip, spot (of dice);** [in compounds] **chances (of winning in dice or the like)**

裏目 うらめ the reverse side of a dice; disappointment

勝ち目 かちめ good chance of winning

⑦ **tooth (of a saw)**

目立て めたて setting of a saw

⑧ **graduations (of a scale)**

目盛り めもり division, scale, graduations

⑨ **eye (of a typhoon)**

台風の目 たいふうのめ eye of a typhoon

⑩ **weight**

目減り めべり loss of weight

目方 めかた weight

⑪ **unclassified compounds**

目安 めやす standard, criterion; aim

お目出度う おめでとう Congratulations!

眼 ⓚ1084

[usu. 目] **eye**

眼鏡 めがね(=がんきょう) glasses, spectacles; judgment, insight

芽 ⓚ1927

bud, sprout, germ

芽生える めばえる bud, sprout; begin

新芽 しんめ sprout, bud, shoot, ratoon

若芽 わかめ young bud

622　めす

雌 ⓚ0971

[sometimes also 牝] (of animals) **female**

雌の狐 めすのきつね vixen, bitch fox

雌犬 めすいぬ female dog, bitch

牝

[usu. 雌] (of animals) **female**

牝犬 めすいぬ female dog, bitch

623　めん

雌 ⓚ0971

[sometimes also 牝] (of animals) **female**

雌鳥(=雌鶏) めんどり hen

牝

[usu. 雌] (of animals) **female**

牝鳥(=牝鶏) めんどり hen

燃える
Ⓚ0995

ⓐ **burn, undergo combustion, blaze**
ⓑ **burn with emotion**

燃え尽きる **もえつきる** burn out [away], be burned up

燃え付く **もえつく** catch fire

萌える
Ⓚ1995

sprout, bud, burst into bud

萌え立つ **もえたつ** sprout, burst into leaf

萌黄色 **もえぎいろ** yellowish green

下萌え **したもえ** sprout of a plant shooting from under the soil

最も
Ⓚ2181

the most

最も重要な事 **もっともじゅうようなこと** the most important thing

尤も
Ⓚ2604

① **right, reasonable, natural**

尤もらしい **もっともらしい** plausible, specious

御尤も **ごもっとも** You are quite right

② **indeed, it is true; but**

尤も例外は有る **もっともれいがいはある** There are, indeed, some exceptions

弄ぶ
Ⓚ2129

① ⓐ **toy [fiddle] with (the hands)**
ⓑ **toy [trifle] with; do (with something) as one pleases**

髪を弄ぶ **かみをもてあそぶ** fiddle with one's hair

人の気持ちを弄ぶ **ひとのきもちをもてあそぶ** toy with people's feelings

② **take pleasure in, appreciate, enjoy as a diversion**

玩ぶ
Ⓚ0778

① ⓐ **toy [fiddle] with (something) with one's hands**
ⓑ **toy [trifle] with; do (with something) as one pleases**

髪を玩ぶ **かみをもてあそぶ** fiddle with one's hair

人の気持ちを玩ぶ **ひとのきもちをもてあそぶ** toy with people's feelings

② **take pleasure in, appreciate, enjoy as a diversion**

詩歌を玩ぶ **しいかをもてあそぶ** enjoy poetry

元
Ⓚ1690

① ⓐ **origin, beginning, genesis**
ⓑ [also suffix] **place of origin, source**
ⓒ **one's origin, one's antecedents, one's past**
ⓓ (something that brings about a result) **origin, cause**

元は **もとは** originally

元元 もともと originally, from the first [outset]; by nature

火の元 ひのもと origin of a fire

製造元 せいぞうもと manufacturer

ガスの元栓を切る がすのもとせんを きる turn the gas off at the main

地元民 じもとみん local people

身元(=身許) みもと one's birth, one's identity, one's background

元を糾す もとをただす inquire into the origin, go to the bottom of an affair

② [also prefix] **former, ex-, one-time, past**

元首相 もとしゅしょう ex-Prime Minister

元の通り もとのとおり as it was before

③ **capital, principal; prime cost**

元手 もとで capital, fund

元が掛かる もとがかかる cost much, be expensive

元を切って売る もとをきってうる sell at a loss, sell under prime cost

④ [formerly also 許] **in the vicinity of, near (a person), with (someone), under (someone's roof)**

⑤ [sometimes also 素] **raw material, base**

本 ⓚ2937

① (the most important thing) **basis, essential thing, principle**

国の本 くにのもと foundation of the country, national principles

②ⓐ **root (of a tree)**
ⓑ **counter for plants with roots**

木の本に きのもとに at the root of a tree

一本の草 ひともとのくさ a blade of grass

③ **first half of a tanka poem**

基 ⓚ2330

(underlying support) **basis, foundation, grounds, authority**

基づく もとづく be based on, be grounded on; originate, be due to

資料を基にする しりょうをもとにする on the basis [grounds] of the data

下 ⓚ2862

① **lower part, bottom**

木の下に きのもとに under a tree

② [in the form of 下に もとに] (subject to the influence of) **under (the supervision of)**

ナポレオンの指揮の下に なぽれおんのしきのもとに under the command of Napoleon

一撃の下に いちげきのもとに by a single blow

許 ⓚ1337

[now usu. 元] **in the vicinity of, near (a person), with (someone), under (someone's roof)**

手許 てもと at hand, within reach; cash at hand

国許 くにもと one's home, one's birthplace

父母の許 ふぼのもと under one's parents' roof

素 ⓚ2171

[now usu. 元] **raw material, base**

味の素 あじのもと AJINOMOTO
(registered trademark)
スープの素 すーぷのもと soup stock

628　もの

物　　　　　　　　　Ⓚ0777

① ⓐ [also suffix] (inanimate material entity) **thing, object, article, something**
ⓑ [also suffix] **commodity, goods, product**
ⓒ **possession, property**
物置き ものおき storeroom
物陰 ものかげ place behind something
建物 たてもの building, structure
品物 しなもの article, thing, goods
本物 ほんもの real thing [stuff], genuine article; expert performance
その物 そのもの the very thing, the thing itself
贈り物 おくりもの present, gift
織物 おりもの cloth, textile, fabric
読み物 よみもの reading matter, book
洗濯物 せんたくもの wash, washing, laundry
売り物 うりもの article for sale, offerings
近海物 きんかいもの shorefish, inshore catch
ハウス物 はうすもの vegetables grown in a hothouse
学校の物 がっこうのもの school property

② [also suffix] **thing(s), matter, something, act**
物語 ものがたり story, tale, legend
物語る ものがたる tell a story; demonstrate, prove

物事 ものごと things, matter; everything
物知り ものしり well-informed person, walking dictionary
物思い ものおもい reverie, meditation, anxiety
笑い物 わらいもの object of ridicule, subject of derision
催し物 もよおしもの (program of) entertainments, amusements
買い物 かいもの shopping, marketing; purchase
捕り物 とりもの capture, arrest
噴飯物 ふんぱんもの something that makes one laugh, quite absurd thing

③ **something, somebody, a success**
物に成る ものになる come to good, prove successful
物の数に入らない もののかずにいらない be insignificant, be off the map
物ともせずに ものともせずに in defiance of, in the face of
大物 おおもの great man, big shot

④ **reason, sense**
物の分かった もののわかった sensible, fair-minded
物心 ものごころ judgment, discretion

者　　　　　　　　　Ⓚ2765

person, fellow, somebody
若者 わかもの young person [fellow], youth
怠け者 なまけもの idle [lazy] fellow
悪者 わるもの bad fellow, ruffian

629　もり

森
Ⓚ2184

[sometimes also 杜] **thick woods, forest**

森の都 もりのみやこ tree-clad town

鎮守の森 ちんじゅのもり grove of the
village shrine

杜
Ⓚ0739

[usu. 森] **grove, small woods (esp. surrounding temples or shrines)**

鎮守の杜 ちんじゅのもり grove of the
village shrine

630　や¹

屋
Ⓚ2669

① [in compounds] **house, dwelling
house**

屋敷 やしき [sometimes also 邸] mansion, residence; residential lot

小屋 こや cottage, hut, cabin; playhouse

部屋 へや room, chamber

母屋(=母家) おもや main house
[wing]

馬屋 うまや [also 厩] horse stable,
horse barn

② [in compounds] **roof**

屋根 やね roof

岩屋 いわや [also 窟] cave, cavern,
hole

③ⓐ [also suffix] **small shop or place of
business, store**

　ⓑ [suffix] **shopkeeper, dealer**

　ⓒ **suffix for forming names of
business establishments**

屋台 やたい stall, stand; float, festival
car

店屋 みせや shop, store

料理屋 りょうりや restaurant

魚屋 さかなや fish shop; fish dealer

花屋 はなや flower shop; florist

本屋 ほんや bookstore; bookseller

不動産屋 ふどうさんや real estate
agent, Realtor

松坂屋 まつざかや Matsuzakaya
Department Store

④ **colloquial occupation suffix—**
sometimes indicates slight contempt or
humility

事務屋 じむや clerk, office worker

何でも屋 なんでもや jack-of-all-
trades

⑤ **colloquial suffix indicating the
peculiarity or idiosyncrasy of a
person**

気取り屋 きどりや affected person,
snob

分からず屋 わからずや obstinate
person, hardhead

恥ずかしがり屋 はずかしがりや shy
person

⑥ [sometimes also 家] **suffix after stage
family names**

音羽屋 おとわや Otowaya (stage
name of a kabuki family)

家
Ⓚ1963

① [also suffix] **house, home**

家主 やぬし house owner, landlord,
landlady

家賃 やちん (house) rent

我が家 わがや one's home [house]

借家 しゃくや house for rent, rented
house

一軒家 いっけんや solitary house;
private home

② [usu. 屋] **suffix after stage family names**
林家正蔵 はやしやしょうぞう Shozo Hayashiya (name of a comic story teller)

★ Both 屋 and 家 refer to a house or dwelling, but they are not used interchangeably in the same compounds.

631 や²

也 Ⓚ2878

[also 哉 or 耶] *classical particle* **rhetorical or interrogative particle like modern か**
これは何ぞ也 これはなんぞや What can this be?

哉 Ⓚ2807

[also 也 or 耶] **classical interrogative or rhetorical particle like modern か**
君迷える哉 きみまよえるや Did you lose your way?

耶 Ⓚ1179

[also 哉 or 也] **classical rhetorical or exclamatory particle**
安ぞ敢えて毒とせん耶 いずくんぞあえてどくとせんや How dare you regard it as poison?

632 やく

焼く Ⓚ0909

① ⓐ [sometimes also 灼く] **burn, set on fire, incinerate; scorch; cauterize**
ⓑ **bake (pottery), fire**
ⓒ **cremate**

炭焼き すみやき charcoal making
焼き物 やきもの pottery, porcelain, earthenware
焼き場 やきば crematory

② **cook by fire: bake, roast, broil, grill, toast**
焼き網 やきあみ toasting grill, broiling grill

③ [sometimes also 妬く] **burn with jealousy, be envious**
焼き餅 やきもち roasted rice cake; jealousy

④ **print (photos)**
焼き付け やきつけ printing (photos)
焼き増し やきまし extra prints

⑤ **take the trouble to do something**
余計な世話を焼く よけいなせわをやく poke one's nose (in) where one is not wanted

妬く Ⓚ0254

[usu. 焼く] **burn with jealousy, be envious**
焼き餅を妬く やきもちをやく be jealous

灼く Ⓚ0741

[usu. 焼く] **scorch, burn; cauterize**

633 やける

焼ける Ⓚ0909

① ⓐ **burn, be burnt, be destroyed by fire; be scorched**
ⓑ (of the sky) **glow, burn**
焼け跡 やけあと ruins of fire
日焼け ひやけ suntan
夕焼け ゆうやけ sunset glow

229

② be cooked by fire: **be baked, be roasted, be broiled, be toasted**
良く焼けた よくやけた well done, done brown
③ [sometimes also 妬ける] **be jealous, burn with jealousy**
焼けて堪まらない やけてたまらない How I envy him!
④ **have heartburn**
胸焼け むねやけ heartburn, sour stomach
⑤ **be subjected to (the trouble of doing something for someone)**
世話の焼ける せわのやける troublesome, annoying

妬ける Ⓚ0254
[usu. 焼ける] **be jealous, burn with jealousy**

優しい Ⓚ0156
①ⓐ **gentle, tender, sweet**
ⓑ **kindhearted, kind**
優男 やさおとこ man of gentle manners
優しい声 やさしいこえ soft voice
優しくする やさしくする be kind to, treat kindly
② **graceful, delicate**

易しい Ⓚ2135
easy, simple
易しさ やさしさ easiness
易しい文章 やさしいぶんしょう easy [simple] writing

邸 Ⓚ1045
[now usu. 屋敷] **mansion, residence**

屋敷 Ⓚ2669
① [sometimes also 邸] **mansion, residence**
② **residential lot**

安い Ⓚ1859
① **inexpensive, cheap, low-priced**
安く やすく inexpensively
安値 やすね low price
安物 やすもの cheap article, bargain
安売り やすうり bargain sale
安っぽい やすっぽい cheapish, flashy
じり安 じりやす gradual decline of stock prices
② **peaceful, quiet, tranquil**
安んじる やすんじる feel at ease, ease a person's mind
安らぎ やすらぎ peace of mind
気安い きやすい friendly

易い Ⓚ2135
ⓐ **easy, simple**
ⓑ [verbal suffix] **easy (to do)**
易易と やすやすと easily, without difficulty
お易い御用 おやすいごよう easy request
壊れ易い こわれやすい break easily, fragile
分かり易い わかりやすい easy to understand

637　やすまる

休まる　Ⓚ0037

[sometimes also 安まる] **feel rested; be set at ease**
体が休まる からだがやすまる be [feel] rested

安まる　Ⓚ1859

[usu. 休まる] **feel rested; be set at ease**
心の安まる時が無い こころのやすまるときがない have no moment of ease

638　やとい

雇　Ⓚ1706

[also 傭] **government employee**

傭　Ⓚ0139

[also 雇] **government employee**

639　やとう

雇う　Ⓚ1706

ⓐ **employ, engage**
ⓑ **hire (as a boat), charter**
雇い やとい employee; employment
雇(=傭) やとい government employee
雇い入れる やといいれる employ, engage
雇い口 やといぐち employment, job
日雇い ひやとい daily employment; day laborer
船を雇う ふねをやとう hire a boat

傭う　Ⓚ0139

ⓐ **hire, employ**
ⓑ **hire (as a boat), charter**
傭い(=雇) やとい employee, government employee; employment

640　やぶれる

破れる　Ⓚ1064

① **tear, be torn, rip open**
破れ目 やぶれめ rent, tear, split
② **be ruined**
国破れて くにやぶれて with one's country in ruins
③ **be baffled, be frustrated**
破れた夢 やぶれたゆめ shattered dream

敗れる　Ⓚ1342

be defeated, be beaten, lose
試合に敗れる しあいにやぶれる lose a game

641　やむ

止む　Ⓚ2545

①ⓐ [sometimes also 已む] **stop, cease, come to an end**
ⓑ **abate, die away**
嵐が止んだ あらしがやんだ The storm has calmed down
② [also 已む] **cease, discontinue; not do**
止むを得ない やむをえない unavoidable, cannot be helped

已む Ⓚ2861

ⓐ [also 止む] (bring to an end) **cease, discontinue; not do**

ⓑ [usu. 止む] (come to an end) **cease, stop**

已むを得ない やむをえない unavoidable, cannot be helped

已む無く やむなく unavoidably, out of necessity

已むに已まれぬ事情 やむにやまれぬ じじょう circumstances beyond one's control

已んぬる哉 やんぬるかな I give up!

死して後已む ししてのちやむ I am determined to do or die

642　　　やめる

辞める Ⓚ1245

resign, retire, quit

会社を辞める かいしゃをやめる leave the company

罷める Ⓚ2272

[in the form of 罷めさせる やめさせる] **fire, discharge**

罷めさせる やめさせる fire, discharge

止める Ⓚ2545

①ⓐ **stop (performing an action), cease, discontinue**

ⓑ **give up, abandon, quit**

仕事を止める しごとをやめる stop [leave off] work

止めになる やめになる be discontinued, be given up

取り止める とりやめる cancel, call off

煙草を止める たばこをやめる give up smoking

② **abolish, do away with**

已める Ⓚ2861

①ⓐ **stop (performing an action), cease, discontinue**

ⓑ **give up, abandon, quit**

② **abolish, do away with**

643　　　やわらか

柔らかな Ⓚ1797

① **soft, tender**

柔らかみ やわらかみ (touch of) softness

② **soft, subdued (color or light)**

柔らかな光 やわらかなひかり soft light

③ **gentle, meek, mild**

柔らかな風 やわらかなかぜ gentle breeze

お手柔らかに おてやわらかに gently, mildly; Don't be hard on me!

軟らかな Ⓚ1345

① **soft, tender**

軟らかな土 やわらかなつち soft earth

② **soft, subdued (color or light)**

軟らかな光 やわらかなひかり soft light

③ **gentle, meek, mild**

軟らかな風 やわらかなかぜ gentle breeze

644 やわらかい

柔らかい   Ⓚ1797

① **soft, tender**
　柔らかい毛布 やわらかいもうふ soft blanket

② **gentle, meek**
　物腰の柔らかい ものごしのやわらかい gentle-mannered

③ **informal**
　柔らかい文章 やわらかいぶんしょう informal style

軟らかい   Ⓚ1345

① **soft, tender**
　軟らかい若葉 やわらかいわかば soft young leaf

② **gentle, meek**
　軟らかく話す やわらかくはなす speak gently

③ **informal**
　軟らかい文章 やわらかいぶんしょう informal style

645 ゆく

行く   Ⓚ0187

literary form of 行く **いく**
　行き帰り ゆきかえり going and returning, both ways
　行方 ゆくえ one's whereabouts

逝く   Ⓚ2673

depart this life, pass away, die

646 ゆるむ

緩む   Ⓚ1272

[sometimes also 弛む] vi **slack(en), loosen, relax; be assuaged, abate, moderate, ease off**
　緩み ゆるみ slackness, looseness; slack
　結び目が緩む むすびめがゆるむ A knot comes loose
　気が緩んで きがゆるんで in lack of vigilance

弛む   Ⓚ0186

ⓐ **slacken, slack, loosen, relax**
ⓑ **be assuaged, abate, moderate, ease off**

647 ゆるめる

緩める   Ⓚ1272

[sometimes also 弛める] vt **loosen, unloose, unfasten; ease (up), mitigate, moderate**
　手綱を緩める たづなをゆるめる slack the reins
　速度を緩める そくどをゆるめる ease up the speed

弛める   Ⓚ0186

ⓐ **loosen, unloose, unfasten**
ⓑ **ease (up), mitigate, moderate**

648 よ

世   Ⓚ2932

①ⓐ **world, society, public**
　ⓑ **this world, life, existence**

世の中 よのなか the world, society, life

この世 このよ this world, present life

あの世 あのよ the other world, world of the dead

② **the times, age**

世に遅れる よにおくれる fall behind the times

代 ⓚ0018

① **era of rule, age**

大正の代 たいしょうのよ Taisho era

明治天皇の代に めいじてんのうのよに under the rule of Emperor Meiji

② **reign, rule**

君が代 きみがよ Imperial reign; title of Japanese national anthem

★ The word よ has a somewhat poetic flavor. Whereas 世 refers to age or times in general, 代 is restricted to a specific era of rule, as under the reign of a particular emperor.

649 よい

良い ⓚ2980

① ⓐ **good, fine, nice, pleasant, excellent**

ⓑ **good-looking, handsome, beautiful, pretty**

ⓒ **good for (one's health), beneficial**

ⓓ (of considerable amount) **good (price)**

良さ よさ merit, virtue, good quality, good point

良く よく well, right(ly), thoroughly, skillfully, carefully, closely; much, usually, often

良い天気 よいてんき fine [fair] weather

良かったら よかったら if you like

ああ良かった ああよかった Thank God!

気分が良い きぶんがよい feel good [pleasant]

良い男 よいおとこ handsome man

健康に良い けんこうによい be good for the health

良い値で よいねで at a good price

② **suitable, proper, fitting; useful**

丁度良い時に ちょうどよいときに just at the right moment

これで良いか これでよいか Will this do?

盗むのは良くない ぬすむのはよくない It's wrong to steal

③ **lucky, auspicious**

良い日を選ぶ よいひをえらぶ choose a lucky [auspicious] day

④ **intimate, friendly**

仲良し なかよし intimacy, familiar terms; bosom friend

⑤ ⓐ **preferable, better**

ⓑ **I wish, I hope**

君はここに居ない方が良い きみはここにいないほうがよい You had better not stay here

助けてくれても良かったのに たすけてくれてもよかったのに You might have helped me

⑥ [following the TE-form of verbs]

ⓐ **may, can, be allowed**

ⓑ **need not (do), do not have to**

入っても良い はいってもよい You may enter

君は行かなくて良い きみはいかなくてよい You need not go

⑦ **do not mind (doing), have no objection**

やって見ても良い やってみてもよい I wouldn't mind trying it

善い

Ⓚ2030

(morally excellent) **good, good-natured, virtuous, upright**
善い行い よいおこない good deed
善く善く よくよく very carefully, very closely; exceedingly

好い

Ⓚ0184

[now usu. 良い] **same as** 良い よい
お人好し おひとよし good-natured person; credulous person

650　　よこいと

緯

Ⓚ1285

[also 横糸 or 緯糸] **woof**

横糸

Ⓚ0979

[also 緯糸 or 緯] **woof**

緯糸

Ⓚ1285

[also 横糸 or 緯] **woof**

651　　よし

葦

Ⓚ2041

common reed, reed
葦簀 よしず reed screen
葦切 よしきり reed warbler
葦鴨 よしがも falcated teal

芦

Ⓚ1897

common reed, reed

652　　よど

澱

[also 淀] **pool, backwater, stagnation**

淀

Ⓚ0467

① [also 澱] **pool, backwater, stagnation**
② **Yodo district (in Kyoto Prefecture)**
淀川 よどがわ Yodo River

653　　よどむ

淀む

Ⓚ0467

① ⓐ **stagnate, be stagnant**
ⓑ **settle, precipitate**
淀み よどみ pool (in river), backwater, stagnation; sedimentation, sediment, deposit; faltering, hesitation, pause
淀んだ空気 よどんだくうき stale air
川底の淀み かわぞこのよどみ sediment on the riverbed
② (of eyes) **become glazed, become glassy**
淀んだ目 よどんだめ glazed eyes
③ **hesitate, stammer, falter**
淀み無い よどみない (of speech) flowing, fluent
言い淀む いいよどむ hesitate to say

澱む

① ⓐ **stagnate, be stagnant**
ⓑ **settle, precipitate**
澱み よどみ pool, backwater, stagnation; sediment, deposit; faltering, hesitation

② (of eyes) **become glazed, become glassy**
③ **hesitate, stammer, falter**

654 よみがえる

蘇る Ⓚ2115

[also 甦る] **revive, resuscitate**
蘇り よみがえり resurrection, resuscitation

甦る

[also 蘇る] **revive, resuscitate**

655 よむ

読む Ⓚ1401

① ⓐ **read**
　ⓑ **read (aloud), recite, chant**
読み よみ reading; reading (of Chinese characters); judgment, foresight, insight
読み物 よみもの reading matter, book
読み手 よみて reader, subscriber; reciter
読み方 よみかた way of reading; reading (of a Chinese character)
楽譜を読む がくふをよむ read music
立ち読み たちよみ browsing (in a bookstore)
読み上げる よみあげる read aloud, read off
経を読む きょうをよむ chant a sutra
② (interpret the meaning of) **read, comprehend, divine, guess, estimate**
読み取る よみとる read (someone's) mind; read (the calibration)

人の心を読む ひとのこころをよむ guess what a person is thinking, read a person's thoughts
票読み ひょうよみ estimation of the number of possible votes a person will get

詠む Ⓚ1360

compose (waka or haiku poems)
詠み人知らず よみびとしらず waka-composer unknown; author unknown
和歌を詠む わかをよむ compose a waka

★ Note that although 詠 means to recite poetry as an element in the formation of *on* compounds, the word 詠む よむ is only used in the sense of composing (not reciting) poetry. Reciting poetry is expressed by 読む よむ.

656 よる

因る Ⓚ2629

[formerly also 由る] **be caused by, be due to**
風邪に因る発熱 かぜによるはつねつ fever caused by a cold

由る Ⓚ2935

[now usu. 因る] **be caused by, be due to**
不注意に由る ふちゅういによる be due to carelessness

依る Ⓚ0065

① **depend on, rely on, hang on**

成功は忍耐の如何に依る せいこうは
にんたいのいかんによる Success
depends upon perseverance

② **do by (means of), resort to, have
recourse to**
彼らの助力に依って かれらの
じょりょくによって by dint of their
help

拠る
⊕0276

① **be based on, be grounded on**
辞書に拠れば じしょによれば based
on [according to] the dictionary

② **occupy (a fortress), hold**
天険に拠る てんけんによる hold a
mountain fortress

寄る
⊕1983

①ⓐ **draw near, draw up, come near,
approach**
　ⓑ **draw aside, step aside**
近寄る ちかよる go near, approach
歩み寄る あゆみよる step up; com-
promise, meet halfway
最寄りの もよりの nearest, nearby
身寄り みより relative, relation,
kinsfolk
思いも寄らない おもいもよらない
unexpected, unforeseen, incon-
ceivable
脇に寄る わきによる draw aside
片寄る かたよる concentrate on one
side [place], go aside

② **draw together, come together,
gather, meet**
寄り合い よりあい meeting, assem-
bly, gathering

③ **drop in, call on**

寄り道する よりみちする drop in on
the way, go out of the way
立ち寄る たちよる drop in for a short
visit, call at

④ **increase, gain**
年寄り としより old [aged] person,
the aged; older councilor
皺が寄る しわがよる wrinkle, crum-
ple

⑤ **lean on, rest against**
壁に寄り掛かる かべによりかかる
rest against the wall

⑥ *sumo* **push one's opponent while
holding his belt**
寄り切り よりきり pushing one's
opponent out of the ring while
holding his belt

⑦ **(of the stock market) open**
寄り付き よりつき opening of a
session

657　　よろこばす

喜ばす
⊕2008

[formerly also 悦ばす] *vt* **please, gladden, make happy**
親を喜ばす おやをよろこばす make
one's parents happy
目を喜ばす めをよろこばす feast
one's eyes (on)

悦ばす
⊕0378

[now usu. 喜ばす] *vt* **please, gladden,
make happy**
親を悦ばす おやをよろこばす make
one's parents happy
目を悦ばす めをよろこばす feast
one's eyes (on)

658 よろこび

喜び   Ⓚ2008
ⓐ [formerly also 悦び] **joy, delight**
ⓑ [sometimes also 慶び] **felicitation, congratulation; matter for congratulation**

悦び   Ⓚ0378
[now usu. 喜び] **joy, delight**

慶び   Ⓚ2739
[usu. 喜び] **felicitation, congratulation; matter for congratulation**

659 よろこぶ

喜ぶ   Ⓚ2008
[formerly also 悦ぶ] *vi* **be happy [glad], be delighted**
    喜び よろこび [formerly also 悦び] joy, delight; [sometimes also 慶び] felicitation, congratulation; matter for congratulation
    喜ばしい よろこばしい joyful, delightful, gratifying
    喜んで よろこんで willingly, with pleasure
    大喜び おおよろこび great joy, delight

悦ぶ   Ⓚ0378
[now usu. 喜ぶ] *vi* **be happy [glad], be delighted**
    悦び よろこび [now usu. 喜び] joy, delight
    悦ばしい よろこばしい joyful, delightful, gratifying

660 わ

輪   Ⓚ1436
① [sometimes also 環] **ring, circle, link**
    輪投げ わなげ quoits, ringtoss
    輪ゴム わごむ rubber band
    輪になって踊る わになっておどる dance in a circle [ring]
    指輪 ゆびわ (finger) ring
② **wheel**

環   Ⓚ1011
[usu. 輪] **ring, circle, link**
    指環 ゆびわ (finger) ring

661 わかつ

分かつ   Ⓚ1713
① **divide, separate**
    分かち難い わかちがたい inseparable
② **distinguish, discriminate**
    昼夜を分かたず ちゅうやをわかたず day and night, by day and night
③ [sometimes also 頒つ] **distribute (things among people)**
    分かち合う わかちあう share (with others)

頒つ   Ⓚ0955
[usu. 分かつ] **distribute (things among people)**
    実費でお頒ちします じっぴでおわかちします It will be offered at actual cost

分かる Ⓚ1713

① ⓐ (grasp the meaning of) **understand, comprehend, see**
ⓑ (be sympathetic toward) **understand, show understanding for (another's feelings)**

分かり わかり understanding
分かり難い わかりにくい hard to understand, incomprehensible, unintelligible
分からず屋 わからずや obstinate person, hardhead
物分かりの良い ものわかりのよい understanding, sensible

② ⓐ **know, tell, recognize**
ⓑ **be made known, be brought to light**

先の事は分からない さきのことはわからない cannot tell what will happen in the future
身元が分かる みもとがわかる be identified

③ **appreciate**

音楽が分かる おんがくがわかる have an ear [appreciation] for music

判る Ⓚ1038

① ⓐ (grasp the meaning of) **understand, comprehend, see**
ⓑ (be sympathetic toward) **understand, show understanding for (another's feelings)**

判り わかり understanding
判り難い わかりにくい hard to understand, incomprehensible, unintelligible
物判りの良い ものわかりのよい understanding; sensible

② ⓐ **know, tell, recognize**
ⓑ **be made known, be brought to light**

先の事は判らない さきのことはわからない cannot tell what will happen in the future
身元が判る みもとがわかる be identified

③ **appreciate**

音楽が判る おんがくがわかる have an ear [appreciation] for music

解る Ⓚ1375

① ⓐ (grasp the meaning of) **understand, comprehend, see**
ⓑ (be sympathetic toward) **understand, show understanding for (another's feelings)**

解り わかり understanding
解り難い わかりにくい hard to understand, incomprehensible, unintelligible
物解りの良い ものわかりのいい understanding; sensible

② ⓐ **know, tell, recognize**
ⓑ **be made known, be brought to light**

先の事は解らない さきのことはわからない cannot tell what will happen in the future
身元が解る みもとがわかる be identified

③ **appreciate**

音楽が解る おんがくがわかる have an ear [appreciation] for music

分かれ Ⓚ1713

branch, offshoot, fork

別れ
® 1032

separation, parting, leave-taking, farewell

664 わかれる

分かれる
® 1713

ⓐ (become separated into parts) **divide, be divided, come apart; disperse**
ⓑ **branch off, branch out, diverge**

分かれ わかれ branch, offshoot, fork
左右に分かれる さゆうにわかれる part right and left
分かれ道 わかれみち branch road, fork

別れる
® 1032

ⓐ **separate, part from, bid farewell**
ⓑ **separate (from one's spouse), divorce**

別れ わかれ separation, parting, leave-taking, farewell
別れ別れに わかれわかれに separately, apart
別れ話 わかればなし talk about divorce
死に別れる しにわかれる be separated from (one's spouse) by death

665 わが

我が–
® 2971

[sometimes also 吾–] *literary* **my; our**

我が輩(=吾輩) わがはい।
我が儘 わがまま selfishness, willfulness
我が国 わがくに our country, Japan
我が家 わがや one's home [house]

吾–
® 2132

[usu. 我が–] *literary* **my; our**

吾輩 わがはい।

666 わき

傍
® 0127

① ⓐ **side**
ⓑ **the other way, another place**
傍に置く わきにおく lay aside
傍視 わきみ looking aside
② **supporting actor [role]**
傍役 わきやく supporting actor [role]

脇
® 0859

① [formerly also 傍]
ⓐ **side**
ⓑ **the other way, another place**
脇腹 わきばら one's side, flank; illegitimate birth
脇差 わきざし short sword
関脇 せきわけ second champion sumo wrestler
両脇 りょうわき both sides
脇見 わきみ looking aside
脇道 わきみち side road; digression
脇目 わきめ looking aside; eyes of an onlooker
② [formerly also 傍] **supporting actor [role]**
脇役 わきやく supporting actor [role]
脇能 わきのう minor piece in noh plays
③ [also 腋]
ⓐ **armpit**
ⓑ **armhole**
脇毛 わきげ hair of the armpit
脇の下 わきのした armpit, axilla

小脇 こわき under one's arm

腋

ⓐ **armpit**
ⓑ **armhole**
腋毛 **わきげ** hair of the armpit
腋の下 **わきのした** armpit, axilla

沸く
Ⓚ0291

① **boil, grow hot**
沸きが早い **わきがはやい** quick to warm up
沸き上がる **わきあがる** boil up; break out, arise; seethe, be in uproar
② **boil over (with excitement), seethe, be excited**
沸き返る **わきかえる** seethe, be in uproar; boil up

湧く
Ⓚ0563

①ⓐ **well up, spring forth, gush out**
ⓑ (of emotions or ideas) **well up, gush out, spring up, appear**
湧き水 **わきみず** spring water
湧き出る **わきでる** well up, spring forth
湧き上がる **わきあがる** arise
降って湧く **ふってわく** take place unexpectedly
② (of insects) **breed, be hatched**
ぼうふらが湧いた **ぼうふらがわいた** Mosquito larvae have hatched

分ける
Ⓚ1713

①ⓐ **divide into parts, part, separate, sever**
ⓑ (group according to kind) **divide, separate, sort, classify**
ⓒ [sometimes also 別ける] (cause to separate) **part, separate, set aside**
二つに分ける **ふたつにわける** divide into two
切り分ける **きりわける** cut and divide
項目別に分ける **こうもくべつにわける** classify by subject
見分ける **みわける** discriminate, distinguish
選り分ける **よりわける** sort out, classify
喧嘩を分ける **けんかをわける** separate quarreling persons
② (parcel out) **divide (up), distribute, apportion, share**
分け前 **わけまえ** share, portion
分け合う **わけあう** share (with a person)
③ **draw (with), end in a tie**
引き分け **ひきわけ** draw; drawn game [match]

別ける
Ⓚ1032

[usu. 分ける] (cause to separate) **part, separate, set aside**
別けて(も) **わけて(も)** above all, in particular

技
Ⓚ0221

① **skill, ability, craft, art**

技を磨く わざをみがく improve one's skill

②*judo*
  ⓐ **trick**
  ⓑ **half point**

業   Ⓚ2265

work, act, deed
業師 わざし tricky wrestler, shrewd fellow
仕業 しわざ act, action, deed, work
人間業 にんげんわざ work of man
軽業 かるわざ acrobatics

670   わざわい

災い   Ⓚ1888

[formerly also 禍] **calamity, misfortune, disaster, evil, serious trouble**
災いする わざわいする be the ruin of (a person)
災い転じて福となる わざわいてんじてふくとなる Good comes out of evil
不測の災い ふそくのわざわい unexpected disaster

禍   Ⓚ0945

[now usu. 災い] **calamity, misfortune, disaster, evil, serious trouble**
禍する わざわいする be the ruin of
口は禍の元 くちはわざわいのもと Out of the mouth comes evil

671   わずらい

患い   Ⓚ2395

illness, sickness

煩い   Ⓚ0937

worry, agony, vexation

672   わずらう

患う   Ⓚ2395

fall ill, be afflicted with
患い わずらい illness, sickness
長患い ながわずらい lingering sickness
胸を患う むねをわずらう have trouble in one's lungs, suffer from pulmonary tuberculosis

煩う   Ⓚ0937

worry about, feel anxious, be vexed
煩い わずらい worry, agony, vexation
煩わしい わずらわしい vexatious, troublesome, complicated
思い煩う おもいわずらう worry about, be vexed

673   わた

綿   Ⓚ1254

ⓐ **cotton plant**
ⓑ **cotton fiber, cotton cloth, cotton wool**
綿の実 わたのみ cotton seed
綿繰り わたくり cotton ginning
綿菓子 わたがし cotton candy

棉

ⓐ **cotton plant**
ⓑ **cotton fiber, cotton cloth, cotton wool**
木棉 きわた cotton fiber; ceiba

渡る ⓚ0560

① **cross (a body of water), ford, cross over, go across**
渡り わたり passage, transit; migration; mutual arrangement, negotiation
綱渡り つなわたり tightrope walking [walker]

② **migrate**
渡り鳥 わたりどり migratory bird
渡り者 わたりもの migratory worker

③ **go through (life), pass**
世渡り よわたり living, subsistence

④ **be transferred, be handed over, be supplied**
人手に渡る ひとでにわたる fall into another's hands
不渡り ふわたり dishonor, nonpayment

亘る ⓚ1697

extend over, extend for, range, span, last
幾年にも亘る いくねんにもわたる extend over so many years
数キロに亘る すうきろにわたる extend over several kilometers

我 ⓚ2971

① **oneself, self, ego**
我知らず われしらず in spite of oneself, unconsciously

② [sometimes also 吾]
ⓐ **I; we**
ⓑ slang **you**
我我 われわれ we

吾 ⓚ2132

ⓐ elegant **I; we**
ⓑ slang **you**
吾等 われら we, I; you

APPENDIXES AND INDEXES
付 録

SYSTEM OF KANJI INDEXING BY PATTERNS
字 型 式 検 字 法

1 INTRODUCTION

The lack of an efficient system for ordering Chinese characters has long been a source of frustration to learners and even native speakers of Chinese and Japanese, posing a major obstacle to the effective use of character dictionaries. The traditional method of looking up characters presupposes a knowledge of kanji elements known as **radicals.** Looking up by radicals is a time-consuming, laborious, and unreliable process that may require weeks of practice to learn. Although many alternative systems have been devised, none has achieved the speed and simplicity required to meet the practical needs of the learner.

To overcome the shortcomings of the traditional methods of ordering characters, the **New Japanese-English Character Dictionary** (Kenkyusha) introduced a new scheme, called the **System of Kanji Indexing by Patterns,** or **SKIP,** that can be used to locate entries as quickly and as accurately as in alphabetical dictionaries. This system, also used in this dictionary, is based on a novel concept: the direct identification of geometrical patterns. With the help of simple rules, each character is unambiguously classified under one of four easy-to-identify **patterns:** ◼1 left-right, ▬2 up-down,

□3 enclosure, and ■4 solid. For example, 相 is classified under pattern ▮1 since it can be divided into left and right parts.

SKIP is a product of seven years of computer-assisted research and experimentation on how kanji elements are intuitively perceived in terms of their parts. Since the system can be learned in a very short time and is easy to use, it has been adopted as the system of choice in a growing number of kanji dictionaries and software applications. SKIP represents a radical departure from all traditional systems, and is rated by Japanese-language experts as an important advance in kanji lexicography. For a more detailed explanation of SKIP, please see the appendix of **The Kodansha Kanji Dictionary.**

2 DESCRIPTION OF THE SYSTEM

2.1 OVERVIEW OF SKIP
The central idea of the **System of Kanji Indexing by Patterns** is the classification of characters into four major categories on the basis of easy-to-identify geometrical **patterns**: ▮1 **left-right** (相), ▬2 **up-down** (字), □3 **enclosure** (進), and ■4 **solid** (下).

SKIP	Acronym of "**System of Kanji Indexing by Patterns.**" A system of classifying characters by geometrical patterns used for the rapid location of entries in this dictionary.

Characters belonging to the first three categories, referred to as the **divisible characters,** are arranged in ascending order of hyphenated numerals called the **subsection number.** The first numeral indicates the number of strokes in the **shaded part,** which corresponds to the shaded segment of the **pattern symbol,** and the second the number of strokes in the **blank part,** which corresponds to the nonshaded segment. The **pattern number** followed by the subsection number is referred to as the **SKIP number.**

To locate a divisible character, first identify the pattern to which it belongs to determine the first part of the SKIP number, then divide it and count the strokes of each part to determine the second and third parts of that number (the subsection number). For example, 格 can be divided into left and right parts and is thus classified under pattern ▮1. Since it contains four strokes in the shaded part (礻) and six strokes in the blank part (各), its SKIP number is ■1-4-6. It thus appears under pattern ■1, subsection 4-6, along with other characters that share the same SKIP number such as 時 and 脂.

Divisible characters in the same **subsection** are divided into **subgroups** containing a shared element (such as 日 and 月), called the **subgroup element,** for maximum lookup speed. The characters within each subgroup are further subdivided into progressively smaller groups until each character is assigned its own position.

Characters that cannot be divided by SKIP rules, called the **indivisible characters,** are classified under pattern ■4 solid. These are arranged by total stroke-count and subclassified into four **solid subpatterns** on the basis of easy-to-identify lines: □**1 top line** (下), □**2 bottom line** (上), ▨**3 through line** (中), and □**4 others** (人). The first part of the subsection number for these characters represents their total stroke-counts, and the second part represents the number of the solid subpattern. 下, for example, is a three-stroke character containing a top line, and is thus classified under pattern ■4, subsection 3-1 (SKIP number ■4-3-1).

Although SKIP rules are simple, a small number of characters may be difficult to locate. To eliminate dead-end searching, many of these are systematically cross-referenced at one or more locations where they might be mistakenly looked for.

The above overview describes the most important elements of the system. Since it is essentially simple, you should be able to look up entries even on the basis of this brief description. Sections §2.2 through §6 below explain the details of looking up entries, summarize the rules for identifying the pattern and dividing the character, and define technical terms.

It is most important that you acquire a clear understanding of the various terms used in a technical sense, particularly the term **division point.** The definitions of technical terms are enclosed in boxes, while terms appearing in the text are printed in **sanserif boldface** whenever it is necessary to draw attention to them, especially the first time they are used in a topic of discussion.

2.2 SKIP PATTERNS

The **System of Kanji Indexing by Patterns** classifies the characters into four major categories on the basis of easy-to-identify geometrical **patterns:** ◧1 left-right, ⬒2 up-down, ☐3 enclosure, and ■4 solid. Each pattern is identified by a **pattern symbol** and **pattern number.** The charts below illustrate and define the various parts and terms associated with SKIP patterns.

Structure of SKIP Patterns

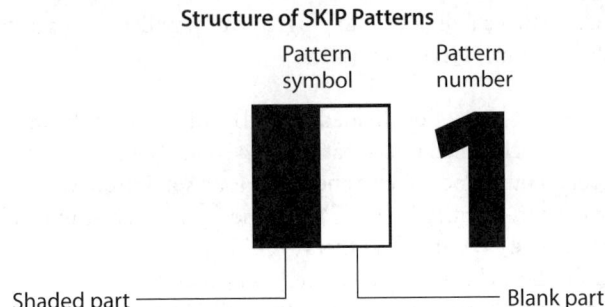

Pattern	A configuration of elements that characterizes the four major groups in the SKIP classification scheme; i.e., ◧1 **left-right,** ⬒2 **up-down,** ☐3 **enclosure,** and ■4 **solid.**
Pattern number	A number that identifies one of the four patterns in the SKIP classification scheme; i.e., 1 = ◧, 2 = ⬒, 3 = ☐, and 4 = ■.
Pattern symbol	A symbol that identifies one of the four patterns in the SKIP classification scheme; i.e., ◧ = 1, ⬒ = 2, ☐ = 3, and ■ = 4. The shaded segment of the first three pattern symbols corresponds to the **shaded part** of the **divisible characters,** and the nonshaded segment to the **blank part** of these characters.

SKIP Patterns

Pattern Number	Pattern Symbol	Pattern Name	Description
1	◧	**LEFT-RIGHT**	Character elements placed side by side. The elements are separated from each other by a **space** (保). The left-right pattern is basically of vertical construction.
2	⬒	**UP-DOWN**	Character elements stacked more or less one on top of the other. The elements are separated from each other by a **space** (示), a **horizontal line** (赤), or a **frame element** (古). The up-down pattern is basically of horizontal construction, but triangular (合) and diagonal (多) divisions are allowed.
3	□	**ENCLOSURE**	A completely exterior element enclosing the rest of a character on two or more sides. The **enclosure element** may be separated from the rest of the character by a **space** (広), or may be in full physical contact (田) with it. The enclosure pattern, which is basically of rectangular construction, is subdivided into **enclosure subpatterns.**
4	■	**SOLID**	A character element or combination of elements that does not constitute a left-right, up-down, or enclosure pattern. Solid characters, such as 口, 由, and 求, cannot be divided according to SKIP rules. Many cannot be divided without breaking through **indivisible units.** The solid pattern is subclassified into **solid subpatterns** (see **§6.2 Solid Subpatterns**).

The chart below has been carefully designed to provide you with a good understanding of SKIP patterns and subpatterns. A glance at the chart will often enable you to locate a character even without a detailed knowledge of SKIP rules.

SKIP Patterns Chart

No.	Pattern	Classification	Examples							
1	▌▐ **LEFT-RIGHT**	clear space	相 4-5	代 2-3	情 3-8	小 1-2	川 1-2	州 2-4	順 1-11	傾 2-11
		conceptual space	扱 3-3	級 6-3	歡 11-4	街 3-9	町 5-2	翻 12-6	髄 10-9	伺 2-5
2	▅ **UP-DOWN**	clear space	示 1-4	二 1-1	三 1-2	言 1-6	公 2-2	谷 2-5	父 2-2	多 3-3
		conceptual space	芳 3-4	合 2-4	響 11-9	桑 2-8	系 1-6	雀 4-7	券 6-2	春 5-4
		horizontal line	寺 3-3	空 3-5	文 2-2	亭 2-7	忘 2-5	学 5-3	索 4-6	義 3-10
		frame element	古 2-3	点 2-7	免 2-6	早 4-2	尭 2-6	当 3-3	南 2-7	支 2-2
3	☐ **ENCLOSURE**	☐	進 3-8	辻 4-2	起 7-3	延 3-5	魅 8-7	直 1-7	匕 1-1	止 1-1
		☐	旬 2-4	載 6-7	刀 1-1	司 1-4	可 2-3	戒 4-3	鳥 7-4	馬 6-4
		☐ ☐	麻 3-8	圧 2-3	尾 3-4	病 5-5	石 2-3	考 4-2	着 7-5	斗 2-2
		☐ ☐	間 8-4	岡 2-6	風 2-7	向 3-3	肉 4-2	凶 2-2	山 2-1	画 2-6
		☐ ☐	医 2-5	臣 3-4	匿 2-9	丑 2-2				
		☐ ☐ ☐	回 3-3	国 3-5	田 3-2	日 3-1	目 3-2	四 3-2	皿 3-2	
4	■ **SOLID**	☐ 1 top line	下 3-1	耳 6-1	雨 8-1	子 3-1	凸 5-1	口 3-1	亜 7-1	爾 14-1
		☐ 2 bottom line	上 3-2	七 2-2	亡 3-2	丘 5-2	由 5-2	自 6-2	坐 7-2	重 9-2
		▐ 3 through line	中 4-3	十 2-3	手 4-3	本 5-3	求 7-3	乗 9-3	毛 4-3	粛 11-3
		☐ 4 others	人 2-4	九 2-4	女 3-4	火 4-4	犬 4-4	成 6-4	寿 7-4	為 9-4

As should be clear from the chart, a pattern is essentially a spatial arrangement of elements. It is important to understand that it is the *position* of the elements in relation to each other, *not their forms,* that determines the pattern. For example, 休 consists of two elements, 亻 and 木, placed side by side and thus constitutes a left-right pattern. The shape of the element 亻, or the fact that it is a radical, is totally irrelevant. Any other elements arranged in a similar manner would equally qualify as a left-right pattern. The pattern is thus independent of the character's form, radical, reading, stroke order, stroke-count, etc. Thus, the user need only identify the *arrangement* of the elements, not their *forms.*

2.3 DIVISIBLE AND INDIVISIBLE CHARACTERS

From the point of view of SKIP rules, the characters are classified into two major groups: **divisible** and **indivisible**. The divisible characters are divided into two parts: the **shaded part,** which corresponds to the shaded segment of the **pattern symbol,** and the **blank part,** which corresponds to the nonshaded segment. The rules for dividing the divisible characters are described in §5 **How to Divide the Character.**

Characters that cannot be divided are referred to as **indivisible** or **solid characters.** These are subclassified according to a principle described in §6 **How to Subclassify the Solid Pattern.**

Divisible characters	Characters that can be divided according to SKIP rules; i.e., characters classified under patterns ▯1, ▬2, and ▯3, such as 相, 字, and 広.
Indivisible characters	Characters that cannot be divided according to SKIP rules; i.e., characters classified under pattern ▮4, such as 雨, 本, and 九.
Shaded part	The part of a **divisible character** corresponding to the shaded segment of the **pattern symbol;** i.e., the part removed at the first **division point.** For example, 扌 is the shaded part of 相 (SKIP number ▯1-4-5). The stroke-count of this part corresponds to the second part of the **SKIP number** and the first part of the **subsection number.**

Blank part	The part of a **divisible character** corresponding to the nonshaded segment of the **pattern symbol;** i.e., the part remaining after the shaded part is removed. For example, 目 is the blank part of 相 (SKIP number ■ 1-4-5). The stroke-count of this part corresponds to the third part of the **SKIP number** and the second part of the **subsection number.**

Structure of Divisible Characters

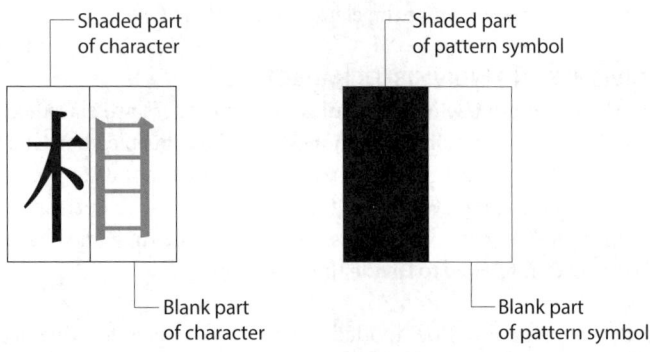

Shaded part of character — Shaded part of pattern symbol

Blank part of character — Blank part of pattern symbol

Structure of Indivisible Characters

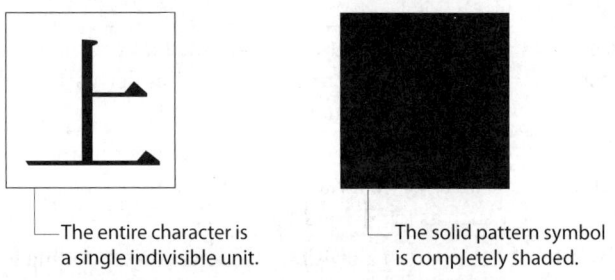

The entire character is a single indivisible unit. — The solid pattern symbol is completely shaded.

2.4 SKIP NUMBER

The **SKIP number** consists of a **pattern symbol** followed by hyphenated numerals used to locate characters according to SKIP rules. The second and third parts of this number are called the **subsection number.** Since the entries of the **Pattern Index** are ordered according to the SKIP number, it is important to get a thorough understanding of how it is formed.

SKIP number	A **pattern symbol** followed by hyphenated numerals consisting of three parts: for the divisible characters, (1) the **pattern number,** (2) the stroke-count of the **shaded part,** and (3) the stroke-count of the **blank part;** for the indivisible characters, (1) the **pattern number,** (2) the total stroke-count, and (3) the **solid subpattern number.** For example, 相 is classified under pattern ▌1 and divided into 木 (shaded part, 4 strokes) and 目 (blank part, 5 strokes), giving a SKIP number of ▌1-4-5. 下 is a three-stroke solid character containing a **top line** (solid subpattern ▭1), giving a SKIP number of ■4-3-1.
Subsection number	Hyphenated numerals used to identify a **subsection** and corresponding to the second and third parts of the SKIP number. For example, the subsection number for 相 (SKIP number ▌1-4-5) is 4-5. This number helps you quickly locate a desired subsection in the **Pattern Index.**

SKIP Number of Divisible Characters

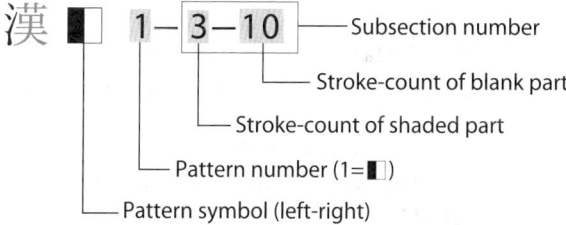

The principle for forming the SKIP number for the divisible characters is as follows:

1. The first part consists of the pattern symbol and the pattern number under which the character is classified; i.e., ▌1, ▀2, or ▭3.
2. The second part indicates the stroke-count of the shaded part and corresponds to the first part of the subsection number.
3. The third part indicates the stroke-count of the blank part and corresponds to the second part of the subsection number.

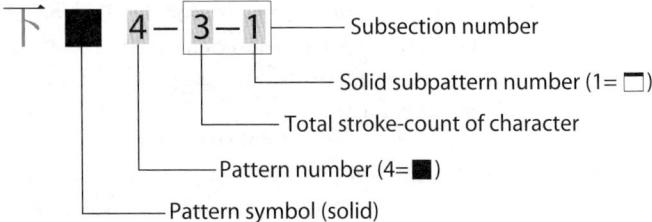

SKIP Number of Indivisible Characters

Ｔ ■ 4 — 3 — 1 ——— Subsection number
└——— Solid subpattern number (1= ▢)
└——— Total stroke-count of character
└——— Pattern number (4= ■)
└——— Pattern symbol (solid)

The principle for forming the SKIP number for the indivisible characters is as follows:

1. The first part consists of the pattern symbol and the pattern number for the solid pattern; i.e., ■4.
2. The second part indicates the total stroke-count of the character and corresponds to the first part of the subsection number.
3. The third part indicates the number of the solid subpattern under which the character is subclassified; i.e., ▢1, ▢2, ▯3, or ▢4 (see §6.2 for details). It corresponds to the second part of the subsection number.

2.5 CLASSIFICATION SCHEME

2.5.1 Subclassification The table below defines some more SKIP elements used in subclassifying characters according to the SKIP system.

Subsection	A subdivision of the **Pattern Index** in which the divisible characters are classified by **subgroup element** and the indivisible characters are classified by **entry type**. The subsections are arranged in ascending order of hyphenated numerals referred to as the **subsection number** (see §2.4). Each subsection is headed by a **subsection guide** for quick reference.
Subgroup	A subdivision of a **subsection** in which a group of **divisible characters** share a common **subgroup element.** Each subgroup is headed by a **subgroup guide,** which indicates the **subgroup element** for quick reference.

Subgroup element	The shared element of a **subgroup,** which corresponds to the **shaded part** of a divisible character. For example, 忄 is the subgroup element for the subgroup consisting of 怖 怪 怜 etc. Many subgroup elements, like 忄 above, are also radicals; others, like 君 in 群, are not. The subgroup elements that are radicals, which are ordered by their radical numbers, precede those that are not.

2.5.2 Classification Keys The order of entries is based on a classification scheme in which the characters are subdivided into progressively smaller groups until each character is assigned its own position. The scheme of SKIP classification keys is shown below.

SKIP Classification Keys

All Entries	
❶ By **SKIP pattern**	
The entry characters are divided into four major categories by **SKIP pattern:**	
1. ◧1 left-right 2. ⬒2 up-down 3. ▢3 enclosure 4. ■4 solid	
◧1 ⬒2 ▢3	**■4**
❷ By stroke-count of **shaded part**	By **total stroke-count**
Divisible characters of identical pattern are ordered by the stroke-counts of their **shaded parts.**	Indivisible characters are ordered by their **total stroke-counts.**
❸ By stroke-count of **blank part**	
Divisible characters of identical shaded-part stroke-count are ordered by the stroke-counts of their **blank parts.**	

❹ By **enclosure subpattern**:	By **solid subpattern**:
Pattern □3 characters of identical blank-part stroke-count are ordered by **enclosure subpattern**: 1. two sides: □ □ □ □ 2. three sides: □ □ □ □ 3. four sides: □ □ □	Indivisible characters of identical total stroke-count are ordered by **solid subpattern**: 1. □1 top line 2. □2 bottom line 3. □3 through line 4. □4 others
❺ By **subgroup element**:	
Divisible characters of identical blank-part stroke-count (and enclosure subpattern) are grouped by **subgroup element** in the following order: 1. **radical elements** by radical number 2. **nonradical elements** by stroke-count and SKIP number	
❻ By **entry type**:	By **entry type**:
Divisible characters of identical subgroup element are grouped by **entry type** in the following order:	Indivisible characters of identical solid subpattern are grouped by **entry type** in the following order:
1. standard entries 2. cross-reference entries	
❼ By **headword reading**:	
The **headwords** under each character are listed in order of their hiragana **readings**.	

2.6 CROSS-REFERENCES

Finding entries by SKIP rules is normally speedy and reliable. However, difficulties may arise in unusual cases, such as characters with difficult-to-identify patterns, characters for which it is difficult to count the strokes, or both. For example, 児 is an up-down character that may be classified as a left-right character by mistakenly considering ⼃ the shaded part, whereas 子 is a three-stroke element that may be incorrectly counted as a two-stroke element.

In the **Pattern Index,** such characters are systematically cross-referenced at one or more **incorrect locations**—that is, locations where they might be mistakenly sought. The **cross-reference entry** that appears there supplies a cross-reference to the corresponding correct location.

The cross-references greatly enhance the value of the system, since they practically eliminate dead-end searching and inform the user of the kind of mistake made.

2.6.1 Cross-Reference Types There are two kinds of cross-reference entries:

1. **Single-character** cross-references consist of one character at an incorrect location.

5-2	田 男	お[1]	109
	目 見	みえ	603
		みる	612
	⽳ 究	きわめる	222[p]

In the example, 究 appears under the incorrect classification ■2-5-2. The entry number 222 points to the correct location. In this case 究 is correctly classified under ■2-3-4. The tiny *p* after the entry number indicates an incorrect pattern classification.

2. **Multiple-character** cross-reference entries are cross-references for a group of two or more characters of similar structure (pattern classification or stroke-count) at an incorrect location.

1-10	⼃ 悼惚etc	→■3-8[p]

If the group consists of two characters, both are given. If the group consists of three or more characters, the first two are given and are followed by **etc.** This indicates that the other members of the group have the same structure as the first two and can also be found at the same correct location. In the example above, **etc** indicates that, in addition to 悼 and 惚, another left-right character sharing the subgroup element 忄, 惟, can be found at the correct location ■3-8.

2.6.2 Incorrect Location refers to a location where a character might be mistakenly looked for. Incorrect locations are of two kinds: (1) locations under an incorrect pattern classification, and (2) locations under an incorrect stroke-count. On rare occasions, an incorrect location may be a combination of both types. Types are shown by the following superscript symbols after the entry numbers:

p incorrect pattern classification
s incorrect stroke-count
ps incorrect pattern classification and incorrect stroke-count

3 INSTRUCTIONS FOR USE

3.1 HOW TO DETERMINE THE SKIP NUMBER

To locate a character by using SKIP, you must first determine its SKIP number. Since determining this number quickly is the key to using the system effectively, you should get a thorough understanding of how it is formed (see **§2.4 SKIP Number**).

The gist of the method is as follows. Identify the **pattern** to get the first part of the SKIP number. To get the second and third parts, count the strokes of the **shaded part** and **blank part** of the divisible characters, or count the total stroke-count and determine the **solid subpattern** of the indivisible characters.

The chart below gives detailed instructions for determining the SKIP number, and includes references to other sections that explain each step in greater detail. Understanding this chart is of crucial importance, so study carefully the examples appearing right after the chart.

DETERMINE THE SKIP NUMBER OF YOUR CHARACTER		
STEP 1	**IDENTIFY PATTERN**	
	Determine to which of the four **patterns** your character belongs to get the first part of the SKIP number (the **pattern number**). If your character belongs to pattern ◧1, ⬓2, or ☐3, carry out the steps in the left column; if it belongs to pattern ◼4, carry out the steps in the right column. ➡ §4 How to Identify the Pattern	
	◧1 ⬓2 ☐3	**◼4**
STEP 2	**DIVIDE CHARACTER** Divide the character into two parts at the first **division point**. ➡ §5 How to Divide the Character	**OMIT** Since **solid characters** cannot be divided, go to STEP 3.
STEP 3	**COUNT STROKES OF SHADED PART** Count the strokes of the **shaded part** to get the second part of the SKIP number.	**DETERMINE TOTAL STROKE-COUNT** Determine the total stroke-count of your character to get the second part of the SKIP number.
STEP 4	**COUNT STROKES OF BLANK PART** Count the strokes of the **blank part** to get the third part of the SKIP number.	**IDENTIFY SOLID SUBPATTERN** Determine to which of the four **solid subpatterns** your character belongs to get the third part of the SKIP number. Select from: ☐1, ⬓2, ◧3, or ☐4. ➡ §6 How to Subclassify the Solid Pattern

SKIP

Example: Determine the SKIP Number of 棚

STEP 1	IDENTIFY PATTERN	Since 棚 can be divided into left and right parts, we identify it as belonging to pattern ◧1 left-right. This gives the first part of the SKIP number as 1: 棚 → ◧1
STEP 2	DIVIDE CHARACTER	Dividing 棚 into two parts at the first **division point** yields 木, the **shaded part**, and 朋, the **blank part**: 棚 → 木 + 朋
STEP 3	COUNT STROKES OF SHADED PART	Counting the strokes of the **shaded part** (木) yields a stroke-count of 4. This gives the second part of the SKIP number as 4: 棚 → ◧1-4-
STEP 4	COUNT STROKES OF BLANK PART	Counting the strokes of the **blank part** (朋) yields a stroke-count of 8. This gives the third part of the SKIP number as 8: 棚 → ◧1-4-8

SKIP number of 棚: ◧1-4-8

Example: Determine the SKIP Number of 下

STEP 1	IDENTIFY PATTERN	Since 下 cannot be divided into parts, we identify it as an **indivisible character** belonging to pattern ■4 solid. This gives the first part of the SKIP number as 4: 下 → ■4
STEP 2	OMIT	Since 下 cannot be divided, go to STEP 3.
STEP 3	DETERMINE TOTAL STROKE-COUNT	Counting the strokes of the entire character yields a stroke-count of 3. This gives the second part of the SKIP number as 3: 下 → ■4-3-

STEP 4	IDENTIFY SOLID SUBPATTERN	Since 下 contains a line on top, we identify it as belonging to subpattern ☐ **1 top line.** This gives the third part of the SKIP number as 1:
		下 → ■4-3-1

SKIP number of 下: ■4-3-1

3.2 THE PATTERN INDEX

After determining the SKIP number of your character, you must locate the entry character in the **Pattern Index** by following the instructions below.

DETERMINE THE ENTRY NUMBER IN THE PATTERN INDEX, THEN LOCATE YOUR ENTRY CHARACTER	
STEP 1	**LOCATE PATTERN**
	Turn the pages of the **Pattern Index** until you locate the **pattern number** (the first part of the SKIP number) which corresponds to your character. Use the **pattern guides** in the upper, outer corners of the pages. ➡How to Use the Pattern Index on p. 306
STEP 2	**LOCATE SUBSECTION**
	Continue turning the pages until you locate the **subsection number** (the second and third parts of the SKIP number) which corresponds to your character. Use the **subsection guides** in the left part of the column. ➡How to Use the Pattern Index on p. 306

	■1 ▬2 ☐3	■4
STEP 3	**LOCATE SUBGROUP**	**OMIT**
	Scan the column of **subgroup guides** until you locate the one which corresponds to the **shaded part** of your character. ➡Pattern Index on p. 309	Since **solid characters** cannot be divided, they are not grouped by subgroup elements.

STEP 4	LOCATE CHARACTER
	Scan the column of characters until you locate your character.
STEP 5	DETERMINE ENTRY NUMBER
	Scan the hiragana readings under your character until you locate the **entry number** for your **headword**.
STEP 6	LOCATE HEADWORD
	Turn the pages of the dictionary until you locate the **entry number** for your **headword**.

4 HOW TO IDENTIFY THE PATTERN

4.1 PATTERN IDENTIFICATION

To locate a character according to SKIP rules, the first task you face is to determine to which of the four patterns your character belongs. The **pattern number** will constitute the first part of the three-part **SKIP number** of your character. For example, 宙 is classified under the up-down pattern ▬2, so the first part of its SKIP number is 2. See **§2.4 SKIP Number** for details.

To identify the pattern, just *look* at the character (or imagine it in your mind's eye) and decide to which pattern it belongs. Most of the time, your intuition will lead you to the correct classification at once. For example, 好, 充, and 尾 look like they belong to patterns ◧1, ▬2, and ◲3 respectively, while 下 and 曲 look like they are indivisible and therefore belong to pattern ◼4. If you have trouble classifying your character, a glance at the various charts below should usually enable you to easily identify the pattern without referring to the rules.

In actual practice, you normally identify the pattern of a character and divide it or subclassify it more or less simultaneously. When you see a character like 相, for example, you identify it as a left-right pattern and, at the same time, decide that it can be divided into 木 and 目. Nevertheless, for the sake of clarity and convenience of presentation, pattern identification and character division are treated here as separate topics.

4.2 PATTERN IDENTIFICATION RULES

	Right	Wrong
❶ DETERMINE TO WHICH OF THE FOUR PATTERNS YOUR CHARACTER BELONGS		
▌1 CHARACTERS THAT CAN BE DIVIDED INTO LEFT AND RIGHT PARTS		
(*a*) The resulting parts must be separated by a **space**.	相 4-5 小 1-2 順 1-11	片 1-3 用 1-4 隹 2-6
(*b*) The resulting division must be more or less vertical.	体 2-5 吹 3-4 扱 3-3	可 3-2 延 3-5 多 3-3
▬2 CHARACTERS THAT CAN BE DIVIDED INTO TOP AND BOTTOM PARTS		
(*a*) The resulting parts must be separated by a **space, horizontal line,** or **frame element**.	二 1-1 寺 3-3 古 2-3	万 1-2 考 4-2
(*b*) The resulting division need not be horizontal.	会 2-4 字 3-3 春 5-4	間 8-4 坐 4-3 凶 2-2
☐3 CHARACTERS THAT CAN BE DIVIDED BY AN **ENCLOSURE ELEMENT**		
(*a*) The resulting parts may be separated by a **space** or be in full physical contact.	進 3-8 問 8-3 国 3-5	入 1-1 伺 3-4 呉 4-3
(*b*) The resulting division must be more or less rectangular.	可 2-3 広 3-2 凶 2-2	吹 4-3 名 3-3 為 5-4
■4 CHARACTERS THAT CANNOT BE CLASSIFIED UNDER PATTERNS **▌1**, **▬2**, OR **☐3**	雨 8-1 丘 5-2 中 4-3 与 3-4	刀 2-1 日 4-1 水 4-3
❷ IF A CHARACTER CAN BE CLASSIFIED UNDER MORE THAN ONE PATTERN, SELECT THE ONE THAT FOLLOWS THE NATURAL CONSTRUCTION OF THE CHARACTER	児 ▬2-5-2 箱 ▬2-6-9	児 ▌1-2-5 箱 ▌1-7-8
❸ DO NOT VIOLATE THE PRINCIPLE OF ELEMENT INTEGRITY		
1. NEVER BREAK THROUGH STROKES	口 ■4-3-1	口 ▬2-1-3
2. NEVER BREAK THROUGH **INDIVISIBLE UNITS**	情 ▌1-3-8	情 ▌1-1-10
3. NEVER MAKE **UNNATURAL DIVISIONS**	箱 ▬2-6-9	箱 ▌1-7-8

SKIP

5 HOW TO DIVIDE THE CHARACTER

5.1 CHARACTER DIVISION

Once you have determined to which of the four patterns your character belongs, you must divide it or subclassify it in order to determine the second and third parts of the **SKIP number.** Characters that can be divided into two or more parts are classified under the first three patterns, i.e., ■1, ▬2, and ☐3. This section explains how to divide these **divisible characters.** Characters that cannot be classified under the above patterns are subclassified according to a different principle described in **§6.1 Subclassification of Solid Pattern.**

The imaginary line that divides the character splits it into a pattern whose shape roughly resembles the pattern symbol. The divisible characters are divided into two parts: the **shaded part** and the **blank part.** The second part of the SKIP number indicates the stroke-count of the former, whereas the third part indicates that of the latter. For example, 相 is divided into 木 (4 strokes) and 目 (5 strokes), giving a SKIP number of ■1-4-5. See **§2.4 SKIP Number** for details.

In the great majority of cases, you should have no problem in identifying the pattern and, at the same time, deciding at which point to divide the character. Sometimes, however, you may identify a character as belonging to a particular pattern but not be sure at which point the division should be made. That is, some characters, like 川, 三, and 磨, may contain several points at which a division could conceivably be made.

To divide such characters correctly and without hesitation, it is important that you get a clear understanding of the concept of **division points,** described in **§5.2** below. The most important thing to remember is: if there is more than one way to divide a character, divide at the first division point.

When dividing a character, be sure not to violate the principle of **element integrity.** This rule prohibits breaking through strokes or **indivisible units.** For example, you must not divide characters like 口 into 丨 and 𠃌, or characters like 情 into 丷 and 情. It also prohibits making **unnatural divisions.** For example, 鬪 should be classified under ☐3, and not be divided into left and right parts, i.e., 丨 and 鬪.

5.2 DIVISION POINTS

The first rule for dividing the pattern is: DIVIDE THE CHARACTER INTO TWO PARTS AT THE *FIRST* DIVISION POINT. That is, if there are several ways in which a character can be divided, always divide at the *first* place possible.

Division point	A **space, horizontal line, frame element,** or **enclosure element** at which it may be possible to divide a character.

A division point is not necessarily the point at which a character is actually divided according to SKIP rules. Whether a character can or cannot be divided at a given point depends on its structure and the particular SKIP rule applying to it.

Space A gap or breaking point between elements. A **clear space** is a clearly visible gap, especially one formed by parallel strokes or elements. A **conceptual space** is a natural breaking point where one would expect a gap; i.e., a gap that may not be visible because the elements are crowded closely together.	川 州 傾 二 言 公 1-2 2-4 2-11 1-2 1-6 2-2 街 町 翻 桑 系 雀 3-9 5-2 12-6 2-8 1-6 4-7

Attachment
 	
One or more usually short strokes, stroke segments, or elements in physical contact, or almost in physical contact, with the main body of an element.
 	
Top attachments are never separated from a main element except when dividing by **frame element. Side** or **end attachments** are never separated from the main element.
 	
    Top attachments
    Side attachments
    End attachments
	
	字 学 美 業 骨 危 度
	年 午 台 情 疒 旬
	軍 字 岩 民

Horizontal line A horizontal, or almost horizontal, stroke not intersected by any other strokes. Division by horizontal line applies only to pattern ▪2.	寺 空 文 亭 学 義 3-3 3-5 2-2 2-7 5-3 3-10

Frame element							
A combination of strokes or stroke segments forming a figure enclosed on two, three, or four sides. Division by frame element applies only to pattern ▬2.	古 2-3	免 2-6	早 4-2	当 3-3	南 2-7	支 2-2	

Enclosure element							
A completely exterior element that encloses the rest of a character on two or more sides. Division by enclosure element applies only to pattern ☐3.	進 3-8	旬 2-4	麻 3-8	間 8-4	医 2-5	回 3-3	

5.3 CHARACTER DIVISION RULES

Main Rules	Right	Wrong
❶ DIVIDE THE CHARACTER INTO TWO PARTS AT THE FIRST DIVISION POINT		
▮1 GOING FROM LEFT TO RIGHT, DIVIDE AT THE FIRST SPACE Divide at the first **clear** or **conceptual space.**	明 4-4　小 1-2　扱 3-3	小 2-1　街 9-3
▬2 GOING FROM TOP TO BOTTOM, DIVIDE AT THE FIRST SPACE, HORIZONTAL LINE, OR FRAME ELEMENT, WHICHEVER COMES FIRST		
(a) Divide at the first **clear** or **conceptual space.**	三 1-2　会 2-4　脅 2-8	三 2-1　会 3-3　脅 6-4
(b) Divide after the first **horizontal line.** The horizontal line, along with its side, top, and end **attachments,** goes to the top.	赤 3-4　空 3-5　業 5-8　年 2-4	赤 2-5　空 5-3　業 8-5
(c) Divide at the first point where the first **frame element** is encountered. **Top attachments** become part of the top (shaded) part.	古 2-3　当 3-3　南 2-7　早 4-2	呂 4-3　免 6-2
(d) When dividing by **horizontal line** or by **frame element,** each part must have at least two strokes.	京 2-6　方 2-2　午 2-2　予 2-2	下 1-2　亡 2-1　了 1-1　白 1-4

□3 GOING FROM THE OUTSIDE TOWARD THE INSIDE, DIVIDE AFTER THE FIRST **ENCLOSURE ELEMENT** Separate the first **enclosure element** from the rest of the character, whether it is separated from it by a **clear** or **conceptual space,** or is in full physical contact with it.	度 進 閉 目 3-6 3-8 8-3 3-2	度 磨 7-2 11-5
❷ DO NOT VIOLATE THE PRINCIPLE OF **ELEMENT INTEGRITY**		
1. NEVER BREAK THROUGH STROKES	凶 □3-2-2	凶 ■1-1-4
2. NEVER BREAK THROUGH **INDIVISIBLE UNITS**	情 ■1-3-8 気 □3-4-2	情 ■1-1-10 気 ■2-2-4
3. NEVER MAKE **UNNATURAL DIVISIONS**	漢 ■1-3-10	漢 ■2-4-9
COROLLARIES		
❶ EACH PART MUST HAVE AT LEAST ONE STROKE	門 ■1-4-4 口 ■4-3-1	門 □3-8-0 口 □3-3-0
❷ THE **SHADED PART** MUST NOT BE FURTHER DIVISIBLE UNDER THE SAME **PATTERN**	測 ■1-3-9 順 ■1-1-11	測 ■1-10-2 順 ■1-3-9

6 HOW TO SUBCLASSIFY THE SOLID PATTERN

6.1 SUBCLASSIFICATION OF SOLID PATTERN

Characters that cannot be divided according to SKIP rules are referred to as **indivisible** or **solid characters** and are classified under pattern ■4. The second and third parts of the **SKIP number** of the divisible characters, i.e., the characters classified under patterns ■1, ■2, or □3, are determined by dividing the character into two parts and counting the strokes of each part. Since the solid characters are, by definition, indivisible, a different principle is required for subclassifying them.

The indivisible characters are arranged in ascending order of their total stroke-counts and are subclassified into four **solid subpatterns** (see §6.2 below). The second part of the SKIP number indicates the total stroke-count of the character, whereas the third part indicates one of the four solid subpatterns. 下, for example, is a three-stroke character containing a **top line** (subpattern □1), giving a SKIP number of ■4-3-1. See §2.4 **SKIP Number** for details.

6.2 SOLID SUBPATTERNS

The solid pattern is classified into four **solid subpatterns** on the basis of easy-to-identify lines located on the top, at the bottom, or in the middle of a character.

Solid subpattern	One of the four groups into which the solid characters are subdivided according to the presence or absence of prominent lines; i.e., ☐1 **top line**, ☐2 **bottom line**, ☐3 **through line**, and ☐4 **others**.
Solid subpattern number	A number that identifies one of the four solid subpatterns; i.e., 1 = ☐, 2 = ☐, 3 = ☐, and 4 = ☐.
Solid subpattern symbol	A symbol that identifies one of the four solid subpatterns; i.e., ☐ = **1**, ☐ = **2**, ☐ = **3**, and ☐ = **4**.

	Solid Subpattern	Examples
☐1	**Top line** A horizontal, or almost horizontal, stroke or stroke segment extending across the very top of a solid character.	下 耳 雨 子 久 3-1 6-1 8-1 3-1 3-1 凸 口 亞 爾 5-1 3-1 7-1 14-1
☐2	**Bottom line** A horizontal, or almost horizontal, stroke or stroke segment extending across the very bottom of a solid character.	七 上 亡 丘 由 2-2 3-2 3-2 5-2 5-2 自 血 垂 重 6-2 6-2 8-2 9-2
☐3	**Through line** A perfectly vertical stroke or stroke segment intersecting another stroke of a solid character and extending over its entire, or almost its entire, length.	中 十 手 本 米 4-3 2-3 4-3 5-3 6-3 車 求 乘 肅 7-3 7-3 9-3 11-3
☐4	**Others** Solid characters that cannot be classified under subpatterns ☐1, ☐2, or ☐3.	人 九 女 火 犬 2-4 2-4 3-4 4-4 4-4 史 成 舟 為 5-4 6-4 6-4 9-4

6.3 PATTERN SUBCLASSIFICATION RULES

❶ DETERMINE TO WHICH OF THE FOUR SOLID SUBPATTERNS YOUR CHARACTER BELONGS	Right	Wrong
☐ **1** CHARACTERS THAT CONTAIN A **TOP LINE**	雨 下 耳 果 8-1 3-1 6-1 8-1	刀 千 垂 丘 2-1 3-1 8-1 5-1
☐ **2** CHARACTERS THAT CONTAIN A **BOTTOM LINE**	上 丘 垂 3-2 5-2 8-2	山 包 者 3-2 5-2 8-2
▥ **3** CHARACTERS THAT CONTAIN A **THROUGH LINE**	中 東 毛 4-3 8-3 4-3	水 寸 午 弟 4-3 3-3 4-3 7-3
☐ **4** CHARACTERS THAT DO NOT CONTAIN A **TOP LINE**, **BOTTOM LINE**, OR **THROUGH LINE**	与 大 寿 3-4 3-4 7-4	糸 久 友 劣 6-4 3-4 4-4 6-4
❷ IF A CHARACTER CAN BE CLASSIFIED UNDER MORE THAN ONE SUBPATTERN, THE SUBPATTERN WITH THE SMALLEST NUMBER TAKES PRECEDENCE	王 己 酉 果 4-1 3-1 7-1 8-1 出 生 甲 5-2 5-2 5-1	王 己 酉 果 4-2 3-2 7-2 8-3 出 生 甲 5-3 5-3 5-3

SKIP

HOW TO USE THE RADICAL INDEX
部 首 索 引 の 使 い 方

For those familiar with the radical system, we have included the **Radical Index,** which lists the characters according to their traditional radicals and additional strokes. It is best not to use this index unless you are well acquainted with the traditional radical system, which is based on the 214 radicals introduced by the 康熙字典 こうきてん (Chinese: kāngxī zìdiǎn), a comprehensive character dictionary published in China in 1716.

1   FORMAT OF RADICAL INDEX
1.1 Scope The **Radical Index** lists all the main entry characters. It also lists nonstandard forms in cases where the original radicals have been lost (see **§3** below).

1.2 Format The heading at the beginning of each section consists of the **radical number** and the **parent radical** in its full traditional form. **Variant forms** are given in parentheses only in cases where the difference between the parent and variant forms is so great as to be difficult to recognize.

For example, Radical 64 手 (扌) includes the variant in parentheses, but Radical 75 木, which has the very common left-side variant 朩, does not, since both forms are so similar that no confusion is likely to arise. The small numerals to the left of the character column indicate the stroke-count of the **nonradical element;** the numerals to the right are the **entry numbers.**

1.3 Order of Entries The radicals appear in order of increasing stroke-count and are numbered from 1 to 214 according to the traditional historical arrangement. Characters sharing the same radical are listed in increasing order of the stroke-counts of their nonradical elements. The characters within a given stroke-count subsection are listed in alphabetical order of their principal *on* readings or, in cases where no *on* reading exists, their principal *kun* readings. The **headwords** under each character are listed in order of their hiragana **readings.**

STEP 1	Determine the **radical** and **radical number** of your character:
	(a) Determine the radical. See **§4 How to Determine the Radical** below.
	(b) Determine the stroke-count of the radical.
	(c) Determine the radical number using the **Quick Reference Radical Chart** on p. 277.
	NOTE: If you have memorized the number of the radical in question, skip steps *(b)* and *(c)*.
STEP 2	Determine the stroke-count of the nonradical element.
STEP 3	Turn to the section of the **Radical Index** that corresponds to your radical number.
STEP 4	Locate your character under the stroke-count of the non-radical element with the aid of the small numerals on the left of the character column.
STEP 5	Scan the column of **readings** under your character until you locate the **entry number** for your **headword.**

Example: Find the headword for 修める

STEP 1	Carrying out STEP 1 as described, determine that the radical of 修 is the 2-stroke element 人 (亻), Radical 9.
STEP 2	Counting the strokes of the nonradical element 修 yields a stroke-count of 8.
STEP 3	Turn to the section headed **Radical 9** 人 (亻).
STEP 4	Under the nonradical stroke-count of 8 appears the character 修.
STEP 5	Scan the readings under 修 until you locate the **entry number** for your **headword** おさめる.

3   CROSS-REFERENCES

The simplification of characters that took place in the postwar period has resulted in the disappearance of the radical element from some characters. For example, 会 is traditionally classified under 曰 (Radical 73) based on its old form 會, but 曰 has completely disappeared from the simplified form 会. These **lost-radical** characters are listed under their traditional radicals, followed by the old form in parentheses. For example, the index entry for 会 appears at its traditional radical 曰 (Radical 73):

9 会(會)　　　　あう　　　　002°

In addition, the lost-radical characters are cross-referenced under another radical based on their simplified forms, which is followed by the number of the traditional radical in square brackets. For example, 会 is cross-referenced under its new radical 人 (Radical 9):

会 [RAD.73]　　　あう　　　　002°

The entry numbers of all lost-radical characters, both at their traditional radicals and at their new radicals, are followed by a small superscript circle (°).

4 HOW TO DETERMINE THE RADICAL

To determine which element of a character is the radical can be a laborious task. The following guidelines should be of help.

4.1 Radical Position The position of the radical within a character may be difficult to predict. A character may contain several radical elements, and to choose between them may require a knowledge of character etymology. 奮, for example, consists of 大, 隹, and 田, all of which are radicals. The general rule is: take the left radical in left-right characters (such as イ in 休), the top radical in up-down characters (such as 宀 in 完), and the enclosing radical in characters containing enclosures (as 广 in 広).

The **Important Radicals** chart below lists the most important radicals, classified by their position within the character. The radicals are shown in the form in which they occur most frequently. The position of many radicals is constant in relation to the rest of the character (though there are exceptions). These are classified in the chart below under the headings **left, right,** etc. The position of other radicals, classified under the heading **others,** is variable.

4.2 Important Radicals Memorizing the most important radicals and their numbers will greatly speed up the lookup process. Since many Japanese and Chinese character dictionaries follow the traditional radical system, those making extensive use of radical indexes will find it worthwhile to memorize the table below.

4.3 Stroke Counting Since the characters within a given radical group are arranged in increasing order of the stroke-counts of their nonradical elements, it is important to learn how to count strokes accurately. Refer to **Appendix 3. How to Count Strokes** in **The Kodansha Kanji Dictionary.**

4.4 Variant Forms Radicals may occur in their unabbreviated **parent form,** or in an abbreviated **variant form.** For example, 犬 (Radical 94) appears in its parent form in 獣, but in its abbreviated form of 犭 in 独. Some radicals, such as 艸 (Radical 140), always occur in their variant forms (in this case ⺾). To use the **Radical Index** effectively, one needs the ability to identify the parent radical from its variant forms. See the **Quick Reference Radical Chart** on p. 277 for information on parent forms and their variants.

4.5 Lost Radicals Since the radicals of some characters are based on the old forms of the characters, a knowledge of the latter may sometimes be necessary in order to identify the radical. See **§3** above for details on how this problem is overcome in this dictionary.

4.6 Quick Reference Radical Chart This chart, which appears on p. 277 immediately before the **Radical Index,** is the quickest way to determine the radical number.

Important Radicals

LEFT RADICALS
◨ 偏 へん

9	亻	120	糸
24	十	128	耳
30	口	130	月
32	土	137	舟
38	女	142	虫
39	子	145	衤
46	山	149	言
57	弓	154	貝
60	彳	157	跙
61	忄	159	車
64	扌	164	酉
75	木	167	金
85	氵	170	阝
86	火	184	食
93	牛	187	馬
94	犭	195	魚
96	王		
112	石		
113	礻		
115	禾		
119	米		

RIGHT RADICALS
◧ 旁 つくり

18	刂
26	卩
62	戈
66	攵

76	欠
163	阝
181	頁

TOP RADICALS
⬒ 冠 かんむり

8	亠
37	大
40	宀
46	山
116	穴
118	竹
122	皿
140	艹
173	雨

BOTTOM RADICALS
⬓ 脚 あし

10	儿
12	八
86	灬
154	貝

ENCLOSURES
❑ 囲 かこい

27	厂
31	囗
44	尸
53	广
104	疒
162	辶
169	門

OTHERS

1	一
19	力
41	寸
50	巾
72	日
74	月
102	田
109	目
172	隹

QUICK REFERENCE RADICAL CHART
部 首 早 見 一 覧

The **Quick Reference Radical Chart** helps the user quickly look up radical numbers as an aid to using the **Radical Index** efficiently.

1. **Format** The left part of each column gives the **radical number** in boldface; the right part shows the **radical** in its **parent form,** followed by the **radical name.**
2. **Order of entries** The radicals and their variants are listed in order of increasing stroke-count of their parent forms. These are numbered consecutively from 1 to 214 according to the traditional historical arrangement. When a radical has more than one form, the parent form is given first, followed by all its variants.
3. **Radical names** When talking about the components of Chinese characters, it is convenient to describe them by naming their constituent radicals. For example, we can say that 洋 consists of 氵 sanzui (the 'water' radical) on the left and 羊 hitsuji (the 'sheep' radical) on the right. Each radical is followed by a romanized version of its most common name in Japanese.
4. **Cross-references** If the stroke-count of a variant differs from that of its parent form, it is cross-referenced under the variant stroke-count to its corresponding parent form. The cross-references appear at the end of a given stroke-count section, and are distinguished by radical numbers in square brackets. For example, Radical 162 has the seven-stroke parent form 辵, one three-stroke variant 辶, and one four-stroke variant 辶. All three forms are listed together under Radical 162, but the variants also appear at the end of the three- and four-stroke sections, respectively.

1 STROKE

1	一	ichi
2	丨	bō
3	、	ten
4	丿	no
	ノ	no
5	乙	otsu
	乚	re
6	亅	hanebō

2 STROKES

7	二	ni
8	亠	nabebuta
9	人	hito
	亻	ninben
	𠆢	hitoyane
10	儿	ninnyō, hitoashi
11	入	iru
12	八	hachigashira
	八	hachi
	丷	hachigashira
13	冂	keigamae
14	冖	wakanmuri
15	冫	nisui
16	几	tsukue
	几	kazagamae
17	凵	kannyō, ukebako
18	刀	katana
	刂	rittō
19	力	chikara
20	勹	tsutsumigamae
21	匕	sajinohi
22	匚	hakogamae
23	匚	kakushigamae
	匸	kakushigamae
24	十	jū

	十	jūhen
25	卜	bokunoto
	卜	bokunoto
26	卩	fushizukuri
	巴	fushizukuri
27	厂	gandare
28	厶	mu
29	又	mata
	又	mata

3 STROKES

30	口	kuchi
	冂	kuchihen
31	囗	kunigamae
32	土	tsuchi
	土	tsuchihen
33	士	samurai
34	夂	fuyugashira
35	夊	suinyō
	夊	natsuashi
36	夕	yūbe
37	大	ōkii, dai
	大	ōkii, dai
38	女	onna
	女	onnahen
39	子	ko
	孑	kohen
40	宀	ukanmuri
41	寸	sun
42	小	chiisai
	小	naogashira
	小	naogashira
43	尢	mageashi
44	尸	shikabane
45	屮	tetsu
46	山	yama
	山	yamahen

	山	yamakanmuri
47	巛	magarigawa
	川	sanbongawa
48	工	takumi
	工	takumihen
49	己	onore
	巳	mi
50	巾	haba
51	干	hosu
52	幺	itogashira
53	广	madare
54	廴	ennyō
	廴	ennyō
55	廾	nijūashi
56	弋	shikigamae
57	弓	yumi
	弓	yumihen
58	彐	keigashira
	彐	keigashira
	彑	keigashira
59	彡	sanzukuri
60	彳	gyōninben
[61]	忄	risshinben
[64]	扌	tehen
[85]	氵	sanzui
[90]	丬	shōhen
[94]	犭	kemonohen
[140]	艹	kusakanmuri
[162]	辶	shinnyō, shinnyū
[163]	阝	ōzato
[170]	阝	kozatohen

4 STROKES

61	心	kokoro
	忄	risshinben
	忝	shitagokoro
62	戈	kanohoko

RADICAL CHART

63	戸 tobiranoto	毛 ke	**5 STROKES**
	戸 tobiranoto	83 氏 uji	95 玄 gen
64	手 te	84 气 kigamae	96 玉 tama
	扌 tehen	85 水 mizu	王 tamahen
65	支 shinyō, jūmata	氵 sanzui	王 ō
	支 shinyō, jūmata	氺 shitamizu	97 瓜 uri
66	攴 bokuzukuri, tomata	86 火 hi	瓜 uri
	攵 nobun	火 hihen	98 瓦 kawara
67	文 bun, bunnyō	灬 rekka	99 甘 amai
	文 bun, bunnyō	87 爪 tsume	100 生 umareru
68	斗 tomasu	爫 notsu	101 用 mochiiru
69	斤 ono	爫 tsumekanmuri	102 田 ta
70	方 kata	88 父 chichi	103 疋 hiki
71	无 munyō	父 chichi	疋 hikihen
	旡 sudenotsukuri	89 爻 meme	104 疒 yamaidare
	旡 sudenotsukuri	爻 meme	105 癶 hatsugashira
72	日 hi	90 爿 shōhen	106 白 shiro
	日 hi	丬 shōhen	107 皮 kegawa
73	曰 hirabi	91 片 kata	108 皿 sara
	曰 hirabi	92 牙 kiba	109 目 me
74	月 tsuki	牙 kiba	110 矛 hoko
	月 tsuki	93 牛 ushi	111 矢 ya
	月 tsuki	牛 ushihen	矢 yahen
75	木 ki	94 犬 inu	112 石 ishi
	朩 kihen	犭 kemonohen	石 ishihen
76	欠 akubi	[96] 王 tamahen	113 示 shimesu
77	止 tomeru	王 ō	礻 nehen, shimesuhen
	止 tomehen	[113] 礻 nehen, shimesuhen	礻 shimesuhen
78	歹 gatsuhen	[122] 罒 yonkashira	114 内 gūnoashi
79	殳 rumata, hokozukuri	[125] 耂 oikanmuri, oigashira	115 禾 nogi
80	毋 nakare	[130] 月 nikuzuki	禾 nogihen
	毌 haha, nakare	月 tsuki	116 穴 ana
	母 haha	[140] 艹 kusakanmuri	穴 anakanmuri
81	比 kuraberu, hi	艹 kusakanmuri	穴 ana
82	毛 ke	[162] 辶 shinnyō, shinnyū	117 立 tatsu

RADICAL CHART

	立	tatsuhen
[71]	旡	sudenotsukuri
[80]	母	haha
[85]	氺	shitamizu
[92]	牙	kiba
[122]	罒	yonkashira
[145]	衤	koromohen

6 STROKES

118	竹	take
	⺮	takekanmuri
119	米	kome
	米	komehen
120	糸	ito
	糹	itohen
121	缶	hotogi
122	网	amigashira
	罒	yonkashira
	罓	yonkashira
123	羊	hitsuji
	𦍌	hitsujikanmuri
	羋	hitsujihen
124	羽	hane
	羽	hane
125	老	oi
	耂	oikanmuri,
		oigashira
126	而	shikashite
127	耒	raisuki
	耒	raihen
	耒	sukihen
128	耳	mimi
	耳	mimihen
129	聿	fudezukuri

130	肉	niku
	月	nikuzuki
	月	tsuki
131	臣	shin
	臣	shin
132	自	mizukara
133	至	itaru
134	臼	usu
	臼	usu
135	舌	shita
	舌	shitahen
136	舛	masu
	舛	maiashi
137	舟	fune
	舟	funehen
138	艮	kon, ushitora
	艮	kon, ushitora
139	色	iro
	色	irozukuri
140	艸	kusa
	艹	kusakanmuri
	艹	kusakanmuri
	艹	kusakanmuri
141	虍	torakanmuri
	虍	torakanmuri
142	虫	mushi
	虫	mushihen
143	血	chi
	血	chihen
144	行	gyō
	行	gyōgamae
145	衣	koromo
	衤	koromohen
	衣	koromo

146	西	nishi
	西	nishi
	西	nishi
[97]	瓜	uri

7 STROKES

147	見	miru
148	角	tsuno
	角	tsunohen
149	言	kotoba
	言	gonben
150	谷	tani
	谷	tanihen
151	豆	mame
	豆	mamehen
152	豕	inoko
	豸	inokohen
153	豸	mujina
154	貝	kai
	貝	kaihen
155	赤	aka
	赤	akahen
156	走	hashiru
	走	sōnyō
157	足	ashi
	𧾷	ashihen
158	身	mi
	身	mihen
159	車	kuruma
	車	kurumahen
160	辛	karai
	辛	karai
161	辰	shinnotatsu
162	辵	shinnyō, shinnyū

	辶	shinnyō, shinnyū	177	革	kawa	
	辶	shinnyō, shinnyū		革	kawahen	
163	邑	mura	178	韋	nameshigawa	
	阝	ōzato		韋	nameshigawa	
164	酉	hiyominotori	179	韭	nira	
	酉	torihen	180	音	oto	
165	釆	nogome		音	oto	
	釆	nogomehen	181	頁	ōgai	
166	里	sato	182	風	kaze	
	里	satohen		風	kaze	
[131]	臣	shin	183	飛	tobu	
[134]	臼	usu	184	食	shoku	
[136]	舛	maiashi		飠	shokuhen	
[168]	镸	nagai		飠	shokuhen	
[199]	麦	bakunyō		食	shoku	
	麦	mugi	185	首	kubi	
			186	香	nioikō	

8 STROKES

10 STROKES

167	金	kane	187	馬	uma	
	釒	kanehen		馬	umahen	
168	長	nagai	188	骨	hone	
	镸	nagai		骨	honehen	
169	門	mon, mongamae	189	高	takai	
170	阜	gifunofu	190	髟	kamikanmuri	
	阝	kozatohen	191	鬥	tōgamae	
171	隶	reizukuri	192	鬯	chō	
172	隹	furutori	193	鬲	kaku	
173	雨	ame		鬲	kaku	
	雨	amekanmuri	194	鬼	oni	
174	靑	ao		鬼	kinyō	
	青	ao	[178]	韋	nameshigawa	
175	非	arazu	[212]	竜	ryū	
[184]	飠	shokuhen				
[210]	斉	sei				

9 STROKES

11 STROKES

176	面	men	
195	魚	uo	
	魚	uohen	

196	鳥	tori	
	鳥	tori	
197	鹵	ro	
198	鹿	shika	
199	麥	baku	
	麥	bakunyō	
	麦	bakunyō	
	麦	mugi	
200	麻	asa	
	麻	asakanmuri	
	麻	asakanmuri	
	麻	asa	
[201]	黄	kiiro	
[203]	黒	kuroi	
[213]	亀	kame	

12 STROKES

201	黄	kiiro	
	黄	kiiro	
202	黍	kibi	
203	黑	kuroi	
	黒	kuroi	
204	黹	futsu	
[211]	歯	hahen	
	歯	ha	

13 STROKES

205	黽	ben	
206	鼎	kanae	
207	鼓	tsuzumi	
208	鼠	nezumi	
	鼠	nezuminyō	

14 STROKES

209	鼻	hana	
	鼻	hanahen	
	鼻	hana	

RADICAL CHART

210 齊 *sei*
斉 *sei*

211 齒 *ha*
歯 *hahen*
齒 *hahen*
歯 *ha*

212 龍 *ryū*
竜 *ryū*
龍 *ryū*

213 龜 *kame*
龜 *kame*
亀 *kame*

214 龠 *yaku*

[213] 龜 *kame*

RADICAL INDEX
部 首 索 引

4	亦	また²	592		使	つかい	390
	亥	い	051			つかう	391
	交	まざる	586	7	係	かかり	158
		まじる	587			かかる	159
		まぜる	590			かかわる	160
6	享	うける	080			がかり	205

RADICAL 9 人 (亻)

					俣	また¹	591
					侵	おかす	115
2	仇	かたき	178	8	値	あたい	021
3	代	かえ	150		倣	ならう	465
		かえる²	154		倦	あきる	010
		かわり	203		倖	しあわせ	292
		かわる	204		修	おさまる	124
		よ	648			おさめる	125
	付	つく¹	395		倉	くら	239
		つける	400		倒	たおす	352
		づけ	410			たおれる	353
	仕	しあわせ	292	9	偽	いつわる	064
	仔	こ¹	247		偏	かたよる	182
	他	ほか	568		偲	しのぶ	300
4	伐	きる	218		側	そば	345
	仲	なか	453		停	とまる	432
	伏	ふす	554			とめる¹	433
		ふせる	556	10	備	そなえ	341
	会 [RAD.73]	あう	002°			そなえる	342
		あわせる	048°		傍	おか	114
	休	やすまる	637			そば	345
	全 [RAD.11]	すべて	325°			はた³	509
5	住	すむ	329			わき	666
	作	つくり	397		偉	えらい	105
		つくる	398		傘	かさ	170
		づくり	409	11	傷	いたむ	061
	伸	のばす	482			いためる	062
		のび	483			きず	213
		のびる	484		傭	やとい	638
		のべる	485			やとう	639
6	併	あわせる	048	15	優	すぐれる	319
	依	よる	656			まさる	585
	価	あたい	021			やさしい	634
	供	そなえ	341				
		そなえる	342		**RADICAL 10 儿**		
		とも	435				
		ども	446	2	元	もと	627
	例	たとえる	374	4	兆	きざし	211
						きざす	212

3 STROKES

9	就	つく[1]	395				
		つける	400		**RADICAL 51** 干		
	RADICAL 44 尸			0	干	ひる	545
						ほす	571
6	屋	や[1]	630	3	年	とし	424
		やしき	635	5	幸	しあわせ	292
12	履	はく[2]	496		**RADICAL 53** 广		
	RADICAL 46 山			2	広	ひろがる	546
5	岩	いわ	078			ひろげる	547
	岡	おか	114			ひろまる	548
7	峰	みね	609			ひろめる	549
	島	しま	304	5	店	たな	375
8	崎	さき	275	7	庫	くら	239
9	嵌	はまる	519		座	すわり	331
		はめる	520			すわる	332
13	嶮	けわしい	246	11	廓	くるわ	244
14	嶺	みね	609		**RADICAL 54** 廴		
	RADICAL 47 巛 (川)			5	延	のばす	482
0	川	かわ[1]	199			のび	483
3	州	す[1]	313			のびる	484
8	巣(巢)	す[3]	315°			のべる	485
	RADICAL 48 工			6	廻	まわす	600
2	巧	うまい	092			まわり	601
		たくみ	355			まわる	602
7	差	さし	279		建	たつ[2]	368
		さす	280			たて[1]	370
	RADICAL 49 己					たてる	373
0	巳	すでに	322			だて	385
		やむ	641		**RADICAL 55** 廾		
		やめる	642	4	弄	もてあそぶ	626
6	巻 [RAD.26]	まく[2]	582°		**RADICAL 57** 弓		
	RADICAL 50 巾			1	引	ひき[1]	535
0	巾	はば	517			ひく	537
4	希	まれ	599	2	弘	ひろまる	548
9	幅	はば	517			ひろめる	549
12	幡	はた[2]	508	3	弛	ゆるむ	646
						ゆるめる	647
				8	張	はる	526

RADICAL 73 日

RADICAL 74 月

RADICAL 75 木

RADICAL 76 欠

	まぜる	590	2 灯	ほ	565
淋	さびしい	284		ともしび	436
	さみしい	286		ともす	437
済	すます	327		ひ²	532
清	きよめる	217		ほ	565
渚	なぎさ	456	3 災	わざわい	670
添	そう	339	灼	やく	632
	みなと	608	4 炎	ほのお	572
9 港	みたす	605	炊	たく	354
満	あたたか	023	5 為 [RAD.87]	なす	462°
温	あたたかい	024		なる	467°
	あたたまる	025	炭	すみ	328
	あたためる	026	点 [RAD.203]	たてる	373°
	しめる¹	307		つく¹	395°
湿	はかる	494		つける	400°
測	みなと	608		ともす	437°
湊	わたる	674	6 烈	はげしい	497
渡	わく	667	焚	たく	354
湧	およぐ	142	無	ない	449
游	こぼす	258		なくす	458
10 溢	こぼれる	259		なくなる	459
	すべる	326	焼	やく	632
滑	ほろびる	576		やける	633
滅	ほろぶ	577	然	しかして	294
	ほろぼす	578		しかも	295
溜	ためる	384	9 煩	わずらい	671
溶	とかす	418		わずらう	672
	とく	420	煉	ねる	474
	とける	422	10 煽	あおぐ	004
11 漬	つける	400	熔	とかす	418
	づけ	410		とける	422
滲	しみる	306	11 熱	あつい¹	029
滴	しずく	297	12 燃	もえる	624
12 澄	すます	327	13 燭	ともしび	436
潮	しお	293			
潰	ついえる	386	**RADICAL 87** 爪 (爫)		
13 澱	よど	652	8 為(爲)	なす	462°
	よどむ	653		なる	467°
激	はげしい	497	**RADICAL 89** 爻		
14 濠	ほり	574			
鴻	おおとり	113	10 爾	なんじ	469
RADICAL 86 火 (灬)			**RADICAL 90** 爿		
0 火	ひ²	532	13 牆	かき	163

RADICAL 91 片

0	片	かたよる	182

RADICAL 93 牛 (牜)

0	牛	うし	081
2	牝	め[1]	620
		めす	622
		めん	623
3	牡	お[1]	109
		おす[2]	128
		おん	148
4	物	もの	628
7	牽	ひく	537

RADICAL 94 犬 (犭)

0	犬	いぬ	066
2	犯	おかす	115
5	狗	いぬ	066
6	独	ひとり	540
	狩	かる	197
8	猪	い	051
9	猶	なお	450
10	猿	さる	289
13	獲	える	108

5 STROKES

RADICAL 96 玉 (王)

0	玉	たま[2]	381
		たまご	383
4	玩	もてあそぶ	626
6	珠	たま[2]	381
7	現	あらわす	043
		あらわれ	044
		あらわれる	045
	球	たま[2]	381
8	琴	こと[2]	256
9	瑞	みず	604
13	璧	たま[2]	381
	環	わ	660

RADICAL 99 甘

0	甘	うまい	092

RADICAL 100 生

0	生	いかす	054
		いきる	055
		いける	057
		うまれる	093
		うみ	094
		うむ	095
		なす	462
		なる	467
		むす	615
6	産	うまれる	093
		うみ	094
		うむ	095
		むす	615
7	甦	よみがえる	654

RADICAL 101 用

2	甫	はじめて	503

RADICAL 102 田

0	申	さる	289
	由	よる	656
2	町	まち	593
	男	お[1]	109
3	画	え	103
		えがく	104
4	畑	はた[1]	507
		はたけ	510
		ばたけ	529
	畏	おそれる	130
5	畠	はた[1]	507
		はたけ	510
		ばたけ	529
	留	とどまる	428
		とどめる	429
		とまる	432
		とめる[1]	433
		とめる[2]	434

RADICAL 116 穴

RADICAL 117 立

6 STROKES

RADICAL 118 竹 (⺮)

RADICAL 119 米

RADICAL 120 糸

RADICAL 134 臼

0	臼	うす	082
6	与(與)	あずかる	020°
9	興	おこす	120
		おこる	121

RADICAL 135 舌

4	舐	なめずる	463
		なめる	464

RADICAL 137 舟

0	舟	ふな	559
		ふね	560
		ぶね	563
5	舵	かじ	171
	船	ふな	559
		ふね	560
		ぶね	563

RADICAL 138 艮

1	良	いい	052
		よい	649

RADICAL 140 艸 (艹)

3	芝	しば	301
4	花	はな¹	512
	芥	ごみ	267
	芦	あし²	019
		よし	651
5	茅	かや	192
	苑	その	344
	芽	め²	621
	茂	しげる	296
6	荒	あら	041
		あらい	042
	草	ぐさ	245
7	莫	なかれ	454
	華	はな¹	512
8	著	あらわす	043
	萌	きざし	211
		きざす	212
		もえる	624
9	萱	かや	192

	葛	かずら	175
	葉	は	492
10	蓄	たくわえ	356
		たくわえる	357
	蓋	おおう	112
	葦	あし²	019
		よし	651
	蒔	まく¹	581
	蒸	むす	615
	蒙	こうむる	250
	蒼	あおい	003
11	蔭	かげ	167
12	蔓	かずら	175
	蔽	おおう	112
	蔵	くら	239
13	薫	かおり	156
		かおる	157
	薦	すすめる	320
	薬	くすり	229
16	蘇	よみがえる	654

RADICAL 141 虍

2	虎	とら	439
5	虚	むなしい	616
	処(處)	ところ	423°
7	虞	おそれ	129

RADICAL 142 虫

10	融	とかす	418
		とける	422

RADICAL 144 行

0	行	いく	056
		ゆく	645
6	街	まち	593
9	衝	つく²	396

RADICAL 145 衣 (衤)

0	衣	きぬ	214
		ぎ	223
2	表	あらわす	043
		あらわれ	044
		あらわれる	045
		おもて	139

8 STROKES

9 STROKES

HOW TO USE THE PATTERN INDEX
字 型 索 引 の 使 い 方

If you don't know the reading of a *kun* word, such as 修める, you can find the **headword** おさめる by locating the headword's first kanji in the **Pattern Index.** This index allows you to quickly locate a character from its SKIP pattern.

1. Determine the **SKIP number** of your character.
2. Determine the **entry number** by locating your character in the **Pattern Index.** Use the **subsection guides** and **subgroup guides.**
3. Locate your **headword** in the dictionary from the **entry number.**

Pattern Index

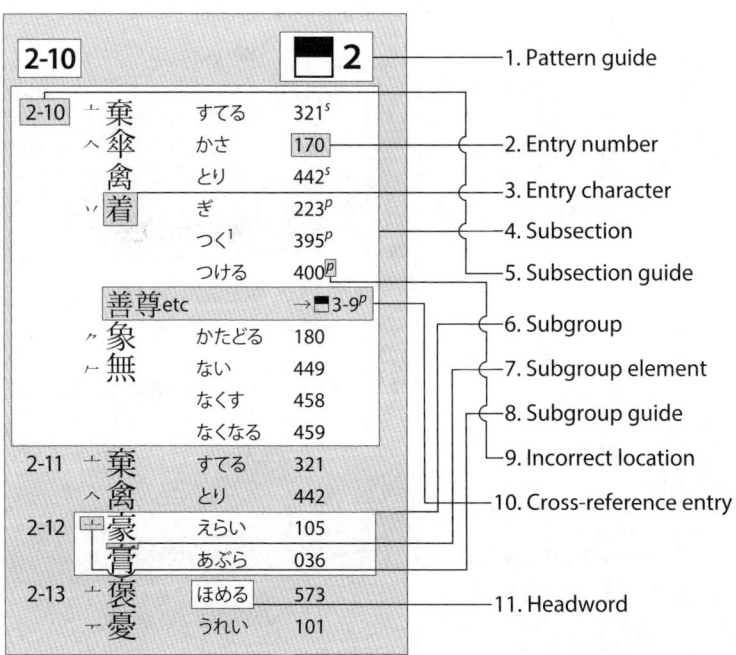

1.	**Pattern guide**	A guide in the upper, outer corner of a page that indicates the **pattern** and **pattern number** for that page.
2.	**Entry number**	A number that uniquely identifies the entry characters of the dictionary. After locating the entry number in the index, turn the pages until you find the corresponding entry character.
3.	**Entry character**	The first kanji of the **headword,** which the character that heads an index entry.
4.	**Subsection**	A subdivision of the **Pattern Index.** The subsections are arranged in ascending order of their **subsection numbers.**
5.	**Subsection guide**	1. Boldface numerals in the upper corner of a page that indicate the **subsection number** for that page. The upper-right guide (on a left page) indicates the subsection number for the first subsection, while the upper-left guide (on a right page) indicates the subsection number for the last subsection on that page. Together they indicate the subsection number range for both pages. 2. Hyphenated numerals in the left part of a column that indicate the subsection number for each subsection. Scanning through the subsection guides enables you to quickly locate the subsection number corresponding to your character.
6.	**Subgroup**	A subdivision of a **subsection** in which a group of **divisible characters** share a common **subgroup element.**
7.	**Subgroup element**	The shared element of a **subgroup,** which corresponds to the **shaded part** of a **divisible character.**

8. Subgroup guide	A guide to the left of the character column that indicates the **subgroup element** for each subgroup. Scanning through the subgroup guides enables you to locate quickly the one corresponding to the **shaded part** of your character.
9. Incorrect location	Location where a character might be mistakenly looked for: *p* incorrect pattern classification *s* incorrect stroke-count *ps* incorrect pattern classification and incorrect stroke-count
10. Cross-reference entry	An entry appearing at an **incorrect location** with a cross-reference to the corresponding correct location. These are of two kinds: 1. Cross-reference for a single character. 2. Cross-references for a group of two or more characters.
11. Headword	The **reading** shared by the members of a homophone group, which appears at the head of the main entries of the dictionary.

PATTERN INDEX
字　型　索　引

309

PATTERN INDEX

PATTERN INDEX

□
ENCLOSURE